Instant Pot Air Fryer Lid Cookbook

600 Easy and Delicious Instant Pot Air Fryer Lid Recipes for Fast and Healthy Meals

Maryer Rosh

Shone Boudar

Table of contents

Introduction

Diversify your culinary experience and bring home a new Instant Pot masterpiece to your home. The new Instant Pot's Air fryer lid is now in the stores. With this lid, the Instant Pot users can change their regular Instant Pot pressure cookers into Air Fryers. Imagine, you don't need to buy another Air fryer which will cost you more money and will definitely take much of the space on your kitchen counter. With its Instant Crispy Technology, this lid is capable of Air frying all of your meals, rendering perfect golden color and a super crispy texture. Using this technology, you can get to cook your meal using both the basic Instant Pot functions and the added Air fryer functions like Air fry, bake, Broil, Reheat, Dehydrate, and Roast. Just switch the lid and see the magic happening yourself.

One appliance and two lids can bring a wide range of possibilities and you will be amazed by the variety of menu you can cook using this kitchen miracle. Whether it is finishing the cooked chops with a crispier touch or Air frying your favorite chips, it's all can be done by switch the lid. Since the users can easily remove the lid from the cooker base, it gives easy and convenient handling and better cleaning. The lid has its own preset function which is given on top along with the display. The touch button system allows you to conveniently choose the right option. You can also customize the temperature and timer settings as per the recipe requirement. This all can be done with a single a lid and the same old Instant Pot cooker base. Don't wait around to try the good crisp at your home, bring the Instant Pot Air Fryer lid home and discover the infinite possibilities.

Chapter 1: Breakfast

Kale Egg Muffins

Preparation Time: 10 minutes; Cooking Time: 35 minutes; Serve: 6

Ingredients:

- 5 eggs
- 1/2 cup coconut milk
- 2 tbsp sausage, sliced
- 2 tbsp kale, chopped
- 2 tbsp sun-dried tomatoes, chopped
- Pepper
- Salt

Directions:

1. In a large bowl, add all ingredients and whisk until well combined.
2. Pour egg mixture into the silicone muffin molds and place it in instant pot air fryer basket. Place basket in the pot.
3. Seal the pot with air fryer basket and select bake mode and cook at 350 F for 30-35 minutes.
4. Serve and enjoy.

Nutritional Value (Amount per Serving):

Calories 115; Fat 9.7 g; Carbohydrates 1.7 g; Sugar 1.1 g; Protein 6 g; Cholesterol 140 mg

Chicken Egg Breakfast Muffins

Preparation Time: 10 minutes; Cooking Time: 15 minutes; Serve: 6

Ingredients:

- 5 eggs
- 1/4 cup green onions, chopped
- 1/2 cup chicken, cooked and chopped
- 1/4 tsp pepper
- 1/2 tsp sea salt

Directions:

1. In a large bowl, whisk eggs with pepper and salt. Add remaining ingredients and stir well.
2. Pour egg mixture into the silicone muffin molds and place it in instant pot air fryer basket. Place basket in the pot.
3. Seal the pot with air fryer basket and select bake mode and cook at 400 F for 15 minutes.
4. Serve and enjoy.

Nutritional Value (Amount per Serving):

Calories 72; Fat 4 g; Carbohydrates 0.7 g; Sugar 0.4 g; Protein 8.1 g; Cholesterol 145 mg

Zucchini Muffins

Preparation Time: 10 minutes; Cooking Time: 20 minutes; Serve: 6

Ingredients:

- 4 eggs
- 1 tbsp parsley, chopped
- 1/2 cup baby spinach, chopped
- 1/2 red bell pepper, diced
- 1/8 cup green onion, chopped
- 6 bacon slices, cooked and crumbled
- 1 small zucchini, sliced
- 1/8 cup coconut milk
- 1/2 tbsp olive oil
- Pepper
- Salt

Directions:

1. Heat olive oil in a pan over medium heat.
2. Add parsley, spinach, green onion, red bell pepper and sauté until spinach is wilted.
3. In a bowl, whisk eggs with coconut milk, pepper, and salt.
4. Add sautéed vegetables, bacon, and zucchini to the egg mixture and stir well.
5. Pour egg mixture into the silicone muffin molds and place it in instant pot air fryer basket. Place basket in the pot.

6. Seal the pot with air fryer basket and select bake mode and cook at 350 F for 20 minutes.
7. Serve and enjoy.

Nutritional Value (Amount per Serving):
Calories 174; Fat 13.3 g; Carbohydrates 2.5 g; Sugar 1.3 g; Protein 11.3 g; Cholesterol 130 mg

Spinach Egg Bites

Preparation Time: 10 minutes; Cooking Time: 20 minutes; Serve: 6
Ingredients:
- 4 eggs
- 1/8 cup coconut milk
- 2 tbsp green onion, chopped
- 1/2 cup spinach, chopped
- 1/2 cup roasted red peppers, chopped
- 1/4 tsp salt

Directions:
1. In a bowl, whisk eggs with coconut milk and salt.
2. Add spinach, green onion, and red peppers to the egg mixture and stir to combine.
3. Pour egg mixture into the silicone muffin molds and place it in instant pot air fryer basket. Place basket in the pot.
4. Seal the pot with air fryer basket and select bake mode and cook at 350 F for 20 minutes.
5. Serve and enjoy.

Nutritional Value (Amount per Serving):
Calories 59; Fat 4.2 g; Carbohydrates 1.7 g; Sugar 1.1 g; Protein 4.1 g; Cholesterol 109 mg

Bacon Egg Muffins

Preparation Time: 10 minutes; Cooking Time: 25 minutes; Serve: 6
Ingredients:
- 6 eggs, lightly beaten
- 1 tbsp fresh parsley, chopped
- 1/4 tsp dry mustard powder
- 1/4 cup coconut milk
- 2 tbsp green onion, chopped
- 4 bacon slices, cooked and crumbled
- Pepper
- Salt

Directions:
1. Spray a muffin tray with cooking spray and set aside.
2. In a bowl, whisk eggs with coconut milk, mustard, pepper, and salt until well combined.
3. Add bacon, green onion, and parsley to the egg mixture and whisk well.
4. Pour egg mixture into the silicone muffin molds and place it in instant pot air fryer basket. Place basket in the pot.
5. Seal the pot with air fryer basket and select bake mode and cook at 375 F for 20-25 minutes.
6. Serve and enjoy.

Nutritional Value (Amount per Serving):
Calories 156; Fat 12.1 g; Carbohydrates 1.3 g; Sugar 0.7 g; Protein 10.6 g; Cholesterol 178 mg

Spinach Tomato Egg Muffins

Preparation Time: 10 minutes; Cooking Time: 20 minutes; Serve: 6
Ingredients:
- 6 eggs, lightly beaten
- 1/2 cup tomatoes, chopped
- 2 tbsp water
- 1/2 tsp Italian seasoning
- 1/2 cup fresh spinach, chopped
- 1/4 tsp pepper
- 1/8 tsp salt

Directions:
1. Whisk eggs in a bowl with water, Italian seasoning, pepper, and salt.
2. Add spinach and tomatoes and whisk well.

3. Pour egg mixture into the silicone muffin molds and place it in instant pot air fryer basket. Place basket in the pot.
4. Seal the pot with air fryer basket and select bake mode and cook at 350 F for 20 minutes.
5. Serve and enjoy.

Nutritional Value (Amount per Serving):

Calories 68; Fat 4.5 g; Carbohydrates 1.1 g; Sugar 0.8 g; Protein 5.8 g; Cholesterol 164 mg

Protein Breakfast Muffins

Preparation Time: 10 minutes; Cooking Time: 25 minutes; Serve: 6

Ingredients:

- 4 eggs
- 4 oz cream cheese
- 1 scoop whey protein powder
- 2 tbsp butter, melted

Directions:

1. Add all ingredients into the bowl and whisk until combined.
2. Pour batter into the silicone muffin molds and place in instant pot air fryer basket. Place basket in the pot.
3. Seal the pot with air fryer basket and select bake mode and cook at 350 F for 25 minutes.
4. Serve and enjoy.

Nutritional Value (Amount per Serving):

Calories 162; Fat 13.7 g; Carbohydrates 1.4 g; Sugar 0.4 g; Protein 8.9 g; Cholesterol 151 mg

Spinach Cheese Quiche

Preparation Time: 10 minutes; Cooking Time: 20 minutes; Serve: 6

Ingredients:

- 8 oz frozen spinach, chopped
- 1/4 cup green pepper, chopped
- 1/4 cup onions, chopped
- 1/2 cup cheddar cheese, shredded
- 3/4 cup liquid egg substitute

Directions:

1. Add spinach to microwave bowl and microwave for 2 minutes.
2. Add the egg substitute, peppers, cheese, spinach and onions in a bowl. Whisk well.
3. Pour batter into the silicone muffin molds and place in instant pot air fryer basket. Place basket in the pot.
4. Seal the pot with air fryer basket and select bake mode and cook at 350 F for 20 minutes.
5. Serve and enjoy.

Nutritional Value (Amount per Serving):

Calories 66; Fat 3.3 g; Carbohydrates 2.3 g; Sugar 0.7 g; Protein 7.3 g; Cholesterol 10 mg

Cheese Spinach Muffins

Preparation Time: 10 minutes; Cooking Time: 25 minutes; Serve: 4

Ingredients:

- 2 eggs
- 1/2 zucchini, grated
- 1/8 cup parmesan cheese, grated
- 1/4 cup feta cheese, crumbled
- 2 onion spring, chopped
- 1/4 cup coconut flour
- 1/4 cup spinach, cooked
- 2 tbsp butter, melted
- 2 tbsp parsley, chopped
- 1/4 tsp nutmeg
- 1/8 cup water
- 1/4 tsp baking powder
- 1/8 tsp black pepper
- 1/8 tsp salt

Directions:

1. In a bowl, whisk together eggs, water, butter, and salt.
2. Add baking soda and coconut flour and mix well.

3. Add onions, nutmeg, parsley, spinach, and zucchini. Mix well.
4. Add parmesan cheese and feta cheese and stir well. Season with pepper and salt.
5. Pour batter into the silicone muffin molds and place in instant pot air fryer basket. Place basket in the pot.
6. Seal the pot with air fryer basket and select bake mode and cook at 400 F for 20-25 minutes.
7. Serve and enjoy.

Nutritional Value (Amount per Serving):
Calories 189; Fat 13.8 g; Carbohydrates 8.4 g; Sugar 1 g; Protein 8.4 g; Cholesterol 114 mg

Rutabaga Noodles

Preparation Time: 10 minutes; Cooking Time: 15 minutes; Serve: 4
Ingredients:
- 25 oz rutabaga, peel, cut and spiralized
- 1/4 cup olive oil
- 1 tsp garlic powder
- 1 tbsp chili powder
- 1 tsp salt

Directions:
1. Add all ingredients into the large bowl and toss until well combined.
2. Line instant pot air fryer basket with parchment paper.
3. Spread rutabaga mixture on parchment paper into the air fryer basket.
4. Seal the pot with air fryer basket and select bake mode and cook at 400 F for 10-15 minutes.
5. Serve and enjoy.

Nutritional Value (Amount per Serving):
Calories 180; Fat 13.3 g; Carbohydrates 14 g; Sugar 10.2 g; Protein 2.5 g; Cholesterol 0 mg

Broccoli Cheese Muffins

Preparation Time: 10 minutes; Cooking Time: 30 minutes; Serve: 6
Ingredients:
- 2 large eggs
- 1 cup almond milk
- 2 cups almond flour
- 1 cup broccoli florets, chopped
- 1 tsp baking powder
- 2 tbsp nutritional yeast
- 1/2 tsp sea salt

Directions:
1. Add all ingredients into the large bowl and whisk until well combined.
2. Pour mixture into the silicone muffin molds and place in instant pot air fryer basket. Place basket in the pot.
3. Seal the pot with air fryer basket and select bake mode and cook at 350 F for 30 minutes.
4. Serve and enjoy.

Nutritional Value (Amount per Serving):
Calories 358; Fat 29.2 g; Carbohydrates 13.3 g; Sugar 1.7 g; Protein 13 g; Cholesterol 62 mg

Tomato Basil Egg Muffins

Preparation Time: 10 minutes; Cooking Time: 15 minutes; Serve: 6
Ingredients:
- 4 eggs
- 1/4 tsp baking powder
- 1/3 cup coconut flour
- 1/4 cup water
- 1/4 cup butter, melted
- 1/2 cup fresh basil, chopped
- 1 cup cherry tomatoes, cut in half
- 1/4 cup parmesan cheese, grated
- 1/4 tsp black pepper
- 1/4 tsp salt

Directions:
1. In a bowl, whisk together eggs, water, butter, pepper, and salt.
2. Add baking soda and coconut flour and whisk until smooth.
3. Add basil, tomatoes, and parmesan cheese and mix well.
4. Pour batter into the silicone muffin molds and place in instant pot air fryer basket. Place basket in the pot.
5. Seal the pot with air fryer basket and select bake mode and cook at 400 F for 15 minutes.
6. Serve and enjoy.

Nutritional Value (Amount per Serving):
Calories 146; Fat 11.6 g; Carbohydrates 6.1 g; Sugar 1 g; Protein 5.4 g; Cholesterol 130 mg

Cheesy Egg Muffins

Preparation Time: 10 minutes; Cooking Time: 25 minutes; Serve: 6
Ingredients:
- 3 eggs
- 1/2 lb ground pork sausage
- 1 1/2 tbsp onion, minced
- 1/4 red pepper, diced
- 1/2 cup egg whites
- 1/4 cup mozzarella cheese
- 1/2 cup cheddar cheese

Directions:
1. Brown sausage over medium-high heat until meat is no pink.
2. Divide red pepper, cheese, cooked sausages, and onion into each silicone muffin molds.
3. In a large bowl, whisk together egg whites, egg, pepper, and salt.
4. Pour egg mixture into each muffin molds.
5. Place muffin molds in instant pot air fryer basket. Place basket in the pot.
6. Seal the pot with air fryer basket and select bake mode and cook at 350 F for 25 minutes.
7. Serve and enjoy.

Nutritional Value (Amount per Serving):
Calories 206; Fat 15.6 g; Carbohydrates 1.1 g; Sugar 0.7 g; Protein 14.4 g; Cholesterol 126 mg

Roasted Cauliflower

Preparation Time: 10 minutes; Cooking Time: 15 minutes; Serve: 4
Ingredients:
- 1 large cauliflower head, cut into florets
- 1/2 tsp garlic powder
- 1 lemon zest
- 3 tbsp olive oil
- 2 tsp lemon juice
- 1/2 tsp Italian seasoning
- 1/4 tsp pepper
- 1/4 tsp salt

Directions:
1. In a bowl, combine together olive oil, lemon juice, Italian seasoning, garlic powder, lemon zest, pepper, and salt.
2. Add cauliflower florets to the bowl and toss well.
3. Line instant pot air fryer basket with parchment paper.
4. Add cauliflower florets into the air fryer basket. Place basket in the pot.
5. Seal the pot with air fryer lid and select roast mode and cook at 400 F for 15 minutes.
6. Serve and enjoy.

Nutritional Value (Amount per Serving):
Calories 151; Fat 10.9 g; Carbohydrates 12.9 g; Sugar 5.6 g; Protein 4.4 g; Cholesterol 0 mg

Mushrooms & Green Beans

Preparation Time: 10 minutes; Cooking Time: 25 minutes; Serve: 4

Ingredients:
- 2 cups mushrooms, sliced
- 2 cups green beans, clean and cut into pieces
- 1/4 cup olive oil
- 1 1/2 tsp garlic, minced
- 1/4 tsp black pepper
- 1/4 tsp sea salt

Directions:
1. Add green beans, mushrooms, oil, pepper, garlic, and salt. Toss well.
2. Line instant pot air fryer basket with parchment paper.
3. Add green beans and mushrooms into the air fryer basket. Place basket in the pot.
4. Seal the pot with air fryer lid and select bake mode and cook at 400 F for 25 minutes.
5. Serve and enjoy.

Nutritional Value (Amount per Serving):
Calories 134; Fat 12.8 g; Carbohydrates 5.5 g; Sugar 1.4 g; Protein 2.2 g; Cholesterol 0 mg

Italian Frittata

Preparation Time: 10 minutes; Cooking Time: 25 minutes; Serve: 6
Ingredients:
- 6 eggs
- 2 tbsp fresh basil, chopped
- 1/4 cup parmesan cheese, grated
- 1/2 cup mozzarella cheese, chopped
- 3/4 cup cherry tomatoes, halved
- 1/2 cup of coconut milk
- 1 tsp Italian seasoning
- Pepper
- Salt

Directions:
1. Pour 1 cup water into the inner pot of instant pot duo crisp and place steamer rack in the pot.
2. Spray an 8-inch baking dish with cooking spray.
3. In a bowl, whisk eggs with remaining ingredients and pour into the baking dish.
4. Place dish on top of the steamer rack.
5. Seal the pot with pressure cooking lid and cook on high for 25 minutes.
6. Once done, release pressure using a quick release. Remove lid.
7. Serve and enjoy.

Nutritional Value (Amount per Serving):
Calories 222; Fat 15 g; Carbohydrates 2.5 g; Sugar 1.7 g; Protein 14 g; Cholesterol 185 mg

Soy Garlic Chicken

Preparation Time: 10 minutes; Cooking Time: 4 hours; Serve: 6
Ingredients:
- 1 1/2 lbs chicken breasts, skinless and boneless
- 4 garlic cloves, minced
- 1/2 tsp ground ginger
- 1/4 cup water
- 1 tsp red pepper flakes
- 3 tbsp soy sauce
- 1/2 onion, chopped

Directions:
1. Place chicken into the inner pot of instant pot duo crisp.
2. Add remaining ingredients over the chicken.
3. Seal the pot with pressure cooking lid and select slow cook mode and cook on high for 4 hours.
4. Shred the chicken using a fork and serve.

Nutritional Value (Amount per Serving):
Calories 252; Fat 8 g; Carbohydrates 8 g; Sugar 6.5 g; Protein 32 g; Cholesterol 101 mg

Creamy Chicken

Preparation Time: 10 minutes; Cooking Time: 4 hours; Serve: 4

Ingredients:

- 1 lb chicken breasts, skinless and boneless
- 1 tbsp garlic, minced
- 2 tbsp olive oil
- 1 tsp chicken bouillon
- 1/2 cup water
- 1/2 cup ricotta cheese
- 4 oz cream cheese
- 1/2 tsp ground pepper
- 1 tsp oregano, dried
- 1 tsp thyme, dried
- 1 tsp rosemary, dried

Directions:

1. Place chicken into the inner pot of instant pot.
2. Top with cream cheese and ricotta cheese.
3. Pour water, oregano, thyme, basil, thyme, rosemary, garlic, oil, bouillon, and pepper over the chicken.
4. Seal the pot with pressure cooking lid and select slow cook mode and cook on high for 4 hours.
5. Serve and enjoy.

Nutritional Value (Amount per Serving):

Calories 425; Fat 26 g; Carbohydrates 3 g; Sugar 0.2 g; Protein 38 g; Cholesterol 142 mg

Mini Frittata

Preparation Time: 10 minutes; Cooking Time: 15 minutes; Serve: 4

Ingredients:

- 6 eggs
- 1/2 small onion, chopped
- 1/2 bell pepper, chopped
- 3 bacon slices, chopped
- 1/4 cup cheddar cheese, shredded
- 1/4 cup coconut milk
- 1/4 tsp black pepper
- 1/2 tsp sea salt

Directions:

1. Add bacon slices on the bottom of each silicone muffin mold. Add chopped vegetables on top of the bacon.
2. In a bowl, whisk eggs with pepper and salt.
3. Pour egg mixture over vegetables.
4. Sprinkle shredded cheddar cheese on top.
5. Place silicone muffin molds into the instant pot air fryer basket and place basket in the pot.
6. Seal the pot with pressure cooking lid and select bake mode and cook at 350 F for 10-15 minutes.
7. Serve and enjoy.

Nutritional Value (Amount per Serving):

Calories 243; Fat 18.5 g; Carbohydrates 3.7 g; Sugar 2.2 g; Protein 15.9 g; Cholesterol 269 mg

Spinach Frittata

Preparation Time: 10 minutes; Cooking Time: 15 minutes; Serve: 4

Ingredients:

- 6 eggs
- 1/4 cup bacon, cooked and chopped
- 1 tomato, chopped
- 1/4 tsp garlic powder
- 3/4 cup fresh spinach
- 1 tsp Italian seasoning
- 1 tbsp heavy cream
- 1/4 tsp pepper
- 1/4 tsp salt

Directions:
1. In a bowl, whisk eggs with spices and heavy cream.
2. Spray a 7-inch baking dish with cooking spray.
3. Add bacon, tomato, and spinach to the prepared dish.
4. Pour egg mixture over the bacon mixture. Cover dish with foil.
5. Pour 1 1/2 cups of water into the inner pot of instant pot then place steamer rack in the pot.
6. Place baking dish on top of the steamer rack.
7. Seal the pot with pressure cooking lid and cook on high for 15 minutes.
8. Once done, release pressure using a quick release. Remove lid.
9. Serve and enjoy.

Nutritional Value (Amount per Serving):
Calories 122; Fat 8.9 g; Carbohydrates 1.8 g; Sugar 1.1 g; Protein 9.2 g; Cholesterol 253 mg

Mushroom Frittata

Preparation Time: 10 minutes; Cooking Time: 15 minutes; Serve: 2

Ingredients:
- 4 eggs
- 1 1/2 cups water
- 1/4 tsp garlic powder
- 4 oz mushrooms, sliced
- 1/8 tsp white pepper
- 1/8 tsp onion powder
- 2 tsp heavy cream
- 2 Swiss cheese slices, cut each slice into 4 pieces
- 1/4 tsp salt

Directions:
1. In a bowl, whisk eggs with spices and heavy cream.
2. Spray a 7-inch baking dish with cooking spray.
3. Add sliced mushrooms to the dish then pour egg mixture over the mushrooms.
4. Arrange cheese slices on top of the mushroom and egg mixture. Cover dish with foil.
5. Pour 1 1/2 cups of water to the instant pot then place steamer rack in the pot.
6. Place dish on top of the steamer rack.
7. Seal the pot with pressure cooking lid and cook on high for 15 minutes.
8. Once done, release pressure using a quick release. Remove lid.
9. Serve and enjoy.

Nutritional Value (Amount per Serving):
Calories 264; Fat 18.5 g; Carbohydrates 4.6 g; Sugar 2.2 g; Protein 20.6 g; Cholesterol 360 mg

Tomato Mozzarella Quiche

Preparation Time: 10 minutes; Cooking Time: 30 minutes; Serve: 6

Ingredients:
- 8 eggs
- 1 red pepper, chopped
- 1/2 cup almond flour
- 1/2 cup almond milk
- 1 1/2 cup mozzarella cheese, shredded
- 2 tbsp green onions, chopped
- 1 cup tomatoes, chopped
- 1/4 tsp pepper
- 1/4 tsp salt

Directions:
1. Pour 1 1/2 cups of water to the instant pot then place steamer rack in the pot.
2. In a large bowl, whisk eggs, almond flour, milk, pepper, and salt.
3. Add vegetables and cheese and stir to combine.
4. Pour egg mixture into the baking dish. Cover dish with foil and place on top of the steamer rack.
5. Seal the pot with pressure cooking lid and cook on high for 30 minutes.

6. Once done, allow to release pressure naturally for 10 minutes then release remaining pressure using a quick release. Remove lid.
7. Serve and enjoy.

Nutritional Value (Amount per Serving):
Calories 219; Fat 16.4 g; Carbohydrates 6.7 g; Sugar 3 g; Protein 12.4; Cholesterol 222 mg

Lemon Butter Brussels sprouts

Preparation Time: 10 minutes; Cooking Time: 5 minutes; Serve: 4
Ingredients:
- 1 lb Brussels sprouts, trimmed and washed
- 1 fresh lemon juice
- 1/4 cup parmesan cheese, grated
- 1/4 tsp garlic powder
- 2 tbsp butter
- 1 cup of water

Directions:
1. Pour water into the inner pot of instant pot duo crisp.
2. Add Brussels sprouts into the steamer basket and place basket in the pot.
3. Seal the pot with pressure cooking lid and cook on high for 2 minutes.
4. Once done, release pressure using a quick release. Remove lid.
5. Drain Brussels sprouts well and place in mixing bowl.
6. Clean the pot. Add butter into the pot and set the pot on sauté mode.
7. Add cooked Brussels sprouts, garlic powder, and lemon juice and sauté for 2-3 minutes.
8. Top with cheese and serve.

Nutritional Value (Amount per Serving):
Calories 123; Fat 7.6 g; Carbohydrates 10.9 g; Sugar 2.7 g; Protein 6.1 g; Cholesterol 20 mg

Creamy Cauliflower Mashed

Preparation Time: 10 minutes; Cooking Time: 15 minutes; Serve: 4
Ingredients:
- 1 medium cauliflower head, cut into florets
- 2 tbsp heavy cream
- 1/4 tsp garlic powder
- 1/4 tsp onion powder
- 4 tbsp butter
- 1 1/2 tbsp ranch seasoning
- 1 cup of water

Directions:
1. Pour water into the instant pot.
2. Add cauliflower florets into the steamer basket and place basket in the pot.
3. Seal the pot with pressure cooking lid and cook on high for 15 minutes.
4. Once done, release pressure using a quick release. Remove lid.
5. Transfer cauliflower florets into the mixing bowl.
6. Add remaining ingredients and mash cauliflower mixture until smooth.
7. Serve and enjoy.

Nutritional Value (Amount per Serving):
Calories 176; Fat 14.4 g; Carbohydrates 8.1 g; Sugar 3.6 g; Protein 3.2 g; Cholesterol 41 mg

Spicy Cabbage

Preparation Time: 10 minutes; Cooking Time: 5 minutes; Serve: 6
Ingredients:
- 1 cabbage head, chopped
- 2 tbsp olive oil
- 1 tsp chili powder
- 3 tbsp soy sauce
- 1/2 onion, diced
- 1 tsp paprika
- 1/2 tsp garlic salt
- 1 cup vegetable stock

- 1/2 tsp salt

Directions:

1. Add oil into the inner pot of instant pot duo crisp and set pot on sauté mode.
2. Add cabbage and sauté for 1-2 minutes.
3. Add remaining ingredients and stir everything well.
4. Seal the pot with pressure cooking lid and cook on high for 3 minutes.
5. Once done, release pressure using a quick release. Remove lid.
6. Stir and serve.

Nutritional Value (Amount per Serving):

Calories 82; Fat 4.9 g; Carbohydrates 9.1 g; Sugar 4.6 g; Protein 2.3 g; Cholesterol 0 mg

Cajun Cheese Zucchini

Preparation Time: 10 minutes; Cooking Time: 1 minute; Serve: 4

Ingredients:

- 4 zucchinis, sliced
- 1/4 cup parmesan cheese, grated
- 1/2 cup water
- 1 tbsp butter
- 1 tsp garlic powder
- 1/2 tsp paprika
- 2 tbsp Cajun seasoning

Directions:

1. Add all ingredients except cheese into the inner pot of instant pot duo crisp and stir well.
2. Seal the pot with pressure cooking lid and cook on high for 1 minute.
3. Once done, release pressure using a quick release. Remove lid.
4. Top with parmesan cheese and serve.

Nutritional Value (Amount per Serving):

Calories 80; Fat 4.6 g; Carbohydrates 7.4 g; Sugar 3.6 g; Protein 4.6 g; Cholesterol 12 mg

Spinach Feta Muffins

Preparation Time: 10 minutes; Cooking Time: 20 minutes; Serve: 6

Ingredients:

- 3 eggs
- 1/2 tsp olive oil
- 1/2 tsp dried oregano
- 1/2 tsp dried basil
- 1 tbsp olives, diced
- 1/4 cup sun-dried tomatoes, diced
- 2 tbsp spinach, cooked
- 1/4 cup egg whites
- 1 tbsp feta cheese, crumbled
- Pepper
- Salt

Directions:

1. In a bowl, whisk eggs, oil, and egg whites until well combined.
2. Add remaining ingredients and stir well.
3. Pour egg mixture into the silicone muffin molds and place it in the air fryer basket. place basket in the pot.
4. Seal the pot with air fryer lid and select bake mode and cook at 350 F for 20 minutes.
5. Serve and enjoy.

Nutritional Value (Amount per Serving):

Calories 55; Fat 3 g; Carbohydrates 1.6 g; Sugar 0.3 g; Protein 4 g; Cholesterol 83 mg

Pesto Cheese Chicken

Preparation Time: 10 minutes; Cooking Time: 35 minutes; Serve: 4

Ingredients:

- 4 chicken breasts, skinless, boneless, and cut in half
- 1 cup mozzarella cheese, shredded
- 2 large tomatoes, sliced

- 1/2 cup basil pesto
- Pepper
- Salt

Directions:
1. Line instant pot air fryer basket with aluminum foil and spray with cooking spray.
2. In a bowl, mix together pesto and chicken until coated.
3. Place chicken in air fryer basket and place basket in the pot.
4. Seal the pot with air fryer lid and select bake mode and cook at 400 F for 35 minutes.
5. Remove chicken from pot and top with cheese and tomatoes.
6. Serve and enjoy.

Nutritional Value (Amount per Serving):
Calories 314; Fat 11 g; Carbohydrates 4 g; Sugar 2 g; Protein 45 g; Cholesterol 134 mg

Meatballs

Preparation Time: 10 minutes; Cooking Time: 25 minutes; Serve: 6
Ingredients:
- 2 lbs ground beef
- 2 tbsp parsley, chopped
- 2 tbsp green onion, chopped
- 1/4 cup bell pepper, roasted and chopped
- 1/4 cup olives, chopped
- 1/4 tsp onion powder
- 1/2 tsp garlic powder
- 1/4 cup feta cheese, crumbled
- 1/4 cup sun-dried tomatoes, chopped
- 1/2 tsp black pepper
- 1/2 tsp salt

Directions:
1. Line instant pot air fryer basket with parchment paper or foil.
2. Add all ingredients into the mixing bowl and mix until combined.
3. Make small meatballs from mixture and place into the air fryer basket. Place basket in the pot.
4. Seal the pot with air fryer lid and select bake mode and cook at 400 F for 25 minutes.
5. Serve and enjoy.

Nutritional Value (Amount per Serving):
Calories 315; Fat 11 g; Carbohydrates 3 g; Sugar 0.7 g; Protein 46 g; Cholesterol 140 mg

Italian Tomato Frittata

Preparation Time: 10 minutes; Cooking Time: 15 minutes; Serve: 4
Ingredients:
- 6 eggs
- 1 cup fresh spinach, chopped
- 1 tsp Italian seasoning
- 2 tsp heavy cream
- 1/4 tsp garlic powder
- 1/4 tsp dried basil
- 2 bacon slices, cooked and chopped
- 1/4 cup cherry tomato, halved
- 1/4 tsp pepper
- 1/4 tsp salt

Directions:
1. In a bowl, whisk eggs with Italian seasoning, garlic powder, basil, heavy cream, pepper, and salt.
2. Spray a 7-inch baking dish with cooking spray.
3. Add tomato, spinach, and bacon into the prepared baking dish.
4. Pour egg mixture over tomato spinach mixture. Cover dish with foil.
5. Pour 1 1/2 cups of water into the instant pot and place steamer rack in the pot.
6. Place baking dish on a top of the steamer rack.
7. Seal the pot with pressure cooking lid and cook on high for 15 minutes.
8. Once done, release pressure using a quick release. Remove lid.
9. Slice and serve.

Nutritional Value (Amount per Serving):
Calories 163; Fat 12 g; Carbohydrates 2 g; Sugar 1.1 g; Protein 12 g; Cholesterol 260 mg

Breakfast Casserole

Preparation Time: 10 minutes; Cooking Time: 30 minutes; Serve: 4
Ingredients:

- 15 oz breakfast sausage
- 2 cups of water
- 1/4 tsp garlic powder
- 1/2 cup coconut milk
- 8 eggs, lightly beaten
- 1 1/2 cups cheddar cheese, shredded
- 1 onion, diced
- 1 bell pepper, diced
- Pepper
- Salt

Directions:

1. Spray a 7-inch baking dish with cooking spray and set aside.
2. Add sausage into the inner pot of instant pot and cook on sauté mode until sausage browned.
3. Add onion and pepper and cook for 2-3 minutes.
4. Transfer sausage mixture into the prepared baking dish. Sprinkle cheese on top of sausage.
5. In a bowl, whisk eggs and milk and pour over sausage mixture. Cover dish with foil.
6. Pour two cups of water into the instant pot then place steamer rack in the pot.
7. Place baking dish on top of the steamer rack.
8. Seal the pot with pressure cooking lid and cook on high for 25 minutes.
9. Once done, release pressure using a quick release. Remove lid.
10. Serve and enjoy.

Nutritional Value (Amount per Serving):
Calories 424; Fat 32 g; Carbohydrates 8 g; Sugar 4 g; Protein 25 g; Cholesterol 458 mg

Healthy Braised Kale

Preparation Time: 10 minutes; Cooking Time: 5 minutes; Serve: 6
Ingredients:

- 1 lb kale, chopped
- 1 tsp garlic, minced
- 1 onion, sliced
- 2 tbsp olive oil
- 14.5 oz can stew tomatoes
- 1 cup vegetable broth
- 1/4 tsp pepper
- 1 tsp salt

Directions:

1. Add oil into the inner pot of instant pot duo crisp and set pot on sauté mode.
2. Add onion and sauté for 3-4 minutes.
3. Add remaining ingredients and stir well.
4. Seal the pot with pressure cooking lid and cook on high for 1 minute.
5. Once done, allow to release pressure naturally. Remove lid.
6. Stir and serve.

Nutritional Value (Amount per Serving):
Calories 110; Fat 5 g; Carbohydrates 13 g; Sugar 3 g; Protein 4 g; Cholesterol 0 mg

Zucchini Chicken Stew

Preparation Time: 10 minutes; Cooking Time: 30 minutes; Serve: 8
Ingredients:

- 2 lbs chicken thighs, cut into pieces
- 2 celery stalk, chopped
- 1 1/2 cups mushrooms, diced
- 2 cups zucchini, diced
- 1 1/2 cups carrots, diced
- 14 oz can tomato, diced

- 1/2 tsp dried thyme
- 1 tbsp garlic, minced
- 1 cup chicken stock
- 2 onion, diced
- Pepper
- Salt

Directions:
1. Add all ingredients into the inner pot of instant pot duo crisp and stir well.
2. Seal the pot with pressure cooking lid and cook on high for 30 minutes.
3. Once done, release pressure using a quick release. Remove lid.
4. Stir and serve.

Nutritional Value (Amount per Serving):
Calories 254; Fat 8 g; Carbohydrates 8 g; Sugar 4 g; Protein 34 g; Cholesterol 100 mg

Tender & Juicy Chicken Breast

Preparation Time: 10 minutes; Cooking Time: 8 minutes; Serve: 4
Ingredients:
- 4 chicken breasts, skinless and boneless
- 1/4 tsp paprika
- 1 tsp Italian seasoning
- 1 1/2 cups chicken stock
- 1 tbsp butter
- 1/4 tsp garlic powder
- 1/8 tsp pepper
- 1/2 tsp salt

Directions:
1. Add the stock into the inner pot of instant pot duo crisp. Place chicken in the pot.
2. In a small bowl, mix Italian seasoning, garlic powder, paprika, pepper, and salt and sprinkle over chicken. Add butter on top.
3. Seal the pot with pressure cooking lid and cook on high for 8 minutes.
4. Once done, allow to release pressure naturally for 10 minutes then release remaining pressure using a quick release. Remove lid.
5. Serve and enjoy.

Nutritional Value (Amount per Serving):
Calories 310; Fat 14 g; Carbohydrates 0.7 g; Sugar 0.4 g; Protein 42 g; Cholesterol 138 mg

Creamy Parmesan Garlic Chicken

Preparation Time: 10 minutes; Cooking Time: 5 minutes; Serve: 4
Ingredients:
- 1 1/2 lbs chicken thighs, skinless and boneless
- 1 tbsp paprika
- 1/2 cup chicken stock
- 2 rosemary sprigs
- 8 garlic cloves
- 2 tbsp olive oil
- 4 tbsp parmesan cheese, grated
- 1/3 cup heavy whipping cream
- Pepper
- Salt

Directions:
1. Season chicken with pepper and salt.
2. Add oil into the inner pot of instant pot duo crisp and set pot on sauté mode.
3. Add chicken and sear until browned. Add rosemary, garlic, paprika, and stock and stir well.
4. Seal the pot with pressure cooking lid and cook on high for 5 minutes.
5. Once done, release pressure using a quick release. Remove lid.
6. Add cheese, cream, and salt and stir well and cook on sauté mode and until sauce thickens.
7. Serve and enjoy.

Nutritional Value (Amount per Serving):

Calories 460; Fat 24 g; Carbohydrates 3 g; Sugar 0.3 g; Protein 52 g; Cholesterol 170 mg

Turkey Breast

Preparation Time: 10 minutes; Cooking Time: 35 minutes; Serve: 6

Ingredients:

- 4 3/4 lbs turkey breasts, bone-in
- 2 cups chicken broth
- 1 1/2 tsp garlic powder
- 1/4 tsp onion powder
- 1 tsp dried sage
- 1 1/2 tsp dried thyme
- 1/2 tsp pepper
- 2 tsp salt

Directions:

1. Season turkey breast with garlic powder, onion powder, thyme, sage, pepper, and salt.
2. Pour broth into the inner pot of instant pot then place steamer rack in the pot.
3. Place turkey breasts on top of the steamer rack.
4. Seal the pot with pressure cooking lid and cook on high for 35 minutes.
5. Once done, allow to release pressure naturally for 10 minutes then release remaining pressure using a quick release. Remove lid.
6. Slice and serve.

Nutritional Value (Amount per Serving):

Calories 411; Fat 7 g; Carbohydrates 14 g; Sugar 14 g; Protein 65 g; Cholesterol 165 mg

Mushroom & Beans

Preparation Time: 10 minutes; Cooking Time: 2 hours 30 minutes; Serve: 8

Ingredients:

- 1 1/2 cups mushrooms, sliced
- 4 cups green beans, trimmed
- 1/4 cup water
- 1/4 cup leeks, sliced
- 6 bacon slices, cooked and sliced
- 2 tbsp butter
- 2 garlic cloves, minced
- 1/4 tsp pepper
- 1/4 tsp salt

Directions:

1. Add all ingredients into the inner pot of instant pot duo crisp and stir well.
2. Seal the pot with pressure cooking lid and select slow cook mode and cook on high for 2 hours 30 minutes.
3. Serve and enjoy.

Nutritional Value (Amount per Serving):

Calories 125; Fat 9 g; Carbohydrates 5.2 g; Sugar 1.1 g; Protein 6.8 g; Cholesterol 23 mg

Creamy Herb Mushrooms

Preparation Time: 10 minutes; Cooking Time: 4 hours; Serve: 4

Ingredients:

- 24 oz criminal mushrooms
- 1 cup vegetable broth
- 1 bay leaf
- 1/4 tsp dried thyme
- 1/2 tsp dried oregano
- 1/2 tsp dried basil
- 2 tbsp parsley, chopped
- 2 tbsp butter
- 1/4 cup half and half
- 1 tbsp garlic, minced
- Pepper
- Salt

Directions:

1. Add mushrooms, bay leaves, thyme, oregano, basil, and garlic into the inner pot of instant pot.
2. Stir in broth and season with pepper and salt.

3. Seal the pot with pressure cooking lid and select slow cook mode and cook on low for 4 hours.
4. Add butter and half and half. Stir well.
5. Garnish with parsley and serve.

Nutritional Value (Amount per Serving):
Calories 123; Fat 8.4 g; Carbohydrates 7.8 g; Sugar 3.2 g; Protein 7.3 g; Cholesterol 21 mg

Cheesy Spinach

Preparation Time: 10 minutes; Cooking Time: 60 minutes; Serve: 4
Ingredients:
- 15 oz baby spinach
- 1/4 tsp garlic powder
- 1/4 tsp onion powder
- 1 cup cheddar cheese, shredded
- 2.5 oz cream cheese
- Pepper
- Salt

Directions:
1. Add all ingredients into the inner pot of instant pot duo crisp and stir well.
2. Seal the pot with pressure cooking lid and select slow cook mode and cook on high for 1 hour.
3. Stir well and serve.

Nutritional Value (Amount per Serving):
Calories 201; Fat 16 g; Carbohydrates 5 g; Sugar 0.7 g; Protein 11.5 g; Cholesterol 49 mg

Herb Chicken

Preparation Time: 10 minutes; Cooking Time: 4 hours; Serve: 6
Ingredients:
- 2 lbs chicken thighs, skinless and boneless
- 1/2 cup chicken stock
- 1 cup olives
- 1 cup roasted red peppers, chopped
- 1 tbsp garlic cloves, minced
- 1 onion, sliced
- 1 tbsp olive oil
- 1 tsp rosemary
- 1 tsp dried thyme
- 1 tsp oregano
- 1 tbsp capers
- Pepper
- Salt

Directions:
1. Add oil into the inner pot of instant pot duo crisp and set pot on sauté mode.
2. Add chicken and sauté until brown.
3. Add garlic and onion and cook for 5 minutes.
4. Add remaining ingredients and stir well.
5. Seal the pot with pressure cooking lid and select slow cook mode and cook on high for 4 hours.
6. Serve and enjoy.

Nutritional Value (Amount per Serving):
Calories 354; Fat 16.1 g; Carbohydrates 6 g; Sugar 2.2 g; Protein 44.7 g; Cholesterol 135 mg

Turkey Breast

Preparation Time: 10 minutes; Cooking Time: 4 hours; Serve: 6
Ingredients:
- 4 lbs turkey breast
- 1 tsp dried oregano
- 1/2 fresh lemon juice
- 1/2 cup sun-dried tomatoes, chopped
- 1/2 cup olives, chopped
- 1 onion, chopped
- 1 cup chicken stock
- 1 tbsp garlic cloves, chopped

- 1/4 tsp pepper
- 1/2 tsp salt

Directions:
1. Add all ingredients into the inner pot of instant pot duo crisp and stir well.
2. Seal the pot with pressure cooking lid and select slow cook mode and cook on high for 4 hours.
3. Stir well and serve.

Nutritional Value (Amount per Serving):
Calories 343; Fat 6.4 g; Carbohydrates 14 g; Sugar 12 g; Protein 52.3 g; Cholesterol 130 mg

Easy Chicken with Mushrooms

Preparation Time: 10 minutes; Cooking Time: 6 hours; Serve: 2
Ingredients:
- 2 chicken breasts, skinless and boneless
- 1 cup chicken stock
- 1/2 tsp thyme, dried
- 1 cup mushrooms, sliced
- 1 onion, sliced
- 1/4 tsp garlic powder
- 1/4 tsp onion powder
- Pepper
- Salt

Directions:
1. Add all ingredients into the inner pot of instant pot duo crisp and stir well.
2. Seal the pot with pressure cooking lid and select slow cook mode and cook on low for 6 hours.
3. Stir well and serve.

Nutritional Value (Amount per Serving):
Calories 315; Fat 11.3 g; Carbohydrates 7.3 g; Sugar 3.5 g; Protein 44.4 g; Cholesterol 130 mg

Baked Zucchini Chicken

Preparation Time: 10 minutes; Cooking Time: 30 minutes; Serve: 4
Ingredients:
- 2 lbs chicken tenders
- 2 dill sprigs
- 1 large zucchini
- 1 cup grape tomatoes
- For topping:
- 1 tbsp olive oil
- 1 tbsp fresh lemon juice
- 1 tbsp fresh dill, chopped
- 2 tbsp feta cheese, crumbled

Directions:
1. Line instant pot air fryer basket with parchment paper and foil.
2. Add chicken, zucchini, dill, and tomatoes into the air fryer basket. Place basket in the pot.
3. Seal the pot with air fryer basket and select bake mode and cook at 400 F for 30 minutes.
4. Meanwhile, in a small bowl, stir together all topping ingredients.
5. Transfer chicken vegetable mixture on the serving plate.
6. Sprinkle topping mixture on top of chicken and vegetables.
7. Serve and enjoy.

Nutritional Value (Amount per Serving):
Calories 499; Fat 21.7 g; Carbohydrates 5.6 g; Sugar 2.9 g; Protein 68 g; Cholesterol 206 mg

Lemon Garlic Chicken

Preparation Time: 10 minutes; Cooking Time: 40 minutes; Serve: 4
Ingredients:
- 2 lbs chicken drumsticks
- 2 tbsp parsley, chopped
- 1 fresh lemon juice
- 10 garlic cloves, sliced
- 2 tbsp olive oil
- Pepper

- Salt

Directions:
1. Line instant pot air fryer basket with parchment paper and foil.
2. Add chicken, parsley, lemon juice, garlic, oil, pepper, and salt into the mixing bowl and toss well.
3. Transfer chicken into the air fryer basket and place basket in the pot.
4. Seal the pot with air fryer basket and select bake mode and cook at 400 F for 35-40 minutes.
5. Serve and enjoy.

Nutritional Value (Amount per Serving):
Calories 458; Fat 20.1 g; Carbohydrates 2.9 g; Sugar 0.4 g; Protein 63 g; Cholesterol 200 mg

Mustard Chicken

Preparation Time: 10 minutes; Cooking Time: 20 minutes; Serve: 4

Ingredients:
- 1 lbs chicken tenders
- 1 tsp paprika
- 2 garlic cloves, minced
- 1/2 oz fresh lemon juice
- 2 tbsp fresh tarragon, chopped
- 1/2 cup whole grain mustard
- 1/2 tsp pepper
- 1/4 tsp kosher salt

Directions:
1. Line instant pot air fryer basket with parchment paper and foil.
2. Add all ingredients except chicken to the large bowl and mix well.
3. Add chicken to the bowl and toss until well coated.
4. Transfer chicken into the air fryer basket and place basket in the pot.
5. Seal the pot with air fryer basket and select bake mode and cook at 400 F for 15-20 minutes.
6. Serve and enjoy.

Nutritional Value (Amount per Serving):
Calories 243; Fat 9.6 g; Carbohydrates 3.5 g; Sugar 0.1 g; Protein 33.3 g; Cholesterol 101 mg

Spicy Shrimp

Preparation Time: 10 minutes; Cooking Time: 50 minutes; Serve: 8

Ingredients:
- 2 lbs large shrimp, peeled and deveined
- 3/4 cup olive oil
- 1 tbsp parsley, minced
- 1/4 tsp red pepper flakes, crushed
- 1 tsp paprika
- 6 garlic cloves, sliced
- 1/4 tsp pepper
- 1 tsp kosher salt

Directions:
1. Add all ingredients except shrimp into the inner pot of instant pot duo crisp and stir well.
2. Seal the pot with pressure cooking lid select slow cook mode and cook on high for 30 minutes.
3. Add shrimp and stir well.
4. Seal the pot with pressure cooking lid select slow cook mode and cook on high for 20 minutes.
5. Stir and serve.

Nutritional Value (Amount per Serving):
Calories 258; Fat 19 g; Carbohydrates 3 g; Sugar 0.1 g; Protein 21.5 g; Cholesterol 162 mg

Greek Salmon

Preparation Time: 10 minutes; Cooking Time: 20 minutes; Serve: 1

Ingredients:
- 4 oz salmon fillet
- 1 tbsp fresh parsley, chopped
- 1 tbsp olive oil
- 1 garlic clove, sliced
- 1/4 onion, diced
- 1/2 lemon juice
- 4 cherry tomatoes
- Pepper
- Salt

Directions:
1. Add all ingredients except lemon juice into the mixing bowl and let sit for 1 hour.
2. Line instant pot air fryer basket with parchment paper or foil.
3. Transfer bowl mixture into the air fryer basket and place basket in the pot.
4. Seal the pot with air fryer lid and select bake mode and cook at 350 F for 20 minutes.
5. Drizzle with lemon juice and serve.
6. Serve and enjoy.

Nutritional Value (Amount per Serving):
Calories 381; Fat 22.3 g; Carbohydrates 3.9 g; Sugar 14.7 g; Protein 27.1 g; Cholesterol 50 mg

Quick Shrimp Scampi

Preparation Time: 10 minutes; Cooking Time: 13 minutes; Serve: 4

Ingredients:
- 1 lb shrimp, peeled and deveined
- 2 tbsp olive oil
- 1/4 cup parmesan cheese, grated
- 8 garlic cloves, peeled
- 1 fresh lemon, cut into wedges
- Pepper
- Salt

Directions:
1. Line instant pot air fryer basket with parchment paper or foil.
2. Add all ingredients except parmesan cheese into the bowl and toss well.
3. Transfer bowl mixture into the air fryer basket and place basket in the pot.
4. Seal the pot with air fryer lid and select bake mode and cook at 400 F for 13 minutes.
5. Sprinkle with parmesan cheese and serve.

Nutritional Value (Amount per Serving):
Calories 234; Fat 10.4 g; Carbohydrates 6.7 g; Sugar 1.1 g; Protein 28.6 g; Cholesterol 243 mg

Stuffed Pork Chops

Preparation Time: 10 minutes; Cooking Time: 35 minutes; Serve: 4

Ingredients:
- 4 pork chops, boneless and thick-cut
- 2 tbsp olives, chopped
- 2 tbsp sun-dried tomatoes, chopped
- 1/2 cup feta cheese, crumbled
- 1 tsp garlic cloves, minced
- 2 tbsp fresh parsley, chopped
- Pepper
- Salt

Directions:
1. Line instant pot air fryer basket with parchment paper or foil.
2. In a bowl, mix together feta cheese, garlic, parsley, olives, and sun-dried tomatoes.
3. Stuff feta cheese mixture all the pork chops. Season with pepper and salt.
4. Place pork chops into the air fryer basket and place basket in the pot.
5. Seal the pot with air fryer lid and select bake mode and cook at 375 F for 35 minutes.
6. Serve and enjoy.

Nutritional Value (Amount per Serving):

Calories 313; Fat 24.4 g; Carbohydrates 1.6 g; Sugar 1 g; Protein 20.8 g; Cholesterol 85 mg

Cauliflower Hash Browns

Preparation Time: 10 minutes; Cooking Time: 15 minutes; Serve: 4
Ingredients:
- 2 1/2 cups cauliflower, grated
- 3/4 cup cheddar cheese, shredded
- 1 large egg, lightly beaten
- 1/4 tsp garlic powder
- 1/4 tsp cayenne pepper
- 1/8 tsp pepper
- 1/2 tsp salt

Directions:
1. Line instant pot air fryer basket with parchment paper or foil.
2. Add all ingredients into the bowl and mix well.
3. Make 4 hash browns from mixture and place on parchment paper into the air fryer basket. Place basket in the pot.
4. Seal the pot with air fryer lid and select bake mode and cook at 400 F for 15 minutes.
5. Serve and enjoy.

Nutritional Value (Amount per Serving):
Calories 82; Fat 4 g; Carbohydrates 3 g; Sugar 1 g; Protein 5 g; Cholesterol 45 mg

Coconut Porridge

Preparation Time: 10 minutes; Cooking Time: 10 minutes; Serve: 6
Ingredients:
- 1 cup shredded coconut, unsweetened
- 1/4 tsp nutmeg
- 1/2 tsp cinnamon
- 1 tsp vanilla
- 4 tbsp psyllium husks
- 4 tbsp coconut flour
- 2 2/3 cups water
- 2 cups almond milk, unsweetened
- 1 tsp liquid stevia

Directions:
1. Add coconut into the inner pot of instant pot duo crisp and set pot on sauté mode.
2. Sauté coconut until toasted.
3. Add water and almond milk and stir well.
4. Seal the pot with pressure cooking lid and select high pressure and set a timer for 0 minutes.
5. Once done, allow to release pressure naturally for 10 minutes then release remaining pressure using a quick release. Remove lid.
6. Add remaining ingredients and stir well.
7. Serve and enjoy.

Nutritional Value (Amount per Serving):
Calories 300; Fat 24 g; Carbohydrates 14 g; Sugar 1 g; Protein 3 g; Cholesterol 0 mg

Coconut Kale Muffins

Preparation Time: 10 minutes; Cooking Time: 30 minutes; Serve: 4
Ingredients:
- 3 large eggs
- 1/4 cup coconut milk
- 1/2 cup kale, chopped
- 1/8 cup chives, chopped
- Pepper
- Salt

Directions:
1. Add all ingredients into the bowl and whisk well.
2. Pour mixture into the silicone muffin molds and place into the air fryer basket. Place basket int the pot.

3. Seal the pot with air fryer lid and select bake mode and cook at 350 F for 30 minutes.
4. Serve and enjoy.

Nutritional Value (Amount per Serving):
Calories 93; Fat 7 g; Carbohydrates 2 g; Sugar 0.8 g; Protein 5 g; Cholesterol 140 mg

Moist Cinnamon Muffins

Preparation Time: 10 minutes; Cooking Time: 15 minutes; Serve: 6
Ingredients:

- 1/4 cup pumpkin puree
- 1/4 cup almond butter
- 1/4 cup coconut oil
- 1/2 tbsp cinnamon
- 1/2 tsp baking powder
- 1 scoop vanilla protein powder
- 1/4 cup almond flour

Directions:
1. In a large bowl, mix together all dry ingredients.
2. Add wet ingredients into the dry ingredients and mix until combined.
3. Pour batter into silicone muffin molds and place into the air fryer basket. Place basket into the pot.
4. Seal the pot with air fryer lid and select bake mode and cook at 350 F for 15 minutes.
5. Serve and enjoy.

Nutritional Value (Amount per Serving):
Calories 80; Fat 7.1 g; Carbohydrates 1.6 g; Sugar 0.4 g; Protein 3.5 g; Cholesterol 0 mg

Meatloaf

Preparation Time: 10 minutes; Cooking Time: 40 minutes; Serve: 8
Ingredients:

- 2 eggs
- 1/2 cup parmesan cheese, grated
- 1/2 cup marinara sauce, sugar-free
- 1 cup cottage cheese
- 1 lb mozzarella cheese, cut into cubes
- 2 lbs ground turkey
- 2 tsp Italian seasoning
- 1/4 cup basil pesto
- 1 tsp salt

Directions:
1. Grease instant pot loaf pan with butter and set aside.
2. Add all ingredients into the mixing bowl and mix until well combined.
3. Transfer bowl mixture into the prepared loaf pan.
4. Pour 1/2 cup water into the instant pot and place steamer rack in the pot.
5. Place loaf pan on top of the steamer rack.
6. Seal the pot with air fryer lid and select bake mode and cook at 400 F for 40 minutes.
7. Slice and serve.

Nutritional Value (Amount per Serving):
Calories 350; Fat 18 g; Carbohydrates 4.5 g; Sugar 1 g; Protein 42 g; Cholesterol 177 mg

Bacon Egg Muffins

Preparation Time: 10 minutes; Cooking Time: 25 minutes; Serve: 6
Ingredients:

- 6 eggs
- 4 bacon slices, cooked and crumbled
- 1 tbsp fresh parsley, chopped
- 1/4 tsp mustard powder
- 1/4 cup heavy cream
- 2 tbsp green onion, chopped
- 2 oz cheddar cheese, shredded
- Pepper
- Salt

Directions:

1. In a bowl, whisk together eggs, mustard powder, heavy cream, pepper, and salt.
2. Divide cheddar cheese, onions, and bacon into the silicone muffin molds then pour egg mixture into each mold.
3. Place silicone muffin molds into the instant pot air fryer basket and place basket in the pot.
4. Seal the pot with air fryer lid and select bake mode and cook at 375 F for 25 minutes.
5. Serve and enjoy.

Nutritional Value (Amount per Serving):
   Calories 116; Fat 8 g; Carbohydrates 1 g; Sugar 0.5 g; Protein 8s g; Cholesterol 178 mg

Zucchini Spinach Muffins

Preparation Time: 10 minutes; Cooking Time: 25 minutes; Serve: 4
Ingredients:

- 2 eggs
- 1/2 zucchini, grated
- 1/8 cup parmesan cheese, grated
- 1/4 cup feta cheese, crumbled
- 2 tbsp onion spring, chopped
- 1/4 cup coconut flour
- 1/8 cup butter, melted
- 2 tbsp parsley, chopped
- 1/4 tsp nutmeg
- 1/8 cup water
- 1/4 tsp baking powder
- 1/4 cup spinach, cooked
- 1/8 tsp black pepper
- 1/8 tsp salt

Directions:
1. In a bowl, whisk together eggs, water, butter, and salt.
2. Add baking soda and coconut flour and mix well.
3. Add onions, nutmeg, parsley, spinach, zucchini, parmesan cheese, feta cheese, pepper, and salt and stir well.
4. Pour batter into the silicone muffin molds.
5. Place silicone muffin molds into the instant pot air fryer basket and place basket in the pot.
6. Seal the pot with air fryer lid and select bake mode and cook at 400 F for 20-25 minutes.
7. Serve and enjoy.

Nutritional Value (Amount per Serving):
   Calories 236; Fat 18 g; Carbohydrates 4 g; Sugar 1 g; Protein 15 g; Cholesterol 135 mg

Baked Coconut Chicken Wings

Preparation Time: 10 minutes; Cooking Time: 55 minutes; Serve: 4
Ingredients:

- 2 lbs chicken wings
- 1/8 tsp paprika
- 2 tsp seasoned salt
- 1/2 cup coconut flour
- 1/4 tsp garlic powder
- 1/2 tsp chili powder

Directions:
1. In a bowl, add all ingredients except chicken wings and mix well.
2. Add chicken wings to the bowl and toss until well coated.
3. Line instant pot air fryer basket with parchment paper or foil.
4. Add chicken wings into the air fryer basket and place basket in the pot.
5. Seal the pot with air fryer lid and select bake mode and cook at 400 F for 55 minutes.
6. Serve and enjoy.

Nutritional Value (Amount per Serving):
   Calories 440; Fat 17 g; Carbohydrates 1 g; Sugar 0.2 g; Protein 66 g; Cholesterol 202 mg

Butter Garlic Chicken

Preparation Time: 10 minutes; Cooking Time: 40 minutes; Serve: 4
Ingredients:

- 2 lbs chicken drumsticks
- 1 fresh lemon juice
- 8 garlic cloves, minced
- 2 tbsp olive oil
- 4 tbsp butter, melted
- 2 tbsp parsley, chopped
- Pepper
- Salt

Directions:

1. Line instant pot air fryer basket with parchment paper or foil.
2. Add chicken into the large bowl and pour remaining ingredients over chicken and toss well.
3. Transfer chicken into the air fryer basket and place basket in the pot.
4. Seal the pot with air fryer lid and select bake mode and cook at 400 F for 35-40 minutes.
5. Serve and enjoy.

Nutritional Value (Amount per Serving):
Calories 560; Fat 31 g; Carbohydrates 3 g; Sugar 0.4 g; Protein 62 g; Cholesterol 230 mg

Sausage Breakfast Muffins

Preparation Time: 10 minutes; Cooking Time: 25 minutes; Serve: 6
Ingredients:

- 3 eggs
- 1/2 lb ground pork sausage
- 2 tbsp onion, minced
- 1/4 red pepper, diced
- 1/2 cup egg whites
- 1/4 cup mozzarella cheese
- 1/2 cup cheddar cheese
- Pepper
- Salt

Directions:

1. Add sausage in a pan and cook over medium-high heat until meat is no pink.
2. Divide red pepper, cheese, cooked sausages, and onion into each silicone muffin molds.
3. In a large bowl, whisk together egg whites, egg, pepper, and salt.
4. Pour egg mixture into each muffin mold.
5. Place silicone muffin molds into the instant pot air fryer basket and place basket in the pot.
6. Seal the pot with air fryer lid and select bake mode and cook at 350 F for 20-25 minutes.
7. Serve and enjoy.

Nutritional Value (Amount per Serving):
Calories 188; Fat 12 g; Carbohydrates 2 g; Sugar 0.7 g; Protein 12 g; Cholesterol 115 mg

Moist Cream Cheese Muffins

Preparation Time: 10 minutes; Cooking Time: 20 minutes; Serve: 5
Ingredients:

- 1 egg
- 1/4 cup Erythritol
- 4 oz cream cheese
- 1/2 tsp ground cinnamon
- 1/4 tsp vanilla

Directions:

1. In a bowl, beat together cream cheese, vanilla, Erythritol, and eggs until fluffy.
2. Pour batter into the silicone muffin molds.
3. Place silicone muffin molds into the instant pot air fryer basket and place basket in the pot.
4. Seal the pot with air fryer lid and select bake mode and cook at 350 F for 20 minutes.

5. Serve and enjoy.

Nutritional Value (Amount per Serving):

Calories 93; Fat 8 g; Carbohydrates 11 g; Sugar 12 g; Protein 2 g; Cholesterol 55 mg

Parmesan Salmon

Preparation Time: 10 minutes; Cooking Time: 15 minutes; Serve: 4

Ingredients:

- 4 salmon fillets
- 1/4 cup parmesan cheese, grated
- 1/4 cup walnuts
- 1 tsp olive oil
- 1 tbsp lemon rind
- Pepper
- Salt

Directions:

1. Line instant pot air fryer basket with parchment paper or foil.
2. Place salmon in the air fryer basket and place basket in the pot.
3. Add walnuts into the food processor and process until finely ground.
4. Mix ground walnuts with cheese, oil, and lemon rind. Stir well.
5. Spread walnut mixture over the salmon fillets and press gently.
6. Seal the pot with air fryer lid and select bake mode and cook at 400 F for 15 minutes.
7. Serve and enjoy.

Nutritional Value (Amount per Serving):

Calories 420; Fat 26 g; Carbohydrates 2 g; Sugar 0.3 g; Protein 45 g; Cholesterol 97 mg

Roasted Cauliflower

Preparation Time: 10 minutes; Cooking Time: 15 minutes; Serve: 4

Ingredients:

- 1 large cauliflower head, cut into florets
- 1 lemon zest
- 3 tbsp olive oil
- 2 tsp lemon juice
- 1/2 tsp Italian seasoning
- 1/2 tsp garlic powder
- 1/4 tsp pepper
- 1/4 tsp salt

Directions:

1. In a bowl, mix together olive oil, lemon juice, Italian seasoning, garlic powder, lemon zest, pepper, and salt.
2. Add cauliflower florets to the bowl and toss well.
3. Add cauliflower florets into the air fryer basket and place basket in the pot.
4. Seal the pot with air fryer lid and select roast mode and cook at 400 F for 15 minutes.
5. Serve and enjoy.

Nutritional Value (Amount per Serving):

Calories 146; Fat 10 g; Carbohydrates 11 g; Sugar 5 g; Protein 4 g; Cholesterol 0 mg

Basil Pesto Salmon

Preparation Time: 10 minutes; Cooking Time: 20 minutes; Serve: 2

Ingredients:

- 2 salmon fillets
- 1/4 cup parmesan cheese, grated
- For pesto:
- 1/4 cup pine nuts
- 1/4 cup olive oil
- 1 1/2 cups fresh basil leaves
- 2 garlic cloves, peeled and chopped
- 1/4 cup parmesan cheese, grated
- 1/2 tsp black pepper
- 1/2 tsp salt

Directions:

1. Add all pesto ingredients to the blender and blend until smooth.

2. Line instant pot air fryer basket with parchment paper or foil.
3. Place salmon fillet on parchment paper in air fryer basket.
4. Spread 2 tablespoons of the pesto on each salmon fillet.
5. Sprinkle cheese on top of the pesto.
6. Seal the pot with air fryer lid and select bake mode and cook at 400 F for 20 minutes.
7. Serve and enjoy.

Nutritional Value (Amount per Serving):
Calories 725; Fat 57 g; Carbohydrates 4 g; Sugar 0.5 g; Protein 50 g; Cholesterol 108 mg

Healthy Garlic Brussels sprouts

Preparation Time: 10 minutes; Cooking Time: 40 minutes; Serve: 8
Ingredients:

- 2 lbs Brussels sprouts, trimmed and quartered
- 2 tbsp coconut oil, melted
- 8 garlic cloves, sliced
- 1/8 tsp black pepper
- 1 tsp salt

Directions:
1. Line instant pot air fryer basket with parchment paper or foil.
2. In a bowl, mix together Brussels sprouts, coconut oil, and garlic.
3. Add Brussels sprouts mixture into the air fryer basket and place basket in the pot.
4. Seal the pot with air fryer lid and select bake mode and cook at 400 F for 40 minutes.
5. Season with pepper and salt.
6. Serve and enjoy.

Nutritional Value (Amount per Serving):
Calories 82; Fat 3.8 g; Carbohydrates 11.1 g; Sugar 32.5 g; Protein 4 g; Cholesterol 0 mg

Stuffed Chicken Jalapenos

Preparation Time: 10 minutes; Cooking Time: 25 minutes; Serve: 6
Ingredients:

- 3 jalapenos, halved
- 1/8 cup green onion, sliced
- 1/8 cup Monterey jack cheese, shredded
- 1/4 cup chicken, cooked and shredded
- 1/8 tsp garlic powder
- 2 oz cream cheese
- 1/8 tsp dried oregano
- 1/8 tsp dried basil
- 1/8 tsp salt

Directions:
1. Line instant pot air fryer basket with parchment paper or foil.
2. Mix all ingredients in a bowl except jalapenos.
3. Spoon 1 tablespoon mixture into each jalapeno halved and place in the air fryer basket. Place basket in the pot.
4. Seal the pot with air fryer lid and select bake mode and cook at 390 F for 25 minutes.
5. Serve and enjoy.

Nutritional Value (Amount per Serving):
Calories 107; Fat 8 g; Carbohydrates 2 g; Sugar 0.7 g; Protein 6 g; Cholesterol 34 mg

Cinnamon Flax Muffins

Preparation Time: 10 minutes; Cooking Time: 20 minutes; Serve: 6
Ingredients:

- 4 eggs, lightly beaten
- 1 tsp cinnamon
- 1 tsp vanilla
- 1/8 cup coconut flour
- 1/4 cup Swerve
- 1/4 cup olive oil

- 1/2 cup walnuts, chopped
- 1/4 tsp baking soda
- 1/2 tsp lemon juice
- 1/2 cup ground flax seed
- Pinch of salt

Directions:
1. Add all ingredients into the large bowl and mix until combined.
2. Pour batter into the silicone muffin molds.
3. Place silicone muffin molds into the air fryer basket and place basket in the pot.
4. Seal the pot with air fryer lid and select bake mode and cook at 325 F for 20 minutes.
5. Serve and enjoy.

Nutritional Value (Amount per Serving):
Calories 219; Fat 20 g; Carbohydrates 6 g; Sugar 1 g; Protein 6 g; Cholesterol 55 mg

Roasted Broccoli

Preparation Time: 10 minutes; Cooking Time: 20 minutes; Serve: 4
Ingredients:
- 1 1/2 lbs broccoli, cut into florets
- 1 tsp garlic cloves, sliced
- 3 tbsp olive oil
- 1/4 cup cheese, grated
- 3 tbsp slivered almonds, toasted
- 1 tbsp lemon juice
- 1/4 tsp pepper
- 1/4 tsp salt

Directions:
1. Line instant pot air fryer basket with parchment paper or foil.
2. Add broccoli, pepper, salt, garlic, and oil in large bowl and toss well.
3. Add broccoli mixture into the air fryer basket and place basket in the pot.
4. Seal the pot with air fryer lid and select roast mode and cook at 400 F for 20 minutes.
5. Add lemon juice, grated cheese, and almonds over broccoli and toss well.
6. Serve and enjoy.

Nutritional Value (Amount per Serving):
Calories 206; Fat 15 g; Carbohydrates 13 g; Sugar 3 g; Protein 7 g; Cholesterol 7 mg

Roasted Broccoli Cauliflower

Preparation Time: 10 minutes; Cooking Time: 15 minutes; Serve: 6
Ingredients:
- 4 cups cauliflower florets
- 6 garlic cloves, minced
- 1/3 cup olive oil
- 4 cups broccoli florets
- 2/3 cup parmesan cheese, grated and divided
- Pepper
- Salt

Directions:
1. Line instant pot air fryer basket with parchment paper or foil.
2. Add cauliflower, broccoli, half cheese, garlic, and olive oil in a bowl and toss well. Season with pepper and salt.
3. Add broccoli and cauliflower mixture into the air fryer basket and place basket in the pot.
4. Seal the pot with air fryer lid and select bake mode and cook at 400 F for 15 minutes.
5. Add cheese and toss well.
6. Serve and enjoy.

Nutritional Value (Amount per Serving):
Calories 81; Fat 6.7 g; Carbohydrates 3.1 g; Sugar 1.1 g; Protein 1.9 g; Cholesterol 5 mg

Zucchini Patties

Preparation Time: 10 minutes; Cooking Time: 15 minutes; Serve: 4
Ingredients:

- 1 egg, beaten
- 1 1/2 cups zucchini, shredded
- 1/4 tsp garlic powder
- 1/4 tsp basil, dried
- 1/4 cup almond flour
- 1/4 cup cheddar cheese, shredded
- 1/8 tsp pepper
- 1/4 tsp salt

Directions:

1. Line instant pot air fryer basket with parchment paper or foil.
2. Place shredded zucchini on a paper towel and pat dry.
3. Add zucchini and remaining ingredients into the bowl and mix well.
4. Make small patties from mixture and place on parchment paper in the air fryer basket.
5. Seal the pot with air fryer lid and select bake mode and cook at 400 F for 15 minutes.
6. Serve and enjoy.

Nutritional Value (Amount per Serving):

Calories 52; Fat 2 g; Carbohydrates 4 g; Sugar 1 g; Protein 3 g; Cholesterol 32 mg

Chapter 2: Beef, Pork & Lamb

Delicious Beef Roast

Preparation Time: 10 minutes; Cooking Time: 8 hours; Serve: 2

Ingredients:
- 1 lb bottom round roast
- 1/2 tsp oregano, dried
- 1/2 tsp rosemary, crushed
- 1/2 tsp fennel seed
- 1 tsp garlic, sliced
- 1/4 cup water
- 1/4 cup onions, caramelized
- 1/2 tsp pepper
- 1/4 tsp salt

Directions:
1. In a bowl, combine together rosemary, fennel seeds, pepper, oregano, and salt.
2. Rub rosemary mixture all over meat and place in the refrigerator for 30 minutes.
3. Place marinated roast into the inner pot of instant pot duo crisp and top with garlic, onions, and water.
4. Seal the pot with pressure cooking lid and select slow cook mode and cook on low for 8 hours.
5. Remove roast from pot and slice.
6. Serve and enjoy.

Nutritional Value (Amount per Serving):
   Calories 334; Fat 12.2 g; Carbohydrates 2.8 g; Sugar 0.6 g; Protein 50.6 g; Cholesterol 151 mg

Spicy Pulled Beef

Preparation Time: 10 minutes; Cooking Time: 8 hours; Serve: 6

Ingredients:
- 2 lbs lean beef eye round, trimmed
- 2 tbsp fresh lime juice
- 1 tbsp Worcestershire sauce
- 1 cup can tomato, diced
- 1/4 cup beef broth
- 2 jalapeno peppers
- 1 onion, diced
- 1/4 tsp coriander
- 1/4 tsp oregano
- 1/2 tsp cumin
- 1 tsp garlic, sliced
- 1 red bell pepper, diced

Directions:
1. Season meat with pepper and salt and place into the inner pot of instant pot duo crisp.
2. Add garlic, red pepper, onion, and jalapeno peppers around the beef.
3. Mix together coriander, lime juice, Worcestershire sauce, tomatoes, oregano, cumin, and broth and pour over meat.
4. Seal the pot with pressure cooking lid and select slow cook mode and cook on low for 8 hours.
5. Remove meat from pot and shred using a fork.
6. Return shredded meat to the pot and stir well.
7. Serve and enjoy.

Nutritional Value (Amount per Serving):
   Calories 278; Fat 6.4 g; Carbohydrates 7.6 g; Sugar 4.1 g; Protein 45.5 g; Cholesterol 83 mg

Tasty Beef Tacos

Preparation Time: 10 minutes; Cooking Time: 8 hours 10 minutes; Serve: 8

Ingredients:
- 3 lbs lean top round roast
- 4 tbsp adobo sauce
- 1 onion, diced
- 1 tbsp garlic, minced
- 2 ancho chili peppers, seeded
- 2 cups vegetable broth

- 1/2 tsp cumin
- 1/2 tsp coriander
- 1 tsp oregano
- Pepper
- Salt

Directions:
1. In a bowl, add dried chilies and broth. Cover and let it sit for 30 minutes.
2. Add broth and dried chilies into the blender along with cumin, coriander, oregano, adobo sauce, onion, and garlic and blend until smooth.
3. Season beef with pepper and salt and place in the inner pot of instant pot duo crisp.
4. Pour blended sauce over beef.
5. Seal the pot with pressure cooking lid and select slow cook mode and cook on low for 8 hours.
6. Remove meat from pot and shred using a fork.
7. Clean the pot. Add shredded meat into the air fryer basket and place basket into the pot.
8. Seal the pot with air fryer lid and select broil mode and cook for 10 minutes.
9. Serve and enjoy.

Nutritional Value (Amount per Serving):
Calories 287; Fat 6.2 g; Carbohydrates 5.6 g; Sugar 3.3 g; Protein 49.5 g; Cholesterol 175 mg

Coconut Beef Curry

Preparation Time: 10 minutes; Cooking Time: 4 hours; Serve: 4
Ingredients:
- 1 lb lean ground beef
- 1 tsp lime zest
- 1 1/2 cups can tomato, sauce
- 1 tbsp curry paste
- 1 tsp ginger
- 1 tsp garlic, minced
- 1 leek, sliced
- 2 tsp lime juice
- 1/2 can coconut milk
- 1 tbsp soy sauce

Directions:
1. Add the meat into the inner pot of instant pot duo crisp and cook on sauté mode until browned.
2. Add remaining ingredients and stir well.
3. Seal the pot with pressure cooking lid and select slow cook mode and cook on low for 4 hours.
4. Stir and serve.

Nutritional Value (Amount per Serving):
Calories 391; Fat 20 g; Carbohydrates 8.9 g; Sugar 2.5 g; Protein 43 g; Cholesterol 122 mg

Lime Garlic Steak Carnitas

Preparation Time: 10 minutes; Cooking Time: 6 hours; Serve: 4
Ingredients:
- 1 1/2 lbs beef chuck, cut into small pieces
- 1 fresh lime juice
- 1 lime zest
- 2 chilies in adobo sauce
- 1 tbsp garlic, minced
- 1 orange juice
- 1 jalapeno pepper, halved

Directions:
1. Add all ingredients into the inner pot of instant pot duo crisp and stir well.
2. Seal the pot with pressure cooking lid and select slow cook mode and cook on low for 6 hours.
3. Serve and enjoy.

Nutritional Value (Amount per Serving):
Calories 346; Fat 11.2 g; Carbohydrates 5.8 g; Sugar 3.2 g; Protein 52 g; Cholesterol 152 mg

Chili Garlic Brisket

Preparation Time: 10 minutes; Cooking Time: 10 hours 10 minutes; Serve: 6

Ingredients:

- 3 lbs brisket
- 1/2 tsp chili powder
- 1 tsp garlic, minced
- 1/4 cup beef broth
- 14.5 oz can tomato, crushed
- 1/4 tsp pepper
- 1/2 tsp sea salt

Directions:

1. Rub spices all over brisket and place in the inner pot of instant pot duo crisp.
2. Pour broth and crushed tomatoes over brisket.
3. Seal the pot with pressure cooking lid and select slow cook mode and cook on low for 10 hours.
4. Remove meat from pot and shred using a fork.
5. Clean the pot. Add shredded meat into the air fryer basket and place basket into the pot.
6. Seal the pot with air fryer lid and select broil mode and cook for 10 minutes.
7. Serve and enjoy.

Nutritional Value (Amount per Serving):

Calories 483; Fat 16 g; Carbohydrates 3.9 g; Sugar 2.4 g; Protein 76.3 g; Cholesterol 156 mg

Taco Pork Roast

Preparation Time: 10 minutes; Cooking Time: 6 hours; Serve: 4

Ingredients:

- 2 lbs pork roasts
- 1 packet taco seasoning
- 14 oz jar salsa

Directions:

1. Season pork roasts with taco seasoning and place in the inner pot of instant pot duo crisp.
2. Pour salsa over pork roast.
3. Seal the pot with pressure cooking lid and select slow cook mode and cook on low for 6 hours.
4. Remove meat from pot and shred using a fork.
5. Return shredded meat to the pot and stir well.
6. Serve and enjoy.

Nutritional Value (Amount per Serving):

Calories 595; Fat 26.5 g; Carbohydrates 13.3 g; Sugar 3.3 g; Protein 69.8 g; Cholesterol 209 mg

Flavorful Pork Chop

Preparation Time: 10 minutes; Cooking Time: 6 hours 10 hours; Serve: 4

Ingredients:

- 4 pork chops
- 1 1/2 cups beef broth
- 2 tbsp butter, melted
- 1 tsp poultry seasoning
- 1 tbsp garlic cloves, minced
- 1 medium onion, chopped
- 1/2 tsp salt

Directions:

1. In a bowl, mix together broth, seasoning, and butter and pour into the inner pot of instant pot duo crisp.
2. Add garlic, onion, and pork chops into the pot.
3. Seal the pot with pressure cooking lid and select slow cook mode and cook on low for 6 hours.

4. Clean the pot. Place pork chops into the air fryer basket and place basket into the pot.
5. Seal the pot with air fryer lid and select broil mode and cook for 10 minutes.
6. Serve and enjoy.

Nutritional Value (Amount per Serving):

Calories 337; Fat 26.2 g; Carbohydrates 3.9 g; Sugar 1.5 g; Protein 20.3 g; Cholesterol 84 mg

Pulled Pork

Preparation Time: 10 minutes; Cooking Time: 8 hours; Serve: 12

Ingredients:

- 4 lbs pork shoulder
- 1 tsp garlic powder
- 1 tsp cayenne pepper
- 1 tsp pepper
- 2 tbsp paprika
- 3/4 cup water
- 1/4 cup apple cider vinegar
- 1 tsp onion powder
- 1 tsp kosher salt

Directions:

1. Add water and vinegar into the inner pot of instant pot duo crisp. Place pork into the pot.
2. Add remaining ingredients into the pot.
3. Seal the pot with pressure cooking lid and select slow cook mode and cook on low for 8 hours.
4. Remove meat from pot and shred using a fork.
5. Serve and enjoy.

Nutritional Value (Amount per Serving):

Calories 448; Fat 32.5 g; Carbohydrates 1.2 g; Sugar 0.3 g; Protein 35.5 g; Cholesterol 136 mg

Cuban Pork

Preparation Time: 10 minutes; Cooking Time: 8 hours 10 minutes; Serve: 6

Ingredients:

- 3 lbs pork shoulder roast
- 1 tsp oregano, dried
- 1 tsp cumin
- 1/2 cup fresh lime juice
- 1/2 cup orange juice
- 1 bay leaf
- 1 onion, sliced
- 1 1/2 garlic cloves, crushed
- 1/4 tsp red chili flakes
- 2 tbsp olive oil
- 1/8 tsp pepper
- 1 1/2 tsp salt

Directions:

1. In a bowl, mix together garlic, pepper, chili flakes, lime juice, orange juice, oil, oregano, cumin, and salt,
2. Place pork into the inner pot of instant pot duo crisp. Pour bowl mixture over pork.
3. Add bay leaf. Seal the pot with pressure cooking lid and select slow cook mode and cook on low for 8 hours.
4. Remove meat from pot and shred using a fork.
5. Clean the pot. Add shredded meat into the air fryer basket and place basket into the pot.
6. Seal the pot with air fryer lid and select broil mode and cook for 10 minutes.
7. Serve and enjoy.

Nutritional Value (Amount per Serving):

Calories 644; Fat 51 g; Carbohydrates 5 g; Sugar 2.6 g; Protein 38.7 g; Cholesterol 161 mg

Pork Tenderloin

Preparation Time: 10 minutes; Cooking Time: 6 hours; Serve: 8

Ingredients:

- 2 lbs pork tenderloin
- 1/2 cup balsamic vinegar
- 1 tbsp garlic cloves, minced
- 1/2 tsp red chili flakes
- 2 tbsp coconut amino
- 1 tbsp Worcestershire sauce
- 1 tbsp olive oil
- 1/2 tsp sea salt

Directions:
1. Add olive oil, garlic, and pork tenderloin into the inner pot of instant pot duo crisp and set pot on sauté mode.
2. In a bowl, mix together remaining ingredients and pour over pork.
3. Seal the pot with pressure cooking lid and select slow cook mode and cook on low for 6 hours.
4. Serve and enjoy.

Nutritional Value (Amount per Serving):
Calories 188; Fat 5.7 g; Carbohydrates 1.6 g; Sugar 0.5 g; Protein 29.8 g; Cholesterol 83 mg

Tasty Chipotle Barbacoa

Preparation Time: 10 minutes; Cooking Time: 1 hour; Serve: 8
Ingredients:
- 3 lbs chuck roast, cut into chunks
- 3 fresh lime juice
- 3 dried chipotle peppers
- 1 tsp pepper
- 1 tbsp oregano
- 4.5 oz green chilies
- 3 garlic cloves
- 1 onion, sliced
- 1/2 cup water
- 1 tbsp cumin
- 3 tbsp coconut vinegar
- 1 tsp salt

Directions:
1. Add all ingredients into the inner pot of instant pot duo crisp and stir well.
2. Seal the pot with pressure cooking lid and cook on high pressure for 60 minutes.
3. Once done, allow to release pressure naturally. Remove lid.
4. Shred the meat using a fork and return to the pot.
5. Stir well and serve.

Nutritional Value (Amount per Serving):
Calories 442; Fat 15.4 g; Carbohydrates 13 g; Sugar 8.3 g; Protein 58.7 g; Cholesterol 172 mg

Easy Pork Roast

Preparation Time: 10 minutes; Cooking Time: 8 hours; Serve: 6
Ingredients:
- 3 lbs pork shoulder roast, boneless and cut into 4 pieces
- 1/2 tbsp cumin
- 1 tbsp fresh oregano
- 1 cup of grapefruit juice
- Pepper
- Salt

Directions:
1. Season meat with pepper and salt and place into the inner pot of instant pot duo crisp.
2. Add oregano, cumin, and grapefruit juice into the blender and blend until smooth.
3. Pour blended mixture over meat.
4. Seal the pot with pressure cooking lid and select slow cook mode and cook on low for 8 hours.
5. Remove meat from pot and shred using a fork.
6. Return shredded meat into the pot and stir well.
7. Serve and enjoy.

Nutritional Value (Amount per Serving):
Calories 599; Fat 46.4 g; Carbohydrates 3.8 g; Sugar 2.7 g; Protein 38.5 g; Cholesterol 161 mg

Ranch Pork Chops

Preparation Time: 10 minutes; Cooking Time: 30 minutes; Serve: 6

Ingredients:

- 6 pork chops, boneless
- 1/4 cup olive oil
- 1 tsp dried parsley
- 2 tbsp ranch seasoning
- Pepper
- Salt

Directions:

1. Line instant pot air fryer basket with parchment paper.
2. Season pork chops with pepper and salt and place on parchment paper into the air fryer basket.
3. Mix together olive oil, parsley, and ranch seasoning.
4. Spoon oil mixture over pork chops.
5. Place air fryer basket in the pot.
6. Seal the pot with air fryer basket and select bake mode and cook at 400 F for 30 minutes.
7. Serve and enjoy.

Nutritional Value (Amount per Serving):

Calories 338; Fat 28.3 g; Carbohydrates 0 g; Sugar 0 g; Protein 18 g; Cholesterol 69 mg

Pork Carnitas

Preparation Time: 10 minutes; Cooking Time: 9 hours; Serve: 6

Ingredients:

- 3 lbs pork shoulder
- 3 tsp cumin
- 2 orange juice
- 1/2 cup water
- 2 tsp olive oil
- 2 tsp ground coriander
- 2 tsp salt

Directions:

1. Place the pork shoulder into the inner pot of instant pot duo crisp.
2. Pour remaining ingredients over the pork shoulder.
3. Seal the pot with pressure cooking lid and select slow cooker mode and cook on low for 9 hours.
4. Remove meat from pot and shred using a fork.
5. Serve and enjoy.

Nutritional Value (Amount per Serving):

Calories 693; Fat 50.4 g; Carbohydrates 3.4 g; Sugar 2.4 g; Protein 53.2 g; Cholesterol 204 mg

Pulled Pork

Preparation Time: 10 minutes; Cooking Time: 50 minutes; Serve: 6

Ingredients:

- 3 lbs pork butt, cut into large chunks
- 1/2 tsp cumin
- 2 tbsp paprika
- 1 tbsp olive oil
- 1/2 cup water
- 1/2 tsp cayenne pepper
- 1 tbsp oregano
- 1 tsp pepper
- 2 tsp salt

Directions:

1. Add the meat into the inner pot of instant pot duo crisp and top with olive oil.
2. In a small bowl, mix together paprika, cayenne, oregano, cumin, pepper, and salt and sprinkle over meat.
3. Add water and stir well.
4. Seal the pot with pressure cooking lid and cook on high for 40 minutes.

5. Once done, allow to release pressure naturally for 10 minutes then release remaining pressure using a quick release. Remove lid.
6. Remove meat from pot and shred using a fork.
7. Return shredded meat to the pot and cook on sauté mode for 10 minutes.
8. Stir and serve.

Nutritional Value (Amount per Serving):
Calories 469; Fat 17.9 g; Carbohydrates 2.2 g; Sugar 0.3 g; Protein 71.1 g; Cholesterol 209 mg

Pork Patties

Preparation Time: 10 minutes; Cooking Time: 15 minutes; Serve: 6
Ingredients:

- 2 lbs ground pork
- 1 tsp red pepper flakes
- 1 tbsp dried parsley
- 1 1/2 tbsp Italian seasoning
- 1 tsp fennel seed
- 1 tsp paprika
- 2 tbsp olive oil
- 2 tsp salt

Directions:
1. Line instant pot air fryer basket with parchment paper.
2. In a large bowl, mix together ground pork, fennel seed, paprika, red pepper flakes, parsley, Italian seasoning, olive oil, pepper, and salt.
3. Make small patties from meat mixture and place on place on parchment paper into the air fryer basket.
4. Place basket into the pot.
5. Seal the pot with air fryer basket and select bake mode and cook at 375 F for 15 minutes.
6. Serve and enjoy.

Nutritional Value (Amount per Serving):
Calories 270; Fat 11.2 g; Carbohydrates 1 g; Sugar 0.4 g; Protein 39.7 g; Cholesterol 113 mg

Herb Pork Tenderloin

Preparation Time: 10 minutes; Cooking Time: 30 minutes; Serve: 4
Ingredients:

- 1 lb pork tenderloin
- 1 tsp oregano, dried
- 1 tsp thyme, dried
- 1 tsp olive oil
- 1/2 tsp onion powder
- 1/2 tsp garlic powder
- 1/2 tsp pepper
- 1/2 tsp salt

Directions:
1. In a small bowl, mix together onion powder, garlic powder, oregano, thyme, pepper and salt.
2. Coat pork with oil then rub with herb mixture and place into the instant pot air fryer basket.
3. Place basket in the pot.
4. Seal the pot with air fryer lid and select roast mode and cook at 400 F for 30 minutes.
5. Slice and serve.

Nutritional Value (Amount per Serving):
Calories 177; Fat 5.2 g; Carbohydrates 1.1 g; Sugar 0.2 g; Protein 29.9 g; Cholesterol 83 mg

Buttery Pork Chops

Preparation Time: 10 minutes; Cooking Time: 10 minutes; Serve: 6
Ingredients:

- 6 pork chops, boneless
- 1 stick butter
- 1 tbsp olive oil
- 1 cup of water

- 1 tbsp ranch seasoning

Directions
1. Add oil into the inner pot of instant pot duo crisp and set pot on sauté mode.
2. Add pork chops and cook until brown. Sprinkle ranch seasoning over pork chops then add butter.
3. Pour water over pork chops.
4. Seal the pot with pressure cooking lid and cook on high for 5 minutes.
5. Once done, allow to release pressure naturally. Remove lid.
6. Serve and enjoy.

Nutritional Value (Amount per Serving):
Calories 410; Fat 37 g; Carbohydrates 2 g; Sugar 1 g; Protein 18 g; Cholesterol 105 mg

Tasty Boneless Pork Chops

Preparation Time: 10 minutes; Cooking Time: 15 minutes; Serve: 2
Ingredients:
- 2 pork chops, boneless
- 1/4 cup beef broth
- 2 tbsp lemon pepper
- ¼ tsp garlic powder

Directions:
1. Set instant pot duo crisp on sauté mode.
2. Place pork chops into the inner pot of instant pot and season with garlic powder and lemon pepper.
3. Cook pork chops until brown.
4. Remove pork chops from pot. Add broth and deglaze the pan.
5. Return pork chops into the pot.
6. Seal the pot with pressure cooking lid and cook on high for 10 minutes.
7. Once done, allow to release pressure naturally. Remove lid.
8. Serve and enjoy.

Nutritional Value (Amount per Serving):
Calories 285; Fat 20 g; Carbohydrates 7 g; Protein 18.7 g; Sugar 3 g; Cholesterol 69 mg

Chipotle Beef

Preparation Time: 10 minutes; Cooking Time: 1 hour 40 minutes; Serve: 4
Ingredients:
- 3 1/2 lbs beef brisket, cut into pieces
- 2 tbsp chipotle powder
- ¼ tsp garlic powder
- 1 tbsp butter
- 1/4 cup cilantro, chopped
- 1 cup chicken broth
- 1 tsp sea salt

Directions:
1. Add butter into the inner pot of instant pot duo crisp and set pot on sauté mode.
2. Add meat and sauté until lightly brown.
3. Add remaining ingredients and stir well.
4. Seal the pot with pressure cooking lid and cook on high for 1 hour 40 minutes.
5. Once done, release pressure using a quick release. Remove lid.
6. Slice and serve.

Nutritional Value (Amount per Serving):
Calories 764; Fat 26 g; Carbohydrates 0.2 g; Protein 121 g; Sugar 0.2 g; Cholesterol 360 mg

Delicious Picadillo

Preparation Time: 10 minutes; Cooking Time: 15 minutes; Serve: 6
Ingredients:

- 2 lbs ground beef
- 14 oz can roasted tomatoes, blended
- 2 cups cherry tomatoes, halved
- 1 bell pepper, diced
- 1/2 cup green olives
- 1/2 tsp ground cumin
- 1/2 cup green onion, chopped
- 1 tbsp olive oil
- 1 tsp salt

Directions:
1. Add oil into the inner pot of instant pot duo crisp and set pot on sauté mode.
2. Add meat and cook until browned, about 5 minutes.
3. Add remaining ingredients and stir well.
4. Seal the pot with pressure cooking lid and cook on high for 10 minutes.
5. Once done, release pressure using a quick release. Remove lid.
6. Stir well and serve.

Nutritional Value (Amount per Serving):
Calories 348; Fat 13 g; Carbohydrates 8 g; Sugar 5 g; Protein 47 g; Cholesterol 135 mg

Lamb Patties

Preparation Time: 10 minutes; Cooking Time: 12 minutes; Serve: 6
Ingredients:
- 1 lb ground lamb
- 1 tsp dried rosemary
- 1 tbsp dried oregano
- 1 tbsp dried thyme
- 1 lb ground beef
- 1/4 cup green onion, chopped
- 2 tbsp olive oil
- 1 tsp cumin
- 1 tsp pepper
- 1 1/2 tsp salt

Directions:
1. Add all ingredients into the large bowl and mix until combined.
2. Make small patties from the meat mixture.
3. Place patties in instant pot air fryer basket and place basket in the pot.
4. Seal the pot with air fryer lid and select bake mode and cook at 360 F for 12 minutes.
5. Serve and enjoy.

Nutritional Value (Amount per Serving):
Calories 329; Fat 15 g; Carbohydrates 1.6 g; Sugar 0.2 g; Protein 44 g; Cholesterol 136 mg

Ranch Seasoned Pork Chops

Preparation Time: 10 minutes; Cooking Time: 35 minutes; Serve: 6
Ingredients:
- 6 pork chops, boneless
- 1/4 cup olive oil
- 1 tsp dried parsley
- 2 tbsp ranch seasoning, homemade
- Pepper
- Salt

Directions:
1. Season pork chops with pepper and salt and place into the instant pot air fryer basket. Place basket in the pot.
2. Mix together olive oil, parsley, and ranch seasoning.
3. Brush pork chops with oil mixture.
4. Seal the pot with air fryer lid and select bake mode and cook at 400 F for 30-35 minutes.
5. Serve and enjoy.

Nutritional Value (Amount per Serving):
Calories 328; Fat 28 g; Carbohydrates 0 g; Sugar 0 g; Protein 18 g; Cholesterol 69 mg

Meatballs

Preparation Time: 10 minutes; Cooking Time: 20 minutes; Serve: 6

Ingredients:
- 2 lbs ground beef
- 1 tsp paprika
- 1 tsp oregano
- 1 tsp cinnamon
- 2 tsp cumin
- 2 tsp coriander
- 1 tsp garlic, minced
- 1 small onion, grated
- 1 egg, lightly beaten
- 1 tbsp fresh mint, chopped
- 1/4 cup fresh parsley, minced
- 1/2 tsp allspice
- 1/4 tsp pepper
- 1/2 tsp salt

Directions:
1. Add all ingredients into the bowl and mix until combined.
2. Make small balls from the meat mixture and place into the instant pot air fryer basket. Place basket in the pot.
3. Seal the pot air fryer lid and select bake mode and cook at 400 F for 15-20 minutes.
4. Serve and enjoy.

Nutritional Value (Amount per Serving):
Calories 304; Fat 10 g; Carbohydrates 2 g; Sugar 0.7 g; Protein 47 g; Cholesterol 162 mg

Spicy Lamb Patties

Preparation Time: 10 minutes; Cooking Time: 8 minutes; Serve: 4
Ingredients:
- 1 lb ground lamb
- 1/4 cup fresh parsley, chopped
- 1 tsp dried oregano
- 1 cup feta cheese, crumbled
- 1 tbsp garlic, minced
- 1/4 cup basil leaves, minced
- 10 mint leaves, minced
- 1 jalapeno pepper, minced
- 1/4 tsp pepper
- 1/2 tsp kosher salt

Directions:
1. Add all ingredients into the bowl and mix until combined.
2. Make small patties from meat mixture and place it into the instant pot air fryer basket. Place basket in the pot.
3. Seal the pot air fryer lid and select air fry mode and cook at 360 F for 15-18 minutes.
4. Serve and enjoy.

Nutritional Value (Amount per Serving):
Calories 317; Fat 16 g; Carbohydrates 3 g; Sugar 1.7 g; Protein 37 g; Cholesterol 135 mg

Chuck Roast

Preparation Time: 10 minutes; Cooking Time: 10 hours; Serve: 6
Ingredients:
- 2 lbs beef chuck roast
- 2 tbsp balsamic vinegar
- 1/2 cup beef broth
- 1/4 cup sun-dried tomatoes, chopped
- 20 garlic cloves, peeled
- 1/4 cup olives, sliced
- 1 tsp Italian seasoning, crushed

Directions:
1. Place meat into the inner pot of instant pot duo crisp.
2. Pour remaining ingredients over meat.
3. Seal the pot with pressure cooking lid and select slow cook mode and cook on low for 10 hours.
4. Remove meat from pot and shred using a fork.
5. Return shredded meat to the pot and stir well.
6. Serve and enjoy.

Nutritional Value (Amount per Serving):

Calories 578; Fat 43 g; Carbohydrates 4 g; Sugar 0.5 g; Protein 40 g; Cholesterol 156 mg

Tomato Beef Brisket

Preparation Time: 10 minutes; Cooking Time: 6 hours 10 minutes; Serve: 6

Ingredients:

- 3 lbs beef brisket
- 1 large onion, chopped
- 1 cup chicken stock
- 28 oz can tomato, diced
- 2 tbsp olive oil
- 4 garlic cloves, minced
- Pepper
- Salt

Directions:

1. Season meat with pepper and salt.
2. Add oil into the inner pot of instant pot duo crisp and set pot on sauté mode.
3. Add meat to the pot and cook until browned. Remove from pot and set aside.
4. Add remaining oil to the pot.
5. Add onion and sauté until softened.
6. Return meat to the pot.
7. Top with tomatoes, garlic, pepper, salt, and stock.
8. Seal the pot with pressure cooking lid and select slow cook mode and cook on low for 6 hours.
9. Slice and serve.

Nutritional Value (Amount per Serving):

Calories 504; Fat 18 g; Carbohydrates 9 g; Sugar 5 g; Protein 70 g; Cholesterol 203 mg

Balsamic Chuck Roast

Preparation Time: 10 minutes; Cooking Time: 55 minutes; Serve: 6

Ingredients:

- 3 lbs chuck roast
- 1 tbsp butter, melted
- 1 tsp rosemary
- 1 tbsp olive oil
- 1 cup chicken stock
- 4 tbsp balsamic vinegar
- 1/4 tsp thyme, dried
- 1/2 tsp pepper
- 1 tsp salt

Directions:

1. In a small bowl, mix together thyme, rosemary, pepper, and salt and rub over meat.
2. Add oil into the inner pot of instant pot duo crisp and set pot on sauté mode.
3. Place meat in the pot and cook until brown, about 5 minutes on each side.
4. Pour broth, butter, and vinegar over meat.
5. Seal the pot with pressure cooking lid and cook on high 40 for minutes.
6. Once done, release pressure using a quick release. Remove lid.
7. Serve and enjoy.

Nutritional Value (Amount per Serving):

Calories 532; Fat 23 g; Carbohydrates 0.5 g; Sugar 0.2 g; Protein 75 g; Cholesterol 234 mg

Classic Pot Roast

Preparation Time: 10 minutes; Cooking Time: 55 minutes; Serve: 6

Ingredients:

- 3 lbs beef chuck roast
- 2 tbsp butter
- 1 tbsp Italian seasoning
- 2 garlic cloves, minced
- 4 large carrots, peeled
- 2 cups chicken stock
- 1 onion, diced
- 1 tsp black pepper
- 1 tsp salt

Directions:
1. Place meat in a large dish and sprinkle with spices.
2. Add oil into the inner pot of instant pot duo crisp and set pot on sauté mode.
3. Add onion and sauté for 5 minutes.
4. Add meat and stock and stir well.
5. Seal the pot with pressure cooking lid and cook on high for 40 minutes.
6. Once done, release pressure using a quick release. Remove lid.
7. Add carrots and stir well.
8. Seal the pot with pressure cooking lid and cook on high for 10 minutes.
9. Once done, release pressure using a quick release. Remove lid.
10. Stir and serve.

Nutritional Value (Amount per Serving):
Calories 897; Fat 67 g; Carbohydrates 7 g; Sugar 3 g; Protein 60 g; Cholesterol 245 mg

Shredded Meat

Preparation Time: 10 minutes; Cooking Time: 60 minutes; Serve: 4

Ingredients:
- 2 lbs beef chuck roast, boneless
- 1 tsp oregano
- 1 tbsp chili powder
- 1 large onion, sliced
- 1/2 cup bone broth
- 1 tbsp lime juice
- 1 tsp garlic powder
- 1 tsp salt

Directions:
1. In a small bowl, mix together, chili powder, oregano, garlic powder, and salt.
2. Rub spice mixture over meat.
3. Add onion into the inner pot of instant pot duo crisp then place the meat on top of the onion.
4. Pour broth and lime juice over the meat.
5. Seal the pot with pressure cooking lid and cook on high for 60 minutes.
6. Once done, allow to release pressure naturally. Remove lid.
7. Shred the meat using a fork and serve.

Nutritional Value (Amount per Serving):
Calories 848; Fat 63 g; Carbohydrates 5 g; Sugar 1 g; Protein 60 g; Cholesterol 234 mg

Beef Fajitas

Preparation Time: 10 minutes; Cooking Time: 4 hours; Serve: 6

Ingredients:
- 18 oz salsa
- 1 onion, sliced
- 2 lbs beef, sliced
- 1 1/2 tbsp fajita seasoning
- 1 red bell pepper, sliced
- 1 green bell pepper, sliced
- Pepper
- Salt

Directions:
1. Add all ingredients into the inner pot of instant pot duo crisp and stir well.
2. Seal the pot with pressure cooking lid and select slow cook mode and cook on high for 4 hours.
3. Serve and enjoy.

Nutritional Value (Amount per Serving):
Calories 332; Fat 9 g; Carbohydrates 11 g; Sugar 5 g; Protein 47 g; Cholesterol 135 mg

Spicy Pepper Beef

Preparation Time: 10 minutes; Cooking Time: 4 hours; Serve: 6

Ingredients:
- 2 lbs beef chuck, sliced
- 1 cup chicken broth
- 1 onion, sliced
- 2 cups bell pepper, chopped
- 1 tsp sriracha sauce
- 1/4 cup parsley, chopped
- 1 tsp garlic cloves, minced
- 1 tsp black pepper
- 2 tsp salt

Directions:
1. Place meat into the inner pot of instant pot duo crisp.
2. Pour remaining ingredients over meat.
3. Seal the pot with pressure cooking lid and select slow cook mode and cook on high for 4 hours.
4. Serve and enjoy.

Nutritional Value (Amount per Serving):
Calories 310; Fat 9 g; Carbohydrates 5 g; Sugar 2 g; Protein 47 g; Cholesterol 135 mg

Slow Cook Beef Roast

Preparation Time: 10 minutes; Cooking Time: 8 hours; Serve: 8
Ingredients:
- 2 1/2 lbs beef round roast
- 1/2 cup red wine
- 1/2 cup beef broth
- 1 onion, sliced
- 1/2 tsp thyme
- 1 tsp basil
- 1/4 tsp black pepper
- 1 tsp kosher salt

Directions:
1. In a small bowl, mix together all spices and rub over meat.
2. Place meat into the inner pot of instant pot duo crisp and top with onion.
3. Pour broth and red over meat.
4. Seal the pot with pressure cooking lid and select slow cook mode and cook on high for 8 hours.
5. Shred meat using a fork and stir well.
6. Serve and enjoy.

Nutritional Value (Amount per Serving):
Calories 286; Fat 11 g; Carbohydrates 1.8 g; Sugar 0.7 g; Protein 39 g; Cholesterol 122 mg

Steak Bites

Preparation Time: 10 minutes; Cooking Time: 8 hours; Serve: 6
Ingredients:
- 3 lbs round steak, cut into 1-inch cubes
- 1/2 cup beef broth
- 1 tsp garlic powder
- 1 tbsp onion, minced
- 4 tbsp butter, sliced
- 1/2 tsp black pepper
- 1/2 tsp salt

Directions:
1. Place meat into the inner pot of instant pot duo crisp.
2. Pour remaining ingredients over meat.
3. Seal the pot with pressure cooking lid and select slow cook mode and cook on high for 8 hours.
4. Serve and enjoy.

Nutritional Value (Amount per Serving):
Calories 564; Fat 29 g; Carbohydrates 0.7 g; Sugar 0.3 g; Protein 69 g; Cholesterol 213 mg

Pepper Sirloin Steak

Preparation Time: 10 minutes; Cooking Time: 6 hours; Serve: 4
Ingredients:

- 1 lb sirloin steak, sliced
- 1 tbsp sesame oil
- 3 tbsp soy sauce
- 1 onion, sliced
- 1 cup mushrooms, sliced
- 1 green bell pepper, sliced
- 1/2 tsp red pepper flakes
- 1 tsp fresh ginger, grated
- 1 garlic clove, minced

Directions:

1. Add steak, onion, mushrooms, and green bell pepper into the inner pot of instant pot duo crisp.
2. In a small bowl, mix together remaining ingredients and pour over meat and vegetables.
3. Seal the pot with pressure cooking lid and select slow cook mode and cook on high for 6 hours.
4. Serve and enjoy.

Nutritional Value (Amount per Serving):
Calories 275; Fat 10 g; Carbohydrates 7 g; Sugar 3 g; Protein 36 g; Cholesterol 101 mg

Spicy Pulled Chuck Roast

Preparation Time: 10 minutes; Cooking Time: 8 hours; Serve: 6
Ingredients:

- 2 1/2 lbs beef chuck roast, trimmed
- 1 onion, sliced
- 4 oz can green chilies, diced
- 6.5 oz can chipotle sauce
- 14 oz can tomato, diced
- 2 tbsp chili powder
- 1 tsp cumin

Directions:

1. Place meat into the inner pot of instant pot duo crisp.
2. Pour remaining ingredients over meat.
3. Seal the pot with pressure cooking lid and select slow cook mode and cook on high for 8 hours.
4. Shred the meat using a fork and serve.

Nutritional Value (Amount per Serving):
Calories 721; Fat 53 g; Carbohydrates 7 g; Sugar 3 g; Protein 50 g; Cholesterol 195 mg

Shredded Mexican Beef

Preparation Time: 10 minutes; Cooking Time: 6 hours; Serve: 6
Ingredients:

- 3 lbs chuck roast, cut into 2-inch pieces
- 1 tsp cumin
- 5 garlic cloves, diced
- 2 tbsp tomato paste
- 1 cup onion, diced
- 1 tbsp olive oil
- 1 cup beef broth
- 1/2 cup salsa
- 1 tsp oregano
- 1 tbsp chili powder
- 1 1/2 tsp sea salt

Directions:

1. Add oil into the inner pot of instant pot duo crisp and set pot on sauté mode.
2. Add meat and cook until browned.
3. Pour remaining ingredients over meat.
4. Seal the pot with pressure cooking lid and select slow cook mode and cook on low for 6 hours.

5. Shred the meat using a fork and serve.

Nutritional Value (Amount per Serving):

Calories 544; Fat 21 g; Carbohydrates 6 g; Sugar 2 g; Protein 76 g; Cholesterol 229 mg

Beef Ribs with Sauce

Preparation Time: 10 minutes; Cooking Time: 8 hours; Serve: 8

Ingredients:

- 2 lbs beef short ribs
- 1/2 cup beef broth
- 3 oz cream cheese, softened
- 1 tsp garlic powder
- 1 tbsp olive oil
- 2 cups mushrooms, sliced
- 1 tsp black pepper
- 1 tsp salt

Directions:

1. Add oil into the inner pot of instant pot duo crisp and set pot on sauté mode.
2. Add ribs and cook until browned.
3. Pour remaining ingredients over meat.
4. Seal the pot with pressure cooking lid and select slow cook mode and cook on low for 8 hours.
5. Serve and enjoy.

Nutritional Value (Amount per Serving):

Calories 293; Fat 15 g; Carbohydrates 1.3 g; Sugar 0.5 g; Protein 34 g; Cholesterol 115 mg

Delicious Goulash

Preparation Time: 10 minutes; Cooking Time: 6 hours; Serve: 6

Ingredients:

- 3 lbs beef stew meat, cut into 1-inch chunks
- 8 garlic cloves, chopped
- 6 oz can tomato paste
- 2 cups beef broth
- 2 tbsp olive oil
- 2 tsp cayenne
- 1/4 cup paprika
- 3 onions, chopped
- 1 tsp salt

Directions:

1. Add oil into the inner pot of instant pot duo crisp and set pot on sauté mode.
2. Add meat, onion, and garlic and cook until meat is browned.
3. Pour remaining ingredients over meat.
4. Seal the pot with pressure cooking lid and select slow cook mode and cook on low for 6 hours.
5. Serve and enjoy.

Nutritional Value (Amount per Serving):

Calories 516; Fat 20 g; Carbohydrates 9 g; Sugar 3 g; Protein 72 g; Cholesterol 203 mg

Balsamic Beef Roast

Preparation Time: 10 minutes; Cooking Time: 8 hours; Serve: 6

Ingredients:

- 2 lbs round beef roast
- 4 tsp garlic, minced
- 2 rosemary stalks, chopped
- 2 tbsp olive oil
- 2 tbsp balsamic vinegar
- 1/2 tsp pepper
- 1 tsp sea salt

Directions:

1. Brush meat with oil.
2. Mix together rosemary, pepper, garlic, and salt and rub over meat.
3. Set instant pot duo crisp on sauté mode.

4. Sear meat in a pot until browned.
5. Pour remaining ingredients over meat.
6. Seal the pot with pressure cooking lid and select slow cook mode and cook on low for 8 hours.
7. Serve and enjoy.

Nutritional Value (Amount per Serving):
Calories 327; Fat 16 g; Carbohydrates 0.8 g; Sugar 0 g; Protein 41 g; Cholesterol 130 mg

Simple Beef Carnitas

Preparation Time: 10 minutes; Cooking Time: 6 hours; Serve: 4
Ingredients:
- 1 lb stew meat
- 1 cup of water
- 1 tbsp olive oil
- 1 cup beef stock
- 1 cup onion, chopped
- 1/2 tsp cumin
- 1 tsp oregano
- 1 tsp garlic powder
- 1/2 tbsp chili powder

Directions:
1. Add oil into the inner pot of instant pot duo crisp and set pot on sauté mode.
2. Add meat and onion and cook until meat is brown and onion is softened.
3. Pour remaining ingredients over meat.
4. Seal the pot with pressure cooking lid and select slow cook mode and cook on low for 6 hours.
5. Shred the meat using a fork.
6. Serve and enjoy.

Nutritional Value (Amount per Serving):
Calories 225; Fat 12 g; Carbohydrates 2 g; Sugar 1 g; Protein 24 g; Cholesterol 80 mg

Beef Curry

Preparation Time: 10 minutes; Cooking Time: 30 minutes; Serve: 2
Ingredients:
- 1/2 lb beef stew meat
- 1/2 cup sun-roasted tomatoes, diced
- 2 tbsp butter
- 2 garlic cloves, crushed
- 1 tbsp fresh ginger, grated
- 1/2 tsp cumin powder
- 1 tsp coriander powder
- 1 tsp garam masala
- 1/2 tsp cayenne pepper
- 1 green chili peppers, chopped
- 1 bell peppers, sliced
- 1 cup of water

Directions:
1. Add all ingredients into the inner pot of instant pot duo crisp and stir well.
2. Seal the pot with pressure cooking lid and cook on high for 30 minutes.
3. Once done, allow to release pressure naturally. Remove lid.
4. Stir well and serve.

Nutritional Value (Amount per Serving):
Calories 350; Fat 19 g; Carbohydrates 8 g; Sugar 3 g; Protein 35 g; Cholesterol 132 mg

Smoked Pork Chops

Preparation Time: 10 minutes; Cooking Time: 10 minutes; Serve: 2
Ingredients:
- 2 pork chops
- 1 cup beef broth
- 1/4 tsp pepper
- 2 tbsp olive oil
- 1 tbsp liquid smoke
- 2 tsp salt

Directions:
1. Season pork chops with pepper and salt.
2. Add oil into the inner pot of instant pot duo crisp and set pot on sauté mode.
3. Add pork chops and sauté until browned.
4. Remove pork chops from the pot and set aside.
5. Add liquid smoke and broth and stir well.
6. Return pork chops to the pot.
7. Seal the pot with pressure cooking lid and cook on high for 10 minutes.
8. Once done, allow to release pressure naturally. Remove lid.
9. Serve and enjoy.

Nutritional Value (Amount per Serving):
Calories 396; Fat 34 g; Carbohydrates 0.6 g; Sugar 0.4 g; Protein 20 g; Cholesterol 69 mg

Asian Pork Roast

Preparation Time: 10 minutes; Cooking Time: 6 hours; Serve: 6
Ingredients:
- 2 lbs pork shoulder roast, boneless
- 1/3 cup chicken broth
- 1/2 tsp red pepper flakes
- 1/2 tsp garlic powder
- 1 tbsp Worcestershire sauce
- 1/3 cup balsamic vinegar
- Salt

Directions:
1. Season meat with pepper garlic powder, salt, and red pepper flakes and place into the inner pot of instant pot duo crisp.
2. In a bowl, mix together vinegar, broth, and Worcestershire sauce and pour over meat.
3. Seal the pot with pressure cooking lid and select slow cook mode and cook on low for 6 minutes.
4. Sliced and serve.

Nutritional Value (Amount per Serving):
Calories 397; Fat 30 g; Carbohydrates 0.9 g; Sugar 0.7 g; Protein 25.8 g; Cholesterol 107 mg

Pork Tacos

Preparation Time: 10 minutes; Cooking Time: 8 hours; Serve: 8
Ingredients:
- 2 lbs pork tenderloin
- 2 tbsp brown sugar
- 2 tbsp ground cumin
- 2 tbsp chili powder
- 24 oz salsa
- 3 tsp garlic powder
- 2 tsp cayenne pepper
- 1 1/2 tsp salt

Directions:
1. Place meat into the inner pot of instant pot duo crisp.
2. Pour remaining ingredients over meat.
3. Seal the pot with pressure cooking lid and select slow cook mode and cook on low for 8 hours.
4. Stir and serve.

Nutritional Value (Amount per Serving):
Calories 210; Fat 4.9 g; Carbohydrates 10.2 g; Sugar 5.3 g; Protein 31.7 g; Cholesterol 83 mg

Lime Tomatillo Pork

Preparation Time: 10 minutes; Cooking Time: 8 hours; Serve: 8
Ingredients:

- 4 lbs pork butt, boneless and trimmed excess fat
- 1 lime juice
- 1/2 cup cilantro, chopped
- 2 cups can tomatillos
- 1 tsp ground cumin
- 2 tsp dried oregano
- 3 garlic cloves, minced
- 1/2 cup onion, chopped
- 1/2 tsp black pepper
- 1 tsp salt

Directions:
1. Place meat into the inner pot of instant pot duo crisp.
2. Pour remaining ingredients over meat.
3. Seal the pot with pressure cooking lid and select slow cook mode and cook on low for 8 hours.
4. Shred the meat using a fork.
5. Stir and serve.

Nutritional Value (Amount per Serving):
Calories 445; Fat 15.3 g; Carbohydrates 1.5 g; Sugar 0.4 g; Protein 70 g; Cholesterol 209 mg

Juicy Pork Carnitas

Preparation Time: 10 minutes; Cooking Time: 8 hours; Serve: 8
Ingredients:
- 4 lb pork shoulder roast
- 1 tsp oregano
- 1 tsp cumin
- 1 tbsp chili powder
- 1 onion, quartered
- 3 garlic cloves, minced
- 1/4 cup lime juice
- 3/4 cup orange juice
- 1 tsp pepper
- 1 tsp salt

Directions:
1. Place meat into the inner pot of instant pot duo crisp.
2. Pour remaining ingredients over meat.
3. Seal the pot with pressure cooking lid and select slow cook mode and cook on low for 8 hours.
4. Shred the meat using a fork. Seal the pot with air fryer lid and select broil mode and cook for 3-5 minutes.
5. Stir and serve.

Nutritional Value (Amount per Serving):
Calories 605; Fat 46 g; Carbohydrates 5 g; Sugar 2.6 g; Protein 38 g; Cholesterol 161 mg

Air Fried Beef Fajitas

Preparation Time: 10 minutes; Cooking Time: 10 minutes; Serve: 6
Ingredients:
- 1 b beef steak, cut into strips
- 1 tsp paprika
- 2 tsp garlic powder
- 1 onion, sliced
- 1 red bell pepper, cut into julienne
- 1 tbsp olive oil
- 2 green bell pepper, cut into julienne
- 1 tsp oregano
- 2 tsp ground cumin
- 1 tsp chili powder
- 1 tsp salt

Directions:
1. Add all ingredients into the large bowl and toss well.
2. Transfer bowl mixture into the instant pot air fryer basket and place basket in the pot.
3. Seal the pot with air fryer lid and select air fry mode and cook at 390 F for 10 minutes.
4. Serve and enjoy.

Nutritional Value (Amount per Serving):

Calories 168; Fat 6 g; Carbohydrates 6 g; Sugar 3 g; Protein 20 g; Cholesterol 58 mg

Tender Pork Chops

Preparation Time: 10 minutes; Cooking Time: 13 minutes; Serve: 4

Ingredients:
- 4 pork chops, boneless
- 1/2 tsp onion powder
- 1/2 tsp garlic powder
- 2 tsp olive oil
- 1/2 tsp parsley
- 1/2 tsp salt

Directions:
1. In a small bowl, mix together onion powder, garlic powder, parsley, oil, and salt and rub over pork chops.
2. Place pork chops in instant pot air fryer basket and place basket in the pot.
3. Seal the pot with air fryer lid and select air fry mode and cook at 350 F for 13 minutes. Turn after 8 minutes.
4. Serve and enjoy.

Nutritional Value (Amount per Serving):
Calories 278; Fat 22.2 g; Carbohydrates 0.5 g; Sugar 0.2 g; Protein 18.1 g; Cholesterol 69 mg

Asian Pork Ribs

Preparation Time: 10 minutes; Cooking Time: 40 minutes; Serve: 4

Ingredients:
- 1 lb baby pork ribs
- 1 tbsp olive oil
- 1 tbsp ginger, minced
- 3 garlic cloves, minced
- 1/2 tbsp soy sauce
- 1 tbsp hoisin sauce

Directions:
1. In a bowl add all ingredients and mix well.
2. Cover bowl and place in the refrigerator for 2 hours.
3. Place marinated ribs in instant pot air fryer basket and place basket in the pot.
4. Seal the pot with air fryer lid and select air fry mode and cook at 320 F for 40 minutes.
5. Serve and enjoy.

Nutritional Value (Amount per Serving):
Calories 369; Fat 30.8 g; Carbohydrates 3.6 g; Sugar 1.2 g; Protein 18.6 g; Cholesterol 90 mg

Easy Pork Roast

Preparation Time: 10 minutes; Cooking Time: 58 minutes; Serve: 6

Ingredients:
- 2 lbs pork shoulder
- 2 tbsp olive oil
- 1 tsp garlic powder
- 2 garlic cloves, minced
- 1 onion, sliced
- 2 cups chicken stock
- 1 tsp pepper
- 1/2 tsp salt

Directions:
1. Coat meat with 1 tbsp oil and season meat with garlic powder, pepper, and salt.
2. Set instant pot duo crisp on sauté mode and add remaining oil in the pot.
3. Place meat in the pot and sear from all the sides, about 5 minutes on each side.
4. Remove meat from pot and set aside.
5. Add stock and stir well.
6. Return meat in the pot.
7. Add garlic and onion on top of the meat.
8. Seal the pot with pressure cooking lid and cook on high for 30 minutes.

9. Once done, allow to release pressure naturally for 10 minutes then release remaining pressure using a quick release. Remove lid.
10. Remove meat from pot and place in the instant pot air fryer basket.
11. Place basket in the pot.
12. Seal the pot with air fryer lid and select air fry mode and cook at 400 F for 10 minutes.
13. Serve and enjoy.

Nutritional Value (Amount per Serving):
Calories 496; Fat 37.2 g; Carbohydrates 2.9 g; Sugar 1.1 g; Protein 35.8 g; Cholesterol 136 mg

Ginger Garlic Ribs

Preparation Time: 10 minutes; Cooking Time: 40 minutes; Serve: 4
Ingredients:
- 1 lb baby pork ribs
- 1 tbsp olive oil
- 1/2 tbsp soy sauce
- 1/2 tbsp Hoisin sauce
- 1 tbsp fresh ginger, minced
- 1 tbsp garlic, minced

Directions:
1. In a mixing bowl add all ingredients and mix well. Cover and place in the refrigerator for 2 hours.
2. Place marinated ribs in the instant pot air fryer basket and place basket in the pot.
3. Seal the pot with air fryer lid and select air fry mode and cook at 320 F for 40 minutes.
4. Serve and enjoy.

Nutritional Value (Amount per Serving):
Calories 364; Fat 30.8 g; Carbohydrates 2.7 g; Sugar 0.7 g; Protein 18.5 g; Cholesterol 90 mg

Meatballs

Preparation Time: 10 minutes; Cooking Time: 15 minutes; Serve: 2
Ingredients:
- 5 oz pork minced
- 1/2 onion, diced
- 1/2 tsp mustard
- 1/2 tsp garlic paste
- 1/2 tbsp cheddar cheese, grated
- 1/2 tbsp fresh basil
- Pepper
- Salt

Directions:
1. Add all ingredients into the bowl and mix until combined.
2. Spray instant pot air fryer basket with cooking spray and place in the pot.
3. Make small balls from mixture and place into the air fryer basket.
4. Seal the pot with air fryer lid and select air fry mode and cook at 390 F for 15 minutes.
5. Serve and enjoy.

Nutritional Value (Amount per Serving):
Calories 243; Fat 20.2 g; Carbohydrates 5.3 g; Sugar 1.3 g; Protein 10.4 g; Cholesterol 51 mg

Meatloaf

Preparation Time: 10 minutes; Cooking Time: 25 minutes; Serve: 6
Ingredients:
- 1 egg
- 1/2 onion, minced
- 1/2 cup breadcrumbs
- 1/4 tsp pepper
- 1/4 cup milk
- 1 lb ground beef
- 1 1/2 carrots, shredded
- 1/2 tsp salt

Directions:
1. Add all ingredients into the bowl and mix until combined.
2. Spray an 8-inch loaf pan with cooking spray.

3. Transfer meat mixture into the loaf pan and cover pan with foil.
4. Pour 2 cups of water into the inner pot of instant pot duo crisp then place steamer rack in the pot.
5. Place loaf pan on top of the steamer rack.
6. Seal the pot with pressure cooking lid and cook on high for 25 minutes.
7. Once done, allow to release pressure naturally. Remove lid.
8. Slice and serve.

Nutritional Value (Amount per Serving):
Calories 202; Fat 6.1 g; Carbohydrates 9.5 g; Sugar 2.2 g; Protein 25.6 g; Cholesterol 96 mg

Butter Cabbage Pork Chops

Preparation Time: 10 minutes; Cooking Time: 30 minutes; Serve: 6
Ingredients:
- 2 lbs pork chops, boneless
- 1 stick butter
- 1 small cabbage head, cut into thick slices
- 2 cups beef stock
- 1/4 tsp garlic powder
- Pepper
- Salt

Directions:
1. Season pork chops with garlic powder, pepper and salt, and place into the inner pot of instant pot duo crisp.
2. Pour remaining ingredients over pork chops.
3. Seal the pot with pressure cooking lid and cook on high for 10 minutes.
4. Once done, allow to release pressure naturally for 10 minutes then release remaining pressure using a quick release. Remove lid.
5. Serve and enjoy.

Nutritional Value (Amount per Serving):
Calories 655; Fat 53.1 g; Carbohydrates 7 g; Sugar 3.9 g; Protein 36.6 g; Cholesterol 171 mg

Beef with Veggie

Preparation Time: 10 minutes; Cooking Time: 45 minutes; Serve: 6
Ingredients:
- 3 lbs beef chuck, cut into 2-inch pieces
- 1/2 tsp black pepper
- 1/2 tsp paprika
- 1/2 tsp cumin
- 1/4 cup ketchup
- 1 tbsp soy sauce
- 1 bay leaf
- 1 cup red wine
- 1 onion, cut into wedges
- 3 carrots, cut into chunks
- 1 tbsp olive oil
- 1 cup beef stock
- 1 tsp sea salt

Directions:
1. Set instant pot duo crisp on sauté mode.
2. Coat meat with oil and season with paprika, cumin, pepper, and salt.
3. Add the meat into the instant pot along with onion and carrots and sauté until meat is brown.
4. Seal the pot with air fryer lid and select air fry mode and cook at 350 F for 10-15 minutes.
5. Add red wine, stock, ketchup, soy sauce, and bay leaf. Stir well.
6. Seal the pot with pressure cooking lid and cook on high for 30 minutes.
7. Once done, release pressure using a quick release. Remove lid.
8. Set pot on sauté mode and cook until sauce reduce.
9. Serve and enjoy.

Nutritional Value (Amount per Serving):

Calories 510; Fat 16.7 g; Carbohydrates 9 g; Sugar 4.9 g; Protein 70.2 g; Cholesterol 203 mg

Beef Roast

Preparation Time: 10 minutes; Cooking Time: 45 minutes; Serve: 2

Ingredients:

- 1 lb beef roast
- 2 whole cloves
- 1/2 tsp ginger, grated
- 1/2 cup of water
- 1/2 tsp garlic powder
- 1/2 tsp thyme
- 1/4 tsp pepper
- 1/4 tsp salt

Directions:

1. Mix together ginger, cloves, thyme, garlic powder, pepper, and salt and rub over meat.
2. Place meat into the inner pot instant pot duo crisp and pour water around the meat.
3. Seal the pot with pressure cooking lid and cook on high for 45 minutes.
4. Once done, release pressure using a quick release. Remove lid.
5. Remove meat from pot and shred using a fork.
6. Serve and enjoy.

Nutritional Value (Amount per Serving):

Calories 433; Fat 14.6 g; Carbohydrates 2.5 g; Sugar 0.2 g; Protein 69.1 g; Cholesterol 203 mg

Cajun Beef

Preparation Time: 10 minutes; Cooking Time: 12 minutes; Serve: 2

Ingredients:

- 1/2 lb ground beef
- 1/2 cup chicken broth
- 5 oz Mexican cheese blend
- 1/2 tbsp Cajun seasoning
- 1/2 tbsp olive oil
- 1 tbsp tomato paste
- Pepper
- Salt

Directions:

1. Add oil into the inner pot of instant pot duo crisp and set pot on sauté mode.
2. Add meat to the pot and cook until browned.
3. Add Cajun seasoning and tomato paste. Stir well.
4. Add broth and stir. Seal the pot with pressure cooking lid and cook on high for 7 minutes.
5. Once done, release pressure using a quick release. Remove lid.
6. Add cheese and stir well. Seal the pot again with pressure cooking lid and cook on high for 5 minutes.
7. Once done, release pressure using a quick release. Remove lid.
8. Serve and enjoy.

Nutritional Value (Amount per Serving):

Calories 279; Fat 33.4 g; Carbohydrates 4.3 g; Sugar 1.1 g; Protein 51 g; Cholesterol 164 mg

Flavorful Short Ribs

Preparation Time: 10 minutes; Cooking Time: 35 minutes; Serve: 2

Ingredients:

- 1 lb beef short ribs
- 1 1/2 tsp garlic, minced
- 2 tbsp swerve
- 2 tbsp coconut amino
- 1/2 cup chicken broth
- 1/2 tbsp ginger, grated
- 1/2 tsp five-spice powder

Directions:

1. Add broth, five-spice powder, garlic, swerve, and coconut amino in the inner pot of instant pot duo crisp and stir well.

2. Place ribs in instant pot.
3. Seal the pot with pressure cooking lid and cook on high for 35 minutes.
4. Once done, allow to release pressure naturally. Remove lid.
5. Serve and enjoy.

Nutritional Value (Amount per Serving):
Calories 502; Fat 20.9 g; Carbohydrates 6.9 g; Sugar 0.2 g; Protein 67 g; Cholesterol 206 mg

Ginger Garlic Beef Roast

Preparation Time: 10 minutes; Cooking Time: 45 minutes; Serve: 2

Ingredients:
- 1 lb beef roast
- 1/2 tsp thyme
- 2 garlic cloves
- 1/2 tsp ginger, grated
- 1/2 cup of water
- 1/2 tsp garlic powder
- 1/4 tsp salt

Directions:
1. In a small bowl, mix together all spices and rub over the meat.
2. Place meat into the inner pot of instant pot duo crisp.
3. Add garlic cloves on top. Pour water around the meat.
4. Seal the pot with pressure cooking lid and cook on high for 45 minutes.
5. Once done, release pressure using a quick release. Remove lid.
6. Remove meat from pot and shred using a fork.
7. Serve and enjoy.

Nutritional Value (Amount per Serving):
Calories 430; Fat 14.2 g; Carbohydrates 2 g; Sugar 0.2 g; Protein 69.2 g; Cholesterol 203 mg

Beef Shank

Preparation Time: 10 minutes; Cooking Time: 37 minutes; Serve: 2

Ingredients:
- 1 lb beef shank
- 1/2 green chili pepper, chopped
- 1 garlic clove, minced
- 1/2 cup mushrooms, sliced
- 1/2 tsp dried thyme
- 1/2 tbsp fresh ginger, grated
- 1/2 tbsp olive oil
- 1 cup beef broth
- 1/2 cup tomatoes, diced
- 1/4 tsp red chili flakes
- 1/2 tsp salt

Directions:
1. Season meat with pepper and salt and set aside.
2. Add oil into the inner pot of instant pot duo crisp and set the pot on sauté mode.
3. Add garlic and green chili and sauté for 2 minutes.
4. Add mushrooms and cook for 3-5 minutes.
5. Add meat to the pot and season with thyme, grated ginger, and chili flakes. Add broth and stir well.
6. Seal the pot with pressure cooking lid and cook on high for 25 minutes.
7. Once done, release pressure using a quick release. Remove lid.
8. Set pot on sauté mode. Add tomatoes and cook for 5 minutes.
9. Stir and serve.

Nutritional Value (Amount per Serving):
Calories 490; Fat 18.6 g; Carbohydrates 4.5 g; Sugar 2 g; Protein 72.4 g; Cholesterol 203 mg

Creamy roast with Mushrooms

Preparation Time: 10 minutes; Cooking Time: 20 minutes; Serve: 2

Ingredients:

- 1/2 lb beef shoulder roast, cut into pieces
- 1/4 cup heavy cream
- 1/2 cup mushrooms, sliced
- 1/2 tsp garlic powder
- 1/4 tsp black pepper
- 1 cup beef broth
- 1/2 tbsp butter
- 1/2 small onion, diced
- 1/2 tsp dried thyme
- 1/2 tsp salt

Directions:

1. Add butter into the inner pot of instant pot duo crisp and set pot on sauté mode.
2. Add mushrooms and onion and season with thyme and salt. Cook for 10 minutes.
3. Add heavy cream and bring to boil, simmer for 3-5 minutes.
4. Pour mushroom mixture to the food processor and process until smooth. Set aside.
5. Add meat to the pot and season with garlic powder, pepper, and salt.
6. Pour broth over meat.
7. Seal the pot with pressure cooking lid and cook on high for 15 minutes.
8. Once done, release pressure using a quick release. Remove lid.
9. Transfer meat on a plate and drizzle with blended mushroom sauce.
10. Serve and enjoy.

Nutritional Value (Amount per Serving):

Calories 281; Fat 17.3 g; Carbohydrates 3.9 g; Sugar 1.6 g; Protein 26.8 g; Cholesterol 98 mg

Shredded Pork

Preparation Time: 10 minutes; Cooking Time: 35 minutes; Serve: 2
Ingredients:

- 1/2 lb pork belly, cut into cubes
- 1/2 cup onion, chopped
- 1/2 cup chicken stock
- 1 tsp thyme
- 3 tbsp water
- 1 1/2 tsp black pepper
- 1/4 tsp salt

Directions:

1. Add all ingredients into the inner pot of instant pot duo crisp and stir well.
2. Seal the pot with pressure cooking lid and cook on high for 35 minutes.
3. Once done, release pressure using a quick release. Remove lid.
4. Remove meat from pot and shred.
5. Serve and enjoy.

Nutritional Value (Amount per Serving):

Calories 543; Fat 30.8 g; Carbohydrates 4.2 g; Sugar 1.4 g; Protein 53.1 g; Cholesterol 131 mg

Italian Pork Chops

Preparation Time: 10 minutes; Cooking Time: 15 minutes; Serve: 2
Ingredients:

- 4 oz pork chops, boneless
- 1/2 tbsp olive oil
- 1/2 tbsp Italian seasoning
- 1/2 tsp garlic powder
- 3 oz goat cheese, crumbled
- 1/4 cup chicken stock
- Pepper
- Salt

Directions:

1. Season pork chops with Italian seasoning, garlic powder, pepper, and salt and set aside.
2. Add oil into the inner pot instant pot and set the pot on sauté mode.
3. Add pork chops into the pot and cook until browned.
4. Pour stock over pork chops.
5. Seal the pot with pressure cooking lid and cook on high for 10 minutes.

6. Once done, allow to release pressure naturally for 10 minutes then release remaining pressure using a quick release. Remove lid.
7. Transfer pork chops on a plate.
8. Add cheese into the pot and stir until melted.
9. Pour pot sauce over pork chops and serve.

Nutritional Value (Amount per Serving):
Calories 418; Fat 33.8 g; Carbohydrates 1.9 g; Sugar 1.5 g; Protein 26 g; Cholesterol 69 mg

Baked Pork Chops

Preparation Time: 10 minutes; Cooking Time: 35 minutes; Serve: 4
Ingredients:
- 4 pork chops, boneless
- 1/2 tsp paprika
- 1/2 tsp garlic powder
- 2 tbsp olive oil
- 1/2 tsp Italian seasoning
- 1/4 tsp pepper
- 1/2 tsp sea salt

Directions:
1. In a small bowl, mix together garlic powder, paprika, Italian seasoning, pepper, and salt.
2. Brush pork chops with oil and season with garlic powder mixture.
3. Place pork chops into the instant pot air fryer basket and place basket in the pot.
4. Seal the pot with air fryer lid and select bake mode and cook at 375 F for 30-35 minutes.
5. Serve and enjoy.

Nutritional Value (Amount per Serving):
Calories 320; Fat 27 g; Carbohydrates 0.5 g; Sugar 0.2 g; Protein 18 g; Cholesterol 69 mg

Garlic Rosemary Pork Chops

Preparation Time: 10 minutes; Cooking Time: 35 minutes; Serve: 4
Ingredients:
- 4 pork chops, boneless
- 1 tsp dried rosemary, crushed
- 1/4 tsp onion powder
- 2 garlic cloves, minced
- 1/4 tsp pepper
- 1/4 tsp sea salt

Directions:
1. Season pork chops with onion powder, pepper, and salt.
2. Mix together rosemary and garlic and rub over pork chops.
3. Place pork chops into the instant pot air fryer basket and place basket in the pot.
4. Seal the pot with air fryer lid and select roast mode and cook at 350 F for 30-35 minutes.
5. Serve and enjoy.

Nutritional Value (Amount per Serving):
Calories 262; Fat 20 g; Carbohydrates 1 g; Sugar 0 g; Protein 19 g; Cholesterol 70 mg

Baked Italian Pork Chops

Preparation Time: 10 minutes; Cooking Time: 30 minutes; Serve: 4
Ingredients:
- 4 pork loin chops, boneless
- 1 tsp Italian seasoning
- 1 tbsp fresh rosemary, chopped
- 2 garlic cloves, minced
- 1/4 tsp black pepper
- 1/2 tsp kosher salt

Directions:
1. Season pork chops with pepper and salt.
2. In a small bowl, mix together garlic, Italian seasoning, and rosemary.
3. Rub Pork chops with garlic and rosemary mixture.
4. Place pork chops into the instant pot air fryer basket and place basket in the pot.

5. Seal the pot with air fryer lid and select roast mode and cook at 400 F for 25-30 minutes.
6. Serve and enjoy.

Nutritional Value (Amount per Serving):
Calories 260; Fat 19 g; Carbohydrates 2 g; Sugar 0 g; Protein 18 g; Cholesterol 68 mg

Paprika Pork Tenderloin

Preparation Time: 10 minutes; Cooking Time: 30 minutes; Serve: 4
Ingredients:
- 1 lb pork tenderloin
- For rub:
- 1 tbsp onion powder
- 1 tbsp paprika
- 1/2 tbsp garlic powder
- 1/4 tbsp salt

Directions:
1. In a small bowl, mix together all rub ingredients and rub over tenderloin.
2. Place tenderloin into the instant pot air fryer basket and place basket in the pot.
3. Seal the pot air fryer lid and select roast mode and cook at 400 F for 25-30 minutes.
4. Sliced and serve.

Nutritional Value (Amount per Serving):
Calories 224; Fat 5 g; Carbohydrates 2 g; Sugar 1 g; Protein 40 g; Cholesterol 45 mg

Delicious Herb Pork Chops

Preparation Time: 10 minutes; Cooking Time: 30 minutes; Serve: 4
Ingredients:
- 4 pork chops, boneless
- 1 tbsp olive oil
- 2 garlic cloves, minced
- 1 tsp dried rosemary, crushed
- 1 tsp oregano
- 1/2 tsp thyme
- 1 tbsp fresh rosemary, chopped
- 1/4 tsp pepper
- 1/4 tsp salt

Directions:
1. Season pork chops with pepper and salt and set aside.
2. Mix together garlic, oil, rosemary, oregano, thyme, and fresh rosemary and rub over pork chops.
3. Place pork chops into the instant pot air fryer basket and place basket in the pot.
4. Seal the pot with air fryer lid and select roast mode and cook at 400 F for 30 minutes.
5. Serve and enjoy.

Nutritional Value (Amount per Serving):
Calories 261; Fat 22 g; Carbohydrates 2.5 g; Sugar 0 g; Protein 19 g; Cholesterol 65 mg

Spicy Baked Pork Tenderloin

Preparation Time: 10 minutes; Cooking Time: 35 minutes; Serve: 4
Ingredients:
- 1 lb pork tenderloin
- 2 garlic cloves, chopped
- Pepper
- Salt
- For the spice mix:
- 1/4 tsp allspice
- 1/4 tsp coriander powder
- 1/4 tsp cayenne
- 1/4 tsp oregano
- 1/4 tsp cloves
- 1/4 tsp cinnamon
- 1/4 tsp cumin

Directions:
1. In a small bowl, mix together all spice ingredients and set aside.
2. Make small cuts on pork tenderloin using a knife and insert chopped garlic into each slit.
3. Rub pork tenderloin with spice mixture.

4. Place pork tenderloin into the instant pot air fryer basket and place basket in the pot.
5. Seal the pot with air fryer lid and select roast mode and cook at 375 F for 30-35 minutes.
6. Slice and serve.

Nutritional Value (Amount per Serving):

Calories 221; Fat 6 g; Carbohydrates 2 g; Sugar 0.1 g; Protein 40 g; Cholesterol 74 mg

Rosemary Thyme Pork Tenderloin

Preparation Time: 10 minutes; Cooking Time: 35 minutes; Serve: 3
Ingredients:
- 1 lb pork tenderloin
- 1/4 tsp thyme
- 1/2 tbsp dried rosemary
- 1 tbsp olive oil
- Pepper
- Salt

Directions:
1. Mix together rosemary, thyme, and olive oil and rub over pork tenderloin.
2. Place pork tenderloin into the instant pot air fryer basket and place basket in the pot.
3. Seal the pot with air fryer lid and select roast mode and cook at 400 F for 30-35 minutes.
4. Slice and serve.

Nutritional Value (Amount per Serving):

Calories 254; Fat 10 g; Carbohydrates 1 g; Sugar 0 g; Protein 40 g; Cholesterol 75 mg

Meatballs

Preparation Time: 10 minutes; Cooking Time: 25 minutes; Serve: 8
Ingredients:
- 3 eggs
- 1/2 cup fresh parsley, minced
- 2 lbs ground beef
- 1 tsp cinnamon
- 1 tsp garlic, minced
- 1 cup almond flour
- 1 onion, grated
- 1 1/2 tsp dried oregano
- 2 tsp cumin
- 1 tsp pepper
- 2 tsp salt

Directions:
1. Add all ingredients into the bowl and mix until combined.
2. Make small meatballs from mixture and place into the instant pot air fryer basket and place basket in the pot.
3. Seal the pot with air fryer lid and select bake mode and cook at 400 F for 20-25 minutes.
4. Serve and enjoy.

Nutritional Value (Amount per Serving):

Calories 324; Fat 16 g; Carbohydrates 6 g; Sugar 2 g; Protein 40 g; Cholesterol 54 mg

Roasted Sirloin Steak

Preparation Time: 10 minutes; Cooking Time: 30 minutes; Serve: 6
Ingredients:
- 2 lbs sirloin steak, cut into 1-inch cubes
- 2 garlic cloves, minced
- 2 tbsp fresh lemon juice
- 2 tsp dried oregano
- 1/4 cup water
- 1/4 cup olive oil
- 2 cups fresh parsley, chopped
- 1/2 tsp black pepper
- 1 tsp salt

Directions:
1. Add all ingredients except meat into the large bowl and mix well.
2. Cover bowl and place in the refrigerator for 1 hour.
3. Place marinated beef into the instant pot air fryer basket and place basket in the pot.

4. Seal the pot with air fryer lid and select bake mode and cook at 400 F for 30 minutes.
5. Serve and enjoy.

Nutritional Value (Amount per Serving):
Calories 365; Fat 18 g; Carbohydrates 2 g; Sugar 1 g; Protein 45 g; Cholesterol 132 mg

Braised Chuck Roast

Preparation Time: 10 minutes; Cooking Time: 8 hours; Serve: 6
Ingredients:

- 2 lbs beef chuck roast
- 2 tbsp arrowroot
- 3 shallots, sliced
- 1 onion, sliced
- 1/4 cup balsamic vinegar
- 1 cup of water
- 1/4 tsp pepper
- 1/2 tsp salt

Directions:

1. Place meat into the inner pot of instant pot duo crisp.
2. Pour remaining ingredients over meat.
3. Seal the pot with pressure cooking lid and select slow cook mode and cook on low for 8 hours.
4. Serve and enjoy.

Nutritional Value (Amount per Serving):
Calories 559; Fat 42 g; Carbohydrates 2.2 g; Sugar 0.8 g; Protein 40 g; Cholesterol 156 mg

Flavors Pork Roast

Preparation Time: 10 minutes; Cooking Time: 30 minutes; Serve: 6
Ingredients:

- 3 lbs pork roast
- 1/2 cup beef broth
- 1 cup of water
- 1 tbsp olive oil
- 1/4 tsp chili powder
- 1/2 tsp garlic powder
- 1/2 tsp onion powder
- 1/2 tsp black pepper
- 1/2 tsp salt

Directions:

1. In a small bowl, mix together all spices and rub over meat.
2. Add oil into the inner pot of instant pot duo crisp and set pot on sauté mode.
3. Add the meat into the pot and cook until brown.
4. Add remaining ingredients and stir well.
5. Seal the pot with pressure cooking lid and cook on high for 25 minutes.
6. Once done, release pressure using a quick release. Remove lid.
7. Serve and enjoy.

Nutritional Value (Amount per Serving):
Calories 500; Fat 23 g; Carbohydrates 2.8 g; Protein 65 g; Sugar 2.1 g; Cholesterol 195 mg

Spicy Pork Stew

Preparation Time: 10 minutes; Cooking Time: 50 minutes; Serve: 8
Ingredients:

- 4 lbs pork loin roast, cut into pieces
- 3 poblanos, diced
- 7 oz can green chilies, diced
- 3/4 cup beef broth
- 1 tbsp paprika
- 2 tbsp chili powder
- 14.5 oz can tomatoes with chilies
- 1 onion, diced
- 1 1/2 tbsp adobo seasoning
- 2 tsp salt

Directions:

1. Add all ingredients into the inner pot of instant pot duo crisp and stir well.

2. Seal the pot with pressure cooking lid and cook on high for 50 minutes.
3. Once done, allow to release pressure naturally. Remove lid.
4. Remove meat from pot and shred using a fork. Return shredded meat to the pot.
5. Stir and serve.

Nutritional Value (Amount per Serving):
Calories 568; Fat 24.2 g; Carbohydrates 13.5 g; Protein 70.9 g; Sugar 1.5 g; Cholesterol 13.5 mg

Shredded Flank Steak

Preparation Time: 10 minutes; Cooking Time: 8 hours; Serve: 4
Ingredients:
- 2 lbs flank steak
- 2 jalapeno, seeded and chopped
- 1 red bell pepper, chopped
- 1 green bell pepper, chopped
- 1 onion, chopped
- For rub:
- 1/4 tsp garlic powder
- 1/4 tsp onion powder
- 1 tsp cumin
- 1/2 tsp black pepper
- 1/4 tsp cayenne pepper
- 2 tsp chili powder
- 1 tsp salt

Directions:
1. In a small bowl, mix together all spice ingredients and rub over flak steak.
2. Place steak into the inner pot of instant pot duo crisp.
3. Add jalapeno pepper, bell peppers, and onion over meat.
4. Seal the pot with pressure cooking lid and select slow cook mode and cook on low for 8 hours.
5. Remove meat from pot and shred using a fork.
6. Return shredded meat to the pot.
7. Stir well and serve.

Nutritional Value (Amount per Serving):
Calories 475; Fat 20 g; Carbohydrates 8 g; Protein 66 g; Sugar 2.5 g; Cholesterol 125 mg

Artichoke Beef

Preparation Time: 10 minutes; Cooking Time: 6 hours; Serve: 6
Ingredients:
- 2 lbs stew beef, cut into 1-inch cubes
- 1 onion, diced
- 1/2 tsp dried basil
- 1/2 tsp dried oregano
- 2 cups can tomato
- 10 oz roasted red peppers, drained and sliced
- 10 oz artichoke hearts, drained
- Pepper
- Salt

Directions:
1. Add all ingredients into the inner pot of instant pot duo crisp and stir well.
2. Seal the pot with pressure cooking lid and select slow cook mode and cook on low for 6 hours.
3. Serve and enjoy.

Nutritional Value (Amount per Serving):
Calories 345; Fat 20 g; Carbohydrates 8 g; Sugar 10 g; Protein 65 g; Cholesterol 66 mg

Greek Beef with Olives

Preparation Time: 10 minutes; Cooking Time: 6 hours; Serve: 6
Ingredients:
- 2 lbs beef stew meat, cut into 1/2-inch pieces
- 1/2 cup feta cheese, crumbled
- 1/2 cup olives, pitted and cut in half

- 28 oz can tomato, diced
- 1/4 tsp pepper
- 1/2 tsp salt

Directions:

1. Add all ingredients into the inner pot of instant pot duo crisp and stir well.
2. Seal the pot with pressure cooking lid and select slow cook mode and cook on high for 6 hours.
3. Serve and enjoy.

Nutritional Value (Amount per Serving):

Calories 370; Fat 14 g; Carbohydrates 9 g; Sugar 5 g; Protein 50 g; Cholesterol 85 mg

Chapter 3: Soups & Stews

Flavorful Broccoli Cheese Soup

Preparation Time: 10 minutes; Cooking Time: 10 minutes; Serve: 4

Ingredients:

- 4 cups broccoli florets
- 1/4 cup water
- 1 cup cheddar cheese, shredded
- 1 3/4 cups heavy cream
- 1 tsp garlic, minced
- 1 1/2 cups carrots, chopped
- 1/2 cup onion, minced
- 3 cups vegetable broth
- 1 1/2 tbsp arrowroot flour
- 1 cup parmesan cheese, shredded
- Pepper
- Salt

Directions:

1. Add broccoli, garlic, carrots, onion, broth, pepper, and salt into the instant pot duo crisp.
2. Seal the pot with pressure cooking lid and cook on high pressure for 2 minutes.
3. Once done, allow to release pressure naturally for 5 minutes then release remaining pressure using a quick release. Remove lid.
4. Add heavy cream and stir well.
5. Set instant pot on sauté mode and cook until soup begins to simmer. Turn off the pot.
6. Add cheddar cheese and parmesan cheese and stir well.
7. In a small bowl, mix together water and arrowroot flour and pour into the soup and stir until thickens.
8. Serve and enjoy.

Nutritional Value (Amount per Serving):

Calories 403; Fat 31.6 g; Carbohydrates 14.8 g; Sugar 4.9 g; Protein 17.2 g; Cholesterol 107 mg

Creamy Basil Tomato Soup

Preparation Time: 10 minutes; Cooking Time: 22 minutes; Serve: 8

Ingredients:

- 28 oz can tomato, diced
- 2 tsp dried basil
- 1/2 cup heavy cream
- 2 cups vegetable broth
- 1 bay leaf
- 1/4 tsp red pepper flakes
- 2 tbsp olive oil
- 2 carrots, diced
- 2 celery stalks, diced
- 1 onion, diced
- 1/4 tsp pepper
- 1 tsp salt

Directions:

1. Add oil into the instant pot duo crisp and set pot on sauté mode.
2. Once the oil is hot then add carrots, celery, and onion and sauté for 5 minutes.
3. Add basil, red pepper flakes, pepper, and salt and sauté for 1-2 minutes.
4. Add tomatoes, bay leaf, and broth and stir well.
5. Seal the pot with pressure cooking lid and cook on high pressure for 15 minutes.
6. Once done, allow to release pressure naturally for 10 minutes then release remaining pressure using a quick release. Remove lid.
7. Discard bay leaf from soup. Using blender puree the soup until smooth.
8. Add cream and stir well.
9. Season with pepper and salt.
10. Serve and enjoy.

Nutritional Value (Amount per Serving):

Calories 100; Fat 6.7 g; Carbohydrates 8.7 g; Sugar 5 g; Protein 2.6 g; Cholesterol 10 mg

Flavorful Fish Stew

Preparation Time: 10 minutes; Cooking Time: 30 minutes; Serve: 5

Ingredients:

- 1 1/2 lbs white fish, remove bones and cut into 1-inch pieces
- 1 tbsp fresh parsley, chopped
- 1 tbsp fresh lime juice
- 2 tbsp coconut oil
- 1/2 tsp cayenne pepper
- 1 tbsp paprika
- 1 tbsp ground cumin
- 6 oz can coconut milk
- 8 oz fish broth
- 14 oz can tomato, crushed
- 1 tbsp garlic, minced
- 1 red bell pepper, sliced
- 1 onion, diced
- 1/4 tsp pepper
- 1 tsp salt

Directions:

1. Add oil into the instant pot duo crisp and set pot on sauté mode.
2. Add garlic, bell pepper, and onion and sauté for 3-5 minutes.
3. Add tomatoes, broth, coconut milk, cumin, paprika, cayenne, pepper, and salt and stir well.
4. Seal the pot with pressure cooking lid and cook on high pressure for 10 minutes.
5. Once done, release pressure using a quick release. Remove lid.
6. Set pot on sauté mode and cook the stew for 10 minutes.
7. Add fish and stir until fish is cooked, about 5 minutes.
8. Turn off the instant pot. Add lime juice and stir well.
9. Garnish with parsley and serve.

Nutritional Value (Amount per Serving):

Calories 620; Fat 53.5 g; Carbohydrates 14.5 g; Sugar 7 g; Protein 24.1 g; Cholesterol 10 mg

Creamy Cauliflower Soup

Preparation Time: 10 minutes; Cooking Time: 10 minutes; Serve: 6

Ingredients:

- 1 medium cauliflower head, cut into florets
- 2 tbsp green onion, chopped
- 1 1/2 cups cheddar cheese, shredded
- 1/2 cup sour cream
- 3 cups vegetable broth
- 1 tsp garlic, minced
- 1 celery stalk, chopped
- 1 onion, chopped
- 1 tbsp olive oil
- 6 bacon slices, cooked and chopped
- Pepper
- Salt

Directions:

1. Add oil into the instant pot and set the pot on sauté mode.
2. Add garlic, celery, onion, pepper, and salt and sauté for 3-5 minutes.
3. Add cauliflower and broth and stir well.
4. Seal the pot with pressure cooking lid and cook on high pressure for 5 minutes.
5. Once done, allow to release pressure naturally for 10 minutes then release remaining pressure using a quick release. Remove lid.
6. Add 1 cup shredded cheese and sour cream and stir well.
7. Blend soup using immersion blender until smooth.
8. Top with bacon, green onion, and remaining cheese.
9. Serve and enjoy.

Nutritional Value (Amount per Serving):

Calories 330; Fat 24.5 g; Carbohydrates 9.1 g; Sugar 3.7 g; Protein 19.3 g; Cholesterol 59 mg

Easy Chicken Soup

Preparation Time: 10 minutes; Cooking Time: 40 minutes; Serve: 8

Ingredients:

- 1 1/2 lbs chicken breasts, boneless and cut into chunks
- 4 cups of water
- 4 cups chicken broth
- 2 tsp thyme
- 2 tsp basil
- 1 onion, chopped
- 1 tbsp garlic, minced
- 2 celery stalks, chopped
- 5 carrots, peeled and chopped
- 1/2 tsp pepper
- 2 tsp salt

Directions:

1. Add all ingredients into the inner pot of instant pot duo crisp. Stir well.
2. Seal the pot with pressure cooking lid and cook on high pressure for 40 minutes.
3. Once done, release pressure using a quick release. Remove lid.
4. Stir well and serve immediately.

Nutritional Value (Amount per Serving):

Calories 205; Fat 7 g; Carbohydrates 6.2 g; Sugar 2.9 g; Protein 27.6 g; Cholesterol 76 mg

Tasty Mexican Chicken Soup

Preparation Time: 10 minutes; Cooking Time: 15 minutes; Serve: 5

Ingredients:

- 1 lb chicken breast, skinless and boneless
- 1 cup cheddar cheese, shredded
- 1/2 cup cream cheese
- 1 cup half and half
- 1 1/2 cups chicken stock
- 1 tsp paprika
- 1 1/2 tsp chili powder
- 1 tsp dried oregano
- 1 1/2 tsp cumin powder
- 1 bell pepper, chopped
- 1 tbsp garlic, minced
- 1 onion, chopped
- 2 tsp olive oil
- 14 oz can fire-roasted tomatoes
- Salt

Directions:

1. Add oil into the instant pot duo crisp and set pot on sauté mode.
2. Add onion and garlic and sauté until onion is softened.
3. Add paprika, oregano, chilli powder, and cumin powder and sauté for 1 minute.
4. Add stock, roasted tomatoes, and salt and stir well. Add chicken breast.
5. Seal the pot with pressure cooking lid and cook on high pressure for 8 minutes.
6. Once done, allow to release pressure naturally for 10 minutes then release remaining pressure using a quick release. Remove lid.
7. Remove chicken from pot and shred using a fork.
8. Return shredded chicken to the pot along with bell pepper, half and half, cheddar cheese, and cream cheese and stir until cheese is melted.
9. Serve and enjoy.

Nutritional Value (Amount per Serving):

Calories 403; Fat 25.9 g; Carbohydrates 12.6 g; Sugar 4.7 g; Protein 29.8 g; Cholesterol 125 mg

Curried Chicken Soup

Preparation Time: 10 minutes; Cooking Time: 10 minutes; Serve: 6

Ingredients:

- 2 lbs chicken breast, boneless and cut into 1-inch cubes
- 1/4 cup fresh cilantro, chopped
- 1 cup of coconut milk
- 2 1/2 cups spinach, chopped
- 1 cup can tomato, diced

- 4 cups chicken broth
- 2 tbsp curry powder
- 1 tbsp ginger, minced
- 1 tbsp garlic, minced
- 1 cup onion, chopped
- 2 tbsp butter
- Pepper
- Salt

Directions:
1. Add butter into the instant pot duo crisp and set pot on sauté mode.
2. Add onion and sauté for 2 minutes.
3. Add ginger and garlic and sauté for 30 seconds.
4. Add remaining ingredients except for spinach, coconut milk, and cilantro and stir well.
5. Seal the pot with pressure cooking lid and cook on high pressure for 5 minutes.
6. Once done, allow to release pressure naturally for 10 minutes then release remaining pressure using a quick release. Remove lid.
7. Set pot on sauté mode. Add coconut milk and spinach and stir until spinach is wilted.
8. Turn off the instant pot.
9. Garnish with cilantro and serve.

Nutritional Value (Amount per Serving):
Calories 355; Fat 18.5 g; Carbohydrates 9.4 g; Sugar 4.1 g; Protein 37.6 g; Cholesterol 107 mg

Buffalo Chicken Soup

Preparation Time: 10 minutes; Cooking Time: 10 minutes; Serve: 6
Ingredients:
- 1 lb chicken, cooked and shredded
- 1/2 cup heavy cream
- 5 oz cream cheese, cubed
- 2 1/2 tbsp buffalo sauce
- 4 cups chicken broth
- 1 tbsp garlic, minced
- 1/2 cup celery, diced
- 1/2 onion, diced
- 1 tbsp olive oil
- Pepper
- Salt

Directions:
1. Add oil into the instant pot duo crisp and set pot on sauté mode.
2. Add celery and onion and sauté until onion is softened about 5 minutes.
3. Add garlic and sauté for a minute. Add shredded chicken, buffalo sauce, and broth and stir well.
4. Seal the pot with pressure cooking lid and cook on high pressure for 5 minutes.
5. Once done, allow to release pressure naturally for 5 minutes then release remaining pressure using a quick release. Remove lid.
6. Transfer 1 cup of soup and cream cheese into the blender and blend until smooth. Return blended soup to the pot.
7. Add heavy cream and stir well.
8. Serve and enjoy.

Nutritional Value (Amount per Serving):
Calories 289; Fat 17.5 g; Carbohydrates 3.9 g; Sugar 1 g; Protein 27.4 g; Cholesterol 98 mg

Creamy & Tasty Chicken Soup

Preparation Time: 10 minutes; Cooking Time: 25 minutes; Serve: 6
Ingredients:
- 1 lb chicken breast, skinless and boneless
- 1 cup cheddar cheese, shredded
- 1/2 cup cream cheese
- 1 cup heavy cream
- 1 1/2 cups chicken broth
- 1 tsp paprika
- 1 tsp chili powder
- 1 tsp dried oregano
- 1 tsp cumin powder

- 1 bell pepper, sliced
- 1 tbsp garlic, minced
- 1 onion, chopped
- 1 tbsp olive oil
- 1 small jar sun-dried tomatoes, drained
- Pepper
- Salt

Directions:
1. Add oil into the instant pot duo crisp and set pot on sauté mode.
2. Add garlic and onion and sauté for 3-5 minutes.
3. Add remaining ingredients except for cheddar cheese, cream cheese, and heavy cream and stir well.
4. Seal the pot with pressure cooking lid and cook on high pressure for 20 minutes.
5. Once done, release pressure using a quick release. Remove lid.
6. Remove chicken from pot and shred using a fork. Return shredded chicken to the pot.
7. Set pot on sauté mode. Add cheddar cheese, cream cheese, and heavy cream and stir until cheese is melted.
8. Season soup with pepper and salt.
9. Serve and enjoy.

Nutritional Value (Amount per Serving):
Calories 372; Fat 25.5 g; Carbohydrates 11 g; Sugar 5.6 g; Protein 25.8 g; Cholesterol 117 mg

No Bean Beef Chili

Preparation Time: 10 minutes; Cooking Time: 45 minutes; Serve: 10
Ingredients:
- 2 1/2 ground beef
- 1 cup beef broth
- 4 oz can green chilies, diced
- 6 oz can tomato paste
- 14 oz can tomato, diced
- 14 oz can fire-roasted tomatoes, diced
- 1 tsp cumin
- 2 tbsp chili powder
- 1 1/2 tbsp garlic, minced
- 1/2 cup onion, diced
- 2 tbsp olive oil
- Pepper
- Salt

Directions:
1. Add oil into the instant pot duo crisp and set pot on sauté mode.
2. Add onion and sauté for 3-5 minutes. Add garlic and sauté for a minute.
3. Add ground meat and cook until browned, about 6-10 minutes.
4. Add remaining ingredients and stir well.
5. Seal the pot with pressure cooking lid and cook on high pressure for 30 minutes.
6. Once done, allow to release pressure naturally. Remove lid.
7. Serve and enjoy.

Nutritional Value (Amount per Serving):
Calories 113; Fat 4.6 g; Carbohydrates 10 g; Sugar 4.8 g; Protein 8.6 g; Cholesterol 19 mg

Vegan Cauliflower Soup

Preparation Time: 10 minutes; Cooking Time: 6 minutes; Serve: 4
Ingredients:
- 5 cups cauliflower florets
- 1 tbsp fresh lemon juice
- 3 cups vegetable broth
- 1/2 tsp cinnamon
- 1/2 tsp turmeric
- 1/2 cup cashews
- 1 tbsp garlic, minced
- 1 onion, diced
- 1 tbsp olive oil
- 1 tsp salt

Directions:
1. Add oil into the instant pot duo crisp and set pot on sauté mode.

2. Add garlic and onion and sauté for 3 minutes.
3. Add broth, cinnamon, turmeric, cashews, cauliflower, and salt and stir well.
4. Seal the pot with pressure cooking lid and cook on high pressure for 3 minutes.
5. Once done, allow to release pressure naturally for 10 minutes then release remaining pressure using a quick release. Remove lid.
6. Add lemon juice and stir well.
7. Blend soup using immersion blender until smooth.
8. Serve and enjoy.

Nutritional Value (Amount per Serving):
Calories 205; Fat 12.7 g; Carbohydrates 16.7 g; Sugar 5.7 g; Protein 9.2 g; Cholesterol 0 mg

Chicken Broccoli Soup

Preparation Time: 10 minutes; Cooking Time: 10 minutes; Serve: 8
Ingredients:
- 6 cups broccoli florets
- 2 cups cooked chicken, chopped
- 1 cup cheddar cheese, shredded
- 1/2 cup coconut milk
- 4 cups chicken stock
- 1 tbsp garlic, minced
- 1/2 onion, chopped
- 2 tbsp coconut oil
- 1/2 tsp sea salt

Directions:
1. Add oil into the instant pot duo crisp and set pot on sauté mode.
2. Add onion, garlic, and cumin and sauté until onion is softened.
3. Add broccoli, stock, pepper, and salt and stir well.
4. Seal the pot with pressure cooking lid and cook on high pressure for 4 minutes.
5. Once done, release pressure using a quick release. Remove lid.
6. Blend soup using immersion blender until smooth.
7. Set pot on sauté mode. Add cheese and chicken and stir until cheese is melted.
8. Serve and enjoy.

Nutritional Value (Amount per Serving):
Calories 206; Fat 13.3 g; Carbohydrates 6.9 g; Sugar 2.4 g; Protein 16.4 g; Cholesterol 42 mg

Broccoli Asparagus Soup

Preparation Time: 10 minutes; Cooking Time: 8 minutes; Serve: 6
Ingredients:
- 15 asparagus spears, cut the ends and chopped
- 1 tsp dried mixed herbs
- 1/4 cup nutritional yeast
- 1/2 cup coconut milk
- 3 1/2 cups vegetable broth
- 2 cups cauliflower florets
- 2 cups broccoli florets
- 2 tsp garlic, chopped
- 1 cup onion, chopped
- 2 tbsp olive oil
- Pepper
- Salt

Directions:
1. Add oil into the instant pot duo crisp and set pot on sauté mode.
2. Add onion and garlic and sauté for 3-5 minutes.
3. Add broth and all vegetables and stir well.
4. Seal the pot with pressure cooking lid and cook on high pressure for 3 minutes.
5. Once done, allow to release pressure naturally. Remove lid.
6. Blend soup using blender until smooth.
7. Add coconut milk, nutritional yeast, herbs, pepper, and salt and stir well.
8. Serve warm and enjoy.

Nutritional Value (Amount per Serving):
Calories 172; Fat 10.8 g; Carbohydrates 13 g; Sugar 4.4 g; Protein 9.5 g; Cholesterol 0 mg

Lemon Asparagus Soup

Preparation Time: 10 minutes; Cooking Time: 7 minutes; Serve: 4
Ingredients:

- 12 oz asparagus, trimmed and chopped
- 1 tsp nutritional yeast
- 2 tsp fresh lemon juice
- 1/4 tsp lemon zest
- 1/4 tsp dried mint
- 2 1/2 cups vegetable stock
- 1 tsp garlic, chopped
- 1 small onion, chopped
- 1 tsp olive oil
- Pepper
- Salt

Directions:

1. Add oil into the instant pot duo crisp and set pot on sauté mode.
2. Add garlic and onion and sauté for 2-3 minutes.
3. Add asparagus, lemon zest, mint, pepper, and salt and sauté for minute.
4. Add stock and stir well.
5. Seal the pot with pressure cooking lid and cook on high pressure for 3 minutes.
6. Once done, release pressure using a quick release. Remove lid.
7. Blend soup using blender until smooth. Add nutritional yeast and lemon juice and stir well.
8. Serve and enjoy.

Nutritional Value (Amount per Serving):
Calories 41; Fat 1.9 g; Carbohydrates 6.2 g; Sugar 2.9 g; Protein 2.5 g; Cholesterol 0 mg

Nutritious Asparagus Soup

Preparation Time: 10 minutes; Cooking Time: 17 minutes; Serve: 4
Ingredients:

- 1 lb asparagus, cut ends and chopped
- 2 turnips, peeled and chopped
- 4 cups vegetable broth
- 1 tsp garlic, minced
- 1 onion, chopped
- 2 tbsp olive oil
- Pepper
- Salt

Directions:

1. Add oil into the instant pot duo crisp and set pot on sauté mode.
2. Add vegetables and sauté for 2 minutes.
3. Add remaining ingredients and stir well.
4. Seal the pot with pressure cooking lid and cook on high pressure for 15 minutes.
5. Once done, allow to release pressure naturally. Remove lid.
6. Blend soup using blender until smooth.
7. Season with pepper and salt.
8. Serve and enjoy.

Nutritional Value (Amount per Serving):
Calories 151; Fat 8.5 g; Carbohydrates 12.1 g; Sugar 6.5 g; Protein 8.2 g; Cholesterol 0 mg

Mushroom Leek Soup

Preparation Time: 10 minutes; Cooking Time: 5 minutes; Serve: 4
Ingredients:

- 2 cups mushrooms, chopped
- 1/3 cup coconut milk
- 1 cup vegetable stock
- 1 tsp white pepper powder
- 1 tsp dried parsley
- 1 cup leeks, chopped

- 2 garlic cloves, chopped
- 1 tbsp olive oil

Directions:
1. Add oil into the instant pot duo crisp and set pot on sauté mode.
2. Add garlic and sauté for 30 seconds. Add leek and mushrooms and sauté for 2 minutes.
3. Add remaining ingredients except for coconut milk and stir well.
4. Seal the pot with pressure cooking lid and cook on high pressure for 2 minutes.
5. Once done, allow to release pressure naturally. Remove lid.
6. Blend soup using blender until smooth.
7. Add coconut milk and stir well.
8. Serve and enjoy.

Nutritional Value (Amount per Serving):
Calories 102; Fat 8.5 g; Carbohydrates 6.5 g; Sugar 2.3 g; Protein 2.2 g; Cholesterol 0 mg

Healthy Pumpkin Soup

Preparation Time: 10 minutes; Cooking Time: 10 minutes; Serve: 6
Ingredients:
- 15 oz can pumpkin puree
- 1 cup of coconut milk
- 2 cups vegetable broth
- 1/2 tsp nutmeg
- 1 tsp garlic, sliced
- 2 tsp ginger, grated
- 1 small onion, chopped
- 1 tbsp olive oil
- Pepper
- Salt

Directions:
1. Add oil into the instant pot duo crisp and set pot on sauté mode.
2. Add onion and sauté until softened.
3. Add ginger and garlic and sauté for 30 seconds.
4. Add remaining ingredients except for coconut milk and stir well.
5. Seal the pot with pressure cooking lid and cook on high pressure for 5 minutes.
6. Once done, allow to release pressure naturally for 5 minutes then release remaining pressure using a quick release. Remove lid.
7. Blend soup using blender until smooth.
8. Add coconut milk and stir well.
9. Serve and enjoy.

Nutritional Value (Amount per Serving):
Calories 166; Fat 12.5 g; Carbohydrates 10.9 g; Sugar 4 g; Protein 3.7 g; Cholesterol 0 mg

Easy Mushroom Soup

Preparation Time: 10 minutes; Cooking Time: 6 minutes; Serve: 6
Ingredients:
- 1 lb mushrooms, chopped
- 2 tbsp arrowroot flour
- 1 cup half and half
- 1 bay leaf
- 1 tsp dried thyme
- 2 cups vegetable broth
- 1 tbsp garlic, minced
- 1 onion, chopped
- 1/4 tsp pepper
- 1/2 tsp sea salt

Directions:
1. Add mushrooms, bay leaf, thyme, broth, garlic, onion, pepper, and salt into the instant pot duo crisp and stir well.
2. Seal the pot with pressure cooking lid and cook on high pressure for 4 minutes.
3. Once done, release pressure using a quick release. Remove lid.
4. Discard bay leaf. In a small bowl, whisk together half and half and arrowroot flour and pour into the pot.

5. Set pot on sauté mode and cook soup until thickens.
6. Serve and enjoy.

Nutritional Value (Amount per Serving):
Calories 94; Fat 5.4 g; Carbohydrates 7.4 g; Sugar 2.4 g; Protein 5.6 g; Cholesterol 15 mg

Curried Pumpkin Soup

Preparation Time: 10 minutes; Cooking Time: 20 minutes; Serve: 4
Ingredients:

- 2 cups can pumpkin puree
- 3 cups vegetable broth
- 1/2 tsp cumin
- 1 tsp curry powder
- 1 tsp ground ginger
- 2 tsp garlic, minced
- 1/2 cup onion, chopped
- 1 tbsp olive oil
- Pepper
- Salt

Directions:
1. Add oil into the instant pot duo crisp and set pot on sauté mode.
2. Add onion and sauté until softened. Add garlic and sauté for a minute.
3. Add remaining ingredients and stir well.
4. Seal the pot with pressure cooking lid and cook on high pressure for 15 minutes.
5. Once done, allow to release pressure naturally. Remove lid.
6. Season soup with pepper and salt.
7. Serve and enjoy.

Nutritional Value (Amount per Serving):
Calories 92; Fat 4.7 g; Carbohydrates 8.2 g; Sugar 3.2 g; Protein 4.5 g; Cholesterol 0 mg

Hearty Kale Sausage Pumpkin Soup

Preparation Time: 10 minutes; Cooking Time: 25 minutes; Serve: 12
Ingredients:

- 15 oz mushrooms, diced
- 1 lb kale, chopped
- 1 cup of coconut milk
- 14 oz can pumpkin puree
- 4 cups chicken broth
- 1/2 cup onion, diced
- 1 lb ground sausage
- 1 tbsp vinegar
- 1 tsp dried thyme
- 1 tbsp garlic, minced
- 2 tbsp olive oil
- Pepper
- Salt

Directions:
1. Add oil into the instant pot duo crisp and set pot on sauté mode.
2. Add mushrooms, pepper, and salt and sauté for 10 minutes.
3. Add garlic, vinegar, and thyme and sauté for 1-2 minutes. Remove mushroom mixture from pot and set aside.
4. Clean instant pot. Add onion and sausage into the pot and cook on sauté mode until sausage is browned.
5. Return mushroom mixture to the pot and stir well.
6. Add remaining ingredients except for coconut milk and stir well.
7. Seal the pot with pressure cooking lid and cook on high pressure for 10 minutes.
8. Once done, release pressure using a quick release. Remove lid.
9. Add coconut milk and stir well.
10. Serve and enjoy.

Nutritional Value (Amount per Serving):
Calories 286; Fat 18.4 g; Carbohydrates 18.9 g; Sugar 6.4 g; Protein 12.9 g; Cholesterol 32 mg

Spicy Mushroom Soup

Preparation Time: 10 minutes; Cooking Time: 10 minutes; Serve: 4
Ingredients:

- 4 cups mushrooms, sliced
- 1 tsp dried thyme
- 1 tbsp garlic, minced
- 1 cup vegetable broth
- 1 jalapeno pepper, chopped
- 3 cups onions, sliced
- 1/2 cup heavy whipping cream
- 1/4 tsp pepper
- 1 tsp salt

Directions:

1. Add all ingredients except cream into the instant pot duo crisp and stir well.
2. Seal the pot with pressure cooking lid and cook on high pressure for 10 minutes.
3. Once done, allow to release pressure naturally for 10 minutes then release remaining pressure using a quick release. Remove lid.
4. Blend soup using blender until smooth.
5. Add cream and stir well.
6. Serve and enjoy.

Nutritional Value (Amount per Serving):
Calories 116; Fat 6.2 g; Carbohydrates 12.2 g; Sugar 5.2 g; Protein 4.9 g; Cholesterol 21 mg

Creamy Celery Soup

Preparation Time: 10 minutes; Cooking Time: 20 minutes; Serve: 6
Ingredients:

- 1 lb chicken breast, skinless, boneless, and cut into pieces
- 3/4 cup heavy cream
- 2 cups chicken broth
- 1 onion, diced
- 2 cups celery, diced
- 2 tbsp olive oil

Directions:

1. Add oil into the instant pot duo crisp and set pot on sauté mode.
2. Add onion and chicken and cook on sauté mode for 3-5 minutes.
3. Add remaining ingredients except for heavy cream and stir well.
4. Seal the pot with pressure cooking lid and cook on high pressure for 20 minutes.
5. Once done, release pressure using a quick release method. Remove lid.
6. Add heavy cream and stir well.
7. Serve and enjoy.

Nutritional Value (Amount per Serving):
Calories 203; Fat 12.7 g; Carbohydrates 3.4 g; Sugar 1.5 g; Protein 18.4 g; Cholesterol 69 mg

Creamy Coconut Zucchini Soup

Preparation Time: 10 minutes; Cooking Time: 2 minutes; Serve: 2
Ingredients:

- 2 zucchinis, chopped
- 1 tsp curry powder
- 3/4 tsp onion powder
- 1/2 tsp garlic powder
- 1 cup of coconut milk
- 1 cup of water
- Pepper
- Salt

Directions:

1. Pour water into the instant pot duo crisp then place steamer rack in the pot.
2. Arrange zucchini on top of the steamer rack.
3. Seal the pot with pressure cooking lid and cook on high pressure for 2 minutes.
4. Once done, release pressure using a quick release. Remove lid.

5. Transfer zucchini into the blender along with remaining ingredients and blend until smooth.
6. Serve and enjoy.

Nutritional Value (Amount per Serving):
Calories 316; Fat 29.1 g; Carbohydrates 15.1 g; Sugar 7.9 g; Protein 5.5 g; Cholesterol 0 mg

Vegan Zucchini Soup

Preparation Time: 10 minutes; Cooking Time: 8 minutes; Serve: 8

Ingredients:
- 4 large zucchinis, chopped
- 1 tbsp apple cider vinegar
- 1/2 cup nutritional yeast
- 1 tsp garlic powder
- 2 tsp paprika
- 1 cup chicken broth
- 1 tbsp garlic, minced
- 2 cups onion, chopped
- 1/4 cup olive oil
- Pepper
- Salt

Directions:
1. Add oil into the instant pot duo crisp and set pot on sauté mode.
2. Add garlic, zucchini, and onion and sauté for 3-5 minutes.
3. Add garlic powder, paprika, broth, and salt and stir well.
4. Seal the pot with pressure cooking lid and cook on high pressure for 3 minutes.
5. Once done, release pressure using a quick release. Remove lid.
6. Add vinegar and nutritional yeast and stir well.
7. Blend soup using blender until smooth.
8. Serve and enjoy.

Nutritional Value (Amount per Serving):
Calories 136; Fat 7.4 g; Carbohydrates 13.7 g; Sugar 4.3 g; Protein 7.7 g; Cholesterol 0 mg

Spinach Soup

Preparation Time: 10 minutes; Cooking Time: 8 minutes; Serve: 3

Ingredients:
- 10 oz fresh spinach, chopped
- 2 tbsp butter
- 1 onion, chopped
- 1 tsp garlic, minced
- 1 cup cream cheese
- 2 cups of water
- Pepper
- Salt

Directions:
1. Add butter into the instant pot duo crisp and set pot on sauté mode.
2. Add onion and garlic and sauté for 2 minutes.
3. Add water and spinach and stir well.
4. Seal the pot with pressure cooking lid and cook on high pressure for 5 minutes.
5. Once done, release pressure using a quick release. Remove lid.
6. Blend soup using blender until smooth.
7. Set pot on sauté mode. Add cream cheese and cook until cheese is melted.
8. Season soup with pepper and salt.
9. Serve and enjoy.

Nutritional Value (Amount per Serving):
Calories 376; Fat 35.1 g; Carbohydrates 9.3 g; Sugar 2.1 g; Protein 9.1 g; Cholesterol 105 mg

Vegan Carrot Soup

Preparation Time: 10 minutes; Cooking Time: 12 minutes; Serve: 4

Ingredients:

- 5 cups carrots, peeled and chopped
- 1 tbsp fresh lime juice
- 14 oz can coconut milk
- 1 tsp dried thyme
- 4 cups vegetable broth
- 2 tbsp ginger, chopped
- 1 tsp garlic, minced
- 1 onion, chopped
- 1 tbsp olive oil
- 1/4 tsp pepper
- 1/2 tsp salt

Directions:
1. Add oil into the instant pot duo crisp and set pot on sauté mode.
2. Add onion and sauté for 5 minutes.
3. Add ginger and garlic and cook for 1-2 minutes.
4. Add remaining ingredients except for coconut milk and lime juice and stir well.
5. Seal the pot with pressure cooking lid and cook on high pressure for 5 minutes.
6. Once done, release pressure using a quick release. Remove lid.
7. Blend soup using blender until smooth.
8. Add lime juice and coconut milk and stir well.
9. Serve and enjoy.

Nutritional Value (Amount per Serving):
Calories 378; Fat 28.7 g; Carbohydrates 25.8 g; Sugar 12.2 g; Protein 8.9 g; Cholesterol 0 mg

Kale Beef Soup

Preparation Time: 10 minutes; Cooking Time: 13 minutes; Serve: 6
Ingredients:
- 1 lb ground beef
- 1/4 tsp chili powder
- 1/2 cup coconut milk
- 8 cups beef broth
- 1 tbsp garlic, minced
- 1 onion, diced
- 3 cups kale, chopped
- Pepper
- Salt

Directions:
1. Add ground beef, garlic, and onion into the instant pot duo crisp and set pot on sauté mode.
2. Cook ground beef until browned.
3. Add chili powder, broth, pepper, and salt and stir well.
4. Seal the pot with pressure cooking lid and cook on high pressure for 8 minutes.
5. Once done, release pressure using a quick release. Remove lid.
6. Add coconut milk and kale and stir until kale is wilted.
7. Serve and enjoy.

Nutritional Value (Amount per Serving):
Calories 264; Fat 11.4 g; Carbohydrates 8.1 g; Sugar 2.4 g; Protein 31.2 g; Cholesterol 68 mg

Cabbage Beef Soup

Preparation Time: 10 minutes; Cooking Time: 30 minutes; Serve: 8
Ingredients:
- 28 oz can tomato, diced
- 1 tsp dried thyme
- 1 tsp dried oregano
- 1 tbsp olive oil
- 1/2 cup carrots, diced
- 1/2 cup onion, diced
- 1 cup cauliflower rice
- 4 cups beef stock
- 5 cups cabbage, chopped
- 1 lb ground beef
- 28 oz can tomato, diced
- 1 1/2 tsp salt

Directions:
1. Add oil into the instant pot duo crisp and set pot on sauté mode.

2. Add meat and cook until browned.
3. Add carrots and onion and cook for 5 minutes.
4. Add remaining ingredients and stir well.
5. Seal the pot with pressure cooking lid and cook on high pressure for 20 minutes.
6. Once done, allow to release pressure naturally. Remove lid.
7. Stir well and serve hot.

Nutritional Value (Amount per Serving):
Calories 249; Fat 5.9 g; Carbohydrates 24.8 g; Sugar 15 g; Protein 23.6 g; Cholesterol 51 mg

Easy Chicken Salsa Soup

Preparation Time: 10 minutes; Cooking Time: 20 minutes; Serve: 6
Ingredients:
- 1 lb chicken breast, skinless and boneless
- 4 cups chicken broth
- 15 oz jar salsa
- Pepper
- Salt

Directions:
1. Add all ingredients into the instant pot duo crisp and stir well.
2. Seal the pot with pressure cooking lid and cook on high pressure for 20 minutes.
3. Once done, allow to release pressure naturally. Remove lid.
4. Remove chicken from pot and shred using a fork.
5. Return shredded chicken to the pot and stir well.
6. Serve and enjoy.

Nutritional Value (Amount per Serving):
Calories 135; Fat 2.8 g; Carbohydrates 5.4 g; Sugar 2.8 g; Protein 19.3 g; Cholesterol 48 mg

Spring Chicken Soup

Preparation Time: 10 minutes; Cooking Time: 8 minutes; Serve: 6
Ingredients:
- 2 cups cooked chicken, shredded
- 1/2 lemon juice
- 2 tbsp basil, chopped
- 1/2 tsp dried rosemary
- 2 tsp Italian seasoning
- 8 cups chicken broth
- 2 cups leeks, sliced
- 1 small onion, diced
- 1 zucchini, diced
- 1 tsp garlic, minced
- 1 tbsp olive oil
- 1/4 tsp pepper
- 1 1/2 tsp salt

Directions:
1. Add oil into the instant pot duo crisp and set pot on sauté mode.
2. Add leeks, onion, zucchini, and garlic and sauté for 3-4 minutes.
3. Add broth, rosemary, Italian seasoning, chicken, pepper, and salt and stir well.
4. Seal the pot with pressure cooking lid and cook on high pressure for 4 minutes.
5. Once done, allow to release pressure naturally for 5 minutes then release remaining pressure using a quick release. Remove lid.
6. Add fresh herbs and lemon juice and stir well.
7. Serve and enjoy.

Nutritional Value (Amount per Serving):
Calories 177; Fat 6.2 g; Carbohydrates 8.2 g; Sugar 3.4 g; Protein 21.1 g; Cholesterol 37 mg

Healthy Lemon Chicken Soup

Preparation Time: 10 minutes; Cooking Time: 10 minutes; Serve: 4
Ingredients:

- 3 lbs chicken breasts, skinless and boneless
- 1 tsp fresh thyme, minced
- 2 cups spinach, chopped
- 1 lemon juice
- 6 cups chicken stock
- 1/4 tsp dried thyme
- 1 tsp garlic powder
- 1/4 tsp lemon pepper
- 3 carrots, diced
- 1 onion, diced
- 1 tsp salt

Directions:
1. Add all ingredients except spinach and lemon juice into the instant pot duo crisp and stir well.
2. Seal the pot with pressure cooking lid and cook on high pressure for 10 minutes.
3. Once done, release pressure using a quick release. Remove lid.
4. Remove chicken from pot and shred using a fork.
5. Return shredded chicken to the pot along with spinach and lemon juice and stir until spinach is wilted.
6. Serve and enjoy.

Nutritional Value (Amount per Serving):
Calories 700; Fat 26.3 g; Carbohydrates 9.7 g; Sugar 5 g; Protein 100.8 g; Cholesterol 303 mg

Hearty Chicken Soup

Preparation Time: 10 minutes; Cooking Time: 11 minutes; Serve: 6
Ingredients:
- 2 chicken breasts, skinless and boneless
- 1/2 cup heavy cream
- 4 oz cream cheese
- 1 1/2 cups broccoli florets
- 1/2 cup celery, diced
- 1 cup carrots, diced
- 1/4 tsp dried dill
- 1/2 tsp dried thyme
- 1 tsp garlic, minced
- 1/2 onion, diced
- 4 cups chicken broth

Directions:
1. Add chicken, dill, thyme, garlic, onion, and broth into the instant pot duo crisp and stir well.
2. Seal the pot with pressure cooking lid and cook on high pressure for 10 minutes.
3. Once done, allow to release pressure naturally for 10 minutes then release remaining pressure using a quick release. Remove lid.
4. Remove chicken from pot and shred using a fork. Return shredded chicken to the pot.
5. Add broccoli, celery, and carrots and stir well.
6. Seal the pot pressure cooking lid and cook on high pressure for 1 minute.
7. Once done, release pressure using a quick release. Remove lid.
8. Add heavy cream and cream cheese and stir well.
9. Serve and enjoy.

Nutritional Value (Amount per Serving):
Calories 236; Fat 14.8 g; Carbohydrates 6 g; Sugar 2.3 g; Protein 19.4 g; Cholesterol 76 mg

Creamy Mushroom Chicken Soup

Preparation Time: 10 minutes; Cooking Time: 15 minutes; Serve: 4
Ingredients:
- 1 lb chicken breasts, skinless and boneless
- 1 tsp Italian seasoning
- 2 1/2 cups chicken stock
- 1 squash, chopped
- 2 cups mushrooms, chopped
- 1 tsp garlic, minced
- 1 onion, sliced
- Pepper
- Salt

Directions:
1. Add all ingredients into the instant pot duo crisp and stir well.
2. Seal the pot with pressure cooking lid and cook on high pressure for 15 minutes.
3. Once done, allow to release pressure naturally for 10 minutes then release remaining pressure using a quick release. Remove lid.
4. Remove chicken from pot and shred using a fork.
5. Blend soup using blender until smooth.
6. Return shredded chicken to the pot and stir well.
7. Serve and enjoy.

Nutritional Value (Amount per Serving):
Calories 253; Fat 9.3 g; Carbohydrates 6.2 g; Sugar 3.2 g; Protein 35.3 g; Cholesterol 102 mg

Vegetable Chicken Soup

Preparation Time: 10 minutes; Cooking Time: 5 minutes; Serve: 4

Ingredients:
- 8 oz shredded chicken
- 12 tsp dried rosemary
- 1 tbsp garlic powder
- 1 tbsp dried parsley
- 1/2 onion, diced
- 1/2 bell pepper, diced
- 2 cups celery, diced
- 2 cups baby carrots
- 2 zucchinis, sliced
- 2 cups chicken stock
- 1/4 tsp pepper
- 1/2 tsp sea salt

Directions:
1. Add all ingredients into the instant pot duo crisp and stir well.
2. Seal the pot with a lid and cook on high pressure for 5 minutes.
3. Once done, allow to release pressure naturally. Remove lid.
4. Stir well and serve.

Nutritional Value (Amount per Serving):
Calories 179; Fat 2.9 g; Carbohydrates 19.5 g; Sugar 9.6 g; Protein 19.2 g; Cholesterol 44 mg

Thai Chicken Coconut Soup

Preparation Time: 10 minutes; Cooking Time: 9 minutes; Serve: 4

Ingredients:
- 2 lbs chicken breast, skinless, boneless, and cut into cubes
- 2 tbsp fresh lime juice
- 1 cup of coconut milk
- 2 tbsp fish sauce
- 5 drops liquid stevia
- 3 cups chicken broth
- 1 red bell pepper, cut into strips
- 2 tbsp Thai curry paste
- 1 small onion, quartered
- 2 tbsp olive oil

Directions:
1. Add oil into the instant pot duo crisp and set pot on sauté mode.
2. Add onion and sauté for 2-3 minutes.
3. Add remaining ingredients except for lime juice and coconut milk and stir well.
4. Seal the pot with pressure cooking lid and cook on high pressure for 6 minutes.
5. Once done, release pressure using a quick release. Remove lid.
6. Add coconut milk and lime juice and stir well.
7. Serve and enjoy.

Nutritional Value (Amount per Serving):
Calories 518; Fat 28.1 g; Carbohydrates 11.6 g; Sugar 6 g; Protein 54.1 g; Cholesterol 145 mg

Flavorful Chicken Drumstick Soup

Preparation Time: 10 minutes; Cooking Time: 30 minutes; Serve: 4

Ingredients:

- 1 1/2 lbs chicken drumsticks
- 4 cups chicken broth
- 1 small onion, diced
- 1 rutabaga, peeled and diced
- 1 parsnip, peeled and diced
- 2 carrots, peeled and diced
- 2 celery ribs, sliced
- 1 bay leaf
- 1/4 tsp pepper
- Salt

Directions:

1. Add all ingredients into the instant pot duo crisp and stir well.
2. Seal the pot with pressure cooking lid and cook on high pressure for 30 minutes.
3. Once done, release pressure using a quick release. Remove lid.
4. Remove chicken drumsticks from the pot. Remove meat from drumsticks and discards the bones.
5. Return meat to the pot and stir well.
6. Serve and enjoy.

Nutritional Value (Amount per Serving):

Calories 413; Fat 11.5 g; Carbohydrates 21.2 g; Sugar 10.5 g; Protein 53.9 g; Cholesterol 150 mg

Garlic Chicken Soup

Preparation Time: 10 minutes; Cooking Time: 13 minutes; Serve: 4

Ingredients:

- 1 lb chicken breasts, skinless and boneless
- 2 tbsp arrowroot flour
- 4 cups chicken broth
- 2 thyme sprigs
- 1/4 cup white wine
- 20 garlic cloves, peeled
- 1 tbsp olive oil
- 1 tbsp butter
- Salt

Directions:

1. Add butter and oil into the instant pot duo crisp and set pot on sauté mode.
2. Add garlic and sauté for 5 minutes.
3. Add remaining ingredients except for arrowroot flour and stir well.
4. Seal the pot with a lid and cook on high pressure for 8 minutes.
5. Once done, release pressure using a quick release. Remove lid.
6. Remove chicken from pot and shred using a fork. Return shredded chicken to the pot.
7. In a small bowl, whisk together 1 cup soup and arrowroot flour and pour into the pot and stir well.
8. Serve and enjoy.

Nutritional Value (Amount per Serving):

Calories 348; Fat 16.3 g; Carbohydrates 7.2 g; Sugar 1 g; Protein 38.9 g; Cholesterol 109 mg

Coconut Squash Soup

Preparation Time: 10 minutes; Cooking Time: 25 minutes; Serve: 4

Ingredients:

- 1 1/4 lbs butternut squash, cubed
- 1 cup of coconut milk
- 2 cups cooked chicken, shredded
- 3 cups chicken broth
- 1 1/2 tbsp curry powder
- 1 tsp ginger, grated
- 1 tsp garlic, crushed
- 1 leek, sliced
- 1 carrot, chopped
- 1 onion, chopped
- 1 tbsp olive oil
- Pepper

- Salt

Directions:
1. Add oil into the instant pot duo crisp and set pot on sauté mode.
2. Add leek, carrot, ginger, garlic, and onion and sauté for 5 minutes.
3. Add remaining ingredients except for chicken and coconut milk and stir well.
4. Seal the pot with pressure cooking lid and cook on high pressure for 15 minutes.
5. Once done, release pressure using a quick release. Remove lid.
6. Blend soup using blender until smooth.
7. Add coconut milk and chicken and stir well. Set pot on sauté mode and cook for 5 minutes.
8. Serve and enjoy.

Nutritional Value (Amount per Serving):
Calories 407; Fat 21.6 g; Carbohydrates 29.7 g; Sugar 8.5 g; Protein 27.9 g; Cholesterol 54 mg

Winter Cauliflower Soup

Preparation Time: 10 minutes; Cooking Time: 4 minutes; Serve: 4
Ingredients:
- 6 cups cauliflower florets
- 1 cup pepper jack cheese, shredded
- 1 1/2 cup cheddar cheese, shredded
- 1 tsp mustard
- 1 cup heavy cream
- 1 small onion, diced
- 1 cup of water
- 2 cups chicken broth
- 1 tsp salt

Directions:
1. Add cauliflower, onion, water, broth, and salt into the instant pot duo crisp. Stir well.
2. Seal the pot with pressure cooking lid and cook on high pressure for 4 minutes.
3. Once done, release pressure using a quick release. Remove lid.
4. Blend cauliflower mixture using blender until smooth.
5. Add cheese, mustard, and heavy cream and stir until cheese is melted.
6. Serve and enjoy.

Nutritional Value (Amount per Serving):
Calories 407; Fat 21.6 g; Carbohydrates 29.7 g; Sugar 8.5 g; Protein 27.9 g; Cholesterol 54 mg

Nutritious Pumpkin Soup

Preparation Time: 10 minutes; Cooking Time: 2 minutes; Serve: 6
Ingredients:
- 3 cups pumpkin, cooked
- 1/4 tsp garlic powder
- 1/2 tbsp chili powder
- 1/2 tbsp curry powder
- 1/2 tbsp turmeric
- 1 1/2 tbsp olive oil
- 3 cups chicken broth
- Pepper
- Salt

Directions:
1. Add all ingredients into the instant pot duo crisp and stir well.
2. Seal the pot with pressure cooking lid and cook on high pressure for 2 minutes.
3. Once done, allow to release pressure naturally. Remove lid.
4. Blend soup using blender until smooth.
5. Serve and enjoy.

Nutritional Value (Amount per Serving):
Calories 97; Fat 4.8 g; Carbohydrates 11.5 g; Sugar 4.5 g; Protein 4 g; Cholesterol 0 mg

Chapter 4: Vegan & Vegetarian

Cheesy Potato Gratin

Preparation Time: 10 minutes; Cooking Time: 30 minutes; Serve: 6

Ingredients:

- 3 medium potatoes, sliced 1/8-inch thick
- 3 cups cheddar cheese, shredded
- 3/4 cup heavy cream
- 3/4 tsp garlic powder
- 1 tbsp butter
- 1/4 tsp pepper
- 1/2 tsp sea salt

Directions:

1. Spray 8-inch round pan with cooking spray.
2. Layer the sliced potatoes in prepared pan.
3. Season each layer with garlic powder, pepper, and salt then pour 1 tablespoon of heavy cream over potato layer and sprinkle thin layer of shredded cheese.
4. Layer sliced potatoes until you have 5 layers.
5. Top with remaining cream and cheese.
6. Pour 1 1/2 cups of water into the instant pot duo crisp then place the trivet in the pot.
7. Place pan on top of the trivet.
8. Seal the pot with pressure cooking lid and cook on pressure cook mode for 25 minutes.
9. Once done, release pressure using a quick release. Remove lid.
10. Seal the pot with air fryer lid and select broil mode for 5 minutes.
11. Once done then remove the pan from instant pot and let it cool for 10 minutes.
12. Serve and enjoy.

Nutritional Value (Amount per Serving):

Calories 371; Fat 26.3 g; Carbohydrates 18.2 g; Sugar 1.6 g; Protein 16.3 g; Cholesterol 85 mg

Crispy Mac & Cheese

Preparation Time: 10 minutes; Cooking Time: 9 minutes; Serve: 6

Ingredients:

- 2 1/2 cups macaroni
- 1/4 tsp garlic powder
- 1 sleeve crackers, crushed
- 1/3 cup parmesan cheese, shredded
- 2 2/3 cups cheddar cheese, shredded
- 1/2 cup butter
- 1 cup heavy cream
- 2 cups vegetable stock
- Pepper
- Salt

Directions:

1. Add stock, heavy cream, 1/4 cup of butter, and macaroni in the instant pot duo crisp and stir well.
2. Seal the pot with pressure cooking lid and cook on high pressure for 4 minutes.
3. Once done, release pressure using a quick release. Remove lid.
4. Add 2 cups of shredded cheddar cheese and stir until cheese is melted.
5. Mix together remaining butter and crushed crackers.
6. Add remaining cheddar cheese, parmesan cheese, and crushed crackers on top of the macaroni mixture.
7. Seal the pot with air fryer lid and air fry for 5 minutes at 400 F.
8. Serve and enjoy.

Nutritional Value (Amount per Serving):

Calories 674; Fat 55 g; Carbohydrates 20 g; Sugar 3 g; Protein 20 g; Cholesterol 160 mg

Crispy Roasted Potatoes

Preparation Time: 10 minutes; Cooking Time: 16 minutes; Serve: 4

Ingredients:
- 2 lbs baby potatoes, scrubbed and pierced with a fork
- 2 tbsp olive oil
- 1 cup vegetable broth
- 2 garlic cloves, peeled
- Pepper
- Salt
- For seasoning:
- 1/8 tsp nutmeg
- 1/2 tsp sage
- 1/2 tsp thyme
- 1/2 tsp oregano
- 1 tsp rosemary
- 1/8 tsp pepper

Directions:
1. Add Baby potatoes, broth, and garlic into the instant pot duo crisp.
2. Seal the pot with pressure cooking lid and cook on pressure cook mode for 11 minutes.
3. Once done, release pressure using a quick release. Remove lid.
4. Drain out the broth and pat dry potatoes.
5. Add oil into the instant pot and set the pot on sauté mode.
6. Once the oil is hot then add potatoes and all seasonings and cook on sauté mode for 5 minutes or until potatoes are lightly brown.
7. Serve and enjoy.

Nutritional Value (Amount per Serving):
Calories 206; Fat 7.7 g; Carbohydrates 29.5 g; Sugar 0.2 g; Protein 7.2 g; Cholesterol 0 mg

Crispy Honey Carrots

Preparation Time: 10 minutes; Cooking Time: 10 minutes; Serve: 2
Ingredients:
- 3 cups carrots, cut into 1/2-inch pieces
- 1 tbsp honey
- 1 tbsp olive oil
- Pepper
- Salt

Directions:
1. Add carrots in a mixing bowl then add honey, oil, pepper, and salt and toss to coat.
2. Transfer carrots into the instant pot duo crisp air fryer basket then place basket in the instant pot.
3. Seal the pot with air fryer lid and air fry carrots for 10 minutes at 400 F. Toss carrots after 5 minutes.
4. Serve and enjoy.

Nutritional Value (Amount per Serving):
Calories 160; Fat 7 g; Carbohydrates 24.9 g; Sugar 16.7 g; Protein 1.4 g; Cholesterol 0 mg

Perfect Mashed Potatoes

Preparation Time: 10 minutes; Cooking Time: 7 minutes; Serve: 6
Ingredients:
- 3 lbs potatoes, peeled and cut into 1 1/2-inch pieces
- 1/4 cup half and half
- 1/4 cup butter
- 1 lb parsnips, cut into 1-inch pieces
- Pepper
- Salt

Directions:
1. Pour 2 cups of water into the instant pot.
2. Add potatoes and parsnips into the air fryer basket then place a basket in the instant pot.
3. Seal the pot with pressure cooking lid and select pressure cook for 7 minutes.
4. Once done, release pressure using a quick release. Remove lid.
5. Transfer potatoes and parsnips into the mixing bowl. Using masher mash until smooth.
6. Add half and half, butter, pepper, and salt and mix well.

7. Serve and enjoy.

Nutritional Value (Amount per Serving):

Calories 294; Fat 9.3 g; Carbohydrates 49.7 g; Sugar 6.3 g; Protein 5.1 g; Cholesterol 24 mg

Ranch Carrots

Preparation Time: 10 minutes; Cooking Time: 3 hours; Serve: 4

Ingredients:

- 2 lbs carrots, cut into fries shape
- 1/4 cup butter
- 1 onion, diced
- 1 tbsp ranch seasoning
- Pepper
- Salt

Directions:

1. Add all ingredients into the inner pot of instant pot duo crisp. Stir well.
2. Seal the pot with pressure cooking lid and select slow cook mode and cook on high for 4 hours.
3. Serve and enjoy.

Nutritional Value (Amount per Serving):

Calories 213; Fat 11.5 g; Carbohydrates 24.9 g; Sugar 12.3 g; Protein 2.3 g; Cholesterol 31 mg

Creamy Sweet Potato Mash

Preparation Time: 10 minutes; Cooking Time: 4 hours; Serve: 6

Ingredients:

- 4 lbs sweet potatoes, peel and diced
- 3/4 tsp curry powder
- 1 cup vegetable stock
- 2 tbsp butter
- 1/4 cup coconut milk
- Pepper
- Salt

Directions:

1. Add sweet potatoes and vegetable stock into the inner pot of instant pot duo crisp.
2. Seal the pot with pressure cooking lid and select slow cook mode and cook on low for 4 hours.
3. Mash sweet potatoes using masher until smooth.
4. Add butter, coconut milk, and curry powder and mix well.
5. Season with pepper and salt.
6. Serve and enjoy.

Nutritional Value (Amount per Serving):

Calories 416; Fat 6.8 g; Carbohydrates 85.2 g; Sugar 2 g; Protein 5 g; Cholesterol 10 mg

Delicious Fruit Salsa

Preparation Time: 10 minutes; Cooking Time: 2 hours; Serve: 6

Ingredients:

- 1/2 red bell pepper, chopped
- 1/2 yellow bell pepper, chopped
- 1/2 green bell pepper, chopped
- 8 oz can pineapple tidbits
- 8 oz can peach, sliced
- 10 oz can oranges
- 3 tbsp cornstarch
- 3 tsp vinegar
- 1 tsp garlic, minced
- 1 medium onion, chopped

Directions:

1. Add all ingredients into the inner pot of instant pot duo crisp and stir well.
2. Seal the pot with pressure cooking lid and select slow cook mode and cook on high for 2 hours.
3. Stir and serve.

Nutritional Value (Amount per Serving):

Calories 101; Fat 0.2 g; Carbohydrates 24.3 g; Sugar 13.7 g; Protein 1.4 g; Cholesterol 0 mg

Easy Dill Carrots

Preparation Time: 10 minutes; Cooking Time: 2 hours; Serve: 4
Ingredients:

- 1 lb carrots, cut round slices
- 1/2 tsp butter
- 3/4 tbsp fresh dill, minced
- 3 tbsp water

Directions:
1. Add all ingredients into the inner pot of instant pot duo crisp and stir well.
2. Seal the pot with pressure cooking lid and select slow cook mode and cook on low for 2 hours.
3. Stir and serve.

Nutritional Value (Amount per Serving):
Calories 52; Fat 0.5 g; Carbohydrates 11.5 g; Sugar 5.6 g; Protein 1.1 g; Cholesterol 1 mg

Tasty Ranch Potatoes

Preparation Time: 10 minutes; Cooking Time: 4 hours; Serve: 4
Ingredients:

- 1 lb potatoes, diced
- 1/2 tsp onion powder
- 3/4 tsp garlic powder
- 1 tsp parsley, dried
- 1/4 cup butter, melted
- 1/4 tsp pepper
- 1/4 tsp dill, dried
- 1/2 tsp sea salt

Directions:
1. In a bowl, add 2 tbsp butter, potatoes, parsley, garlic powder, onion powder, sea salt, dill, and pepper. Toss well.
2. Transfer potato mixture to a foil piece and fold foil to cover potato mixture and place in the inner pot of instant pot duo crisp.
3. Seal the pot with pressure cooking lid and select slow cook mode and cook on low for 4 hours.
4. Open foil carefully and add remaining butter and mix well.
5. Serve and enjoy.

Nutritional Value (Amount per Serving):
Calories 183; Fat 11.6 g; Carbohydrates 18.6 g; Sugar 1.6 g; Protein 2.2 g; Cholesterol 31 mg

Healthy Summer Vegetables

Preparation Time: 10 minutes; Cooking Time: 4 hours; Serve: 4
Ingredients:

- 1 1/2 cups zucchini, sliced
- 1 tsp butter
- 1/2 cup okra, diced
- 1/4 cup lemon juice
- 1 1/2 cups yellow squash, sliced
- 1 medium onion, sliced
- 1 tbsp thyme, minced
- 1/4 tsp pepper
- 1/4 tsp salt

Directions:
1. Add the onion in the inner pot of instant pot duo crisp then top with yellow squash, zucchini, pepper, lemon juice, thyme, and salt.
2. Seal the pot with pressure cooking lid and select slow cook mode and cook on low for 3 1/2 hours.
3. Add butter and okra and stir well.
4. Seal the pot again with pressure cooking lid and select slow cook mode and cook on high for 30 minutes more.

5. Serve and enjoy.

Nutritional Value (Amount per Serving):

Calories 45; Fat 1.3 g; Carbohydrates 7.8 g; Sugar 3.1 g; Protein 1.9 g; Cholesterol 3 mg

Stewed Okra

Preparation Time: 10 minutes; Cooking Time: 2 hours; Serve: 4

Ingredients:

- 1 1/2 cups okra, diced
- 14 oz can tomato, crushed
- 1 tsp hot sauce
- 1 tsp garlic, minced
- 1 small onion, diced

Directions:

1. Add all ingredients into the inner pot of instant pot duo crisp and stir well.
2. Seal the pot with pressure cooking lid and select slow cook mode and cook on low for 2 hours.
3. Stir well and serve.

Nutritional Value (Amount per Serving):

Calories 44; Fat 0.1 g; Carbohydrates 9.7 g; Sugar 4.7 g; Protein 1.9 g; Cholesterol 0 mg

Roasted Vegetables

Preparation Time: 10 minutes; Cooking Time: 45 minutes; Serve: 3

Ingredients:

- 4 carrots, peeled and cut into 3-inch pieces
- 5 potatoes, quartered
- 3 shallots, peeled and cut into half
- 1 tbsp olive oil
- 1/4 tsp garlic powder
- Pepper
- Salt

Directions:

1. Add carrots, potatoes, and shallots to the mixing bowl. Add oil, garlic powder, pepper, and salt over vegetables and toss well.
2. Line instant pot duo crisp air fryer basket with parchment paper or foil.
3. Add vegetables into the air fryer basket then place basket in the pot.
4. Seal the pot with air fryer lid and select roast mode and cook at 400 F for 45 minutes.
5. Serve and enjoy.

Nutritional Value (Amount per Serving):

Calories 326; Fat 5 g; Carbohydrates 65.6 g; Sugar 8.1 g; Protein 6.9 g; Cholesterol 0 mg

Delicious Potato Wedges

Preparation Time: 10 minutes; Cooking Time: 17 minutes; Serve: 6

Ingredients:

- 1 1/2 lbs russet potatoes, cut into wedges
- 3/4 tsp garlic powder
- 1/2 tsp onion powder
- 1/4 cup olive oil
- 1 cup vegetable broth
- 1 tsp paprika
- 1/4 tsp pepper
- 1 tsp sea salt

Directions:

1. Add oil into the inner pot of instant pot duo crisp and set pot on sauté mode.
2. Add potatoes and sauté for 3-5 minutes.
3. Add remaining ingredients and stir well.
4. Seal the pot with pressure cooking lid and cook on high pressure for 7 minutes.
5. Once done, release pressure using a quick release. Remove lid.
6. Remove potato wedges from the pot and clean the pot.

7. Add potato wedges into the air fryer basket and place basket in the pot.
8. Seal the pot with air fryer lid and select broil and cook for 5 minutes.
9. Serve and enjoy.

Nutritional Value (Amount per Serving):
Calories 160; Fat 8.8 g; Carbohydrates 18.6 g; Sugar 1.6 g; Protein 2.9 g; Cholesterol 0 mg

Crispy Ranch Potatoes

Preparation Time: 10 minutes; Cooking Time: 10 minutes; Serve: 2
Ingredients:
- 1/2 lb potatoes, cut into 1-inch pieces
- 1 tbsp ranch seasoning
- 1/2 tbsp olive oil

Directions:
1. Add all ingredients into the bowl and toss well.
2. Transfer potato into the instant pot air fryer basket and place basket in the pot.
3. Seal the pot with air fryer lid and select air fry mode and cook at 375 F for 10 minutes.
4. Serve and enjoy.

Nutritional Value (Amount per Serving):
Calories 123; Fat 3.6 g; Carbohydrates 17.8 g; Sugar 1.3 g; Protein 1.9 g; Cholesterol 0 mg

Healthy Roasted Vegetables

Preparation Time: 10 minutes; Cooking Time: 45 minutes; Serve: 4
Ingredients:
- 2 potatoes, cut into chunks
- 3 medium carrots, peeled and cut into chunks
- 1 small rutabaga, peeled and cut into chunks
- 2 parsnips, peeled and cut into chunks
- 1/4 cup olive oil
- Pepper
- Salt

Directions:
1. In a large bowl, toss vegetable with oil.
2. Transfer vegetables into the instant pot air fryer basket and season with pepper and salt.
3. Place air fryer basket in the pot.
4. Seal the pot with air fryer lid and select roast mode and cook at 400 F for 35-45 minutes.

Nutritional Value (Amount per Serving):
Calories 267; Fat 13 g; Carbohydrates 37.1 g; Sugar 9.4 g; Protein 3.6 g; Cholesterol 0 mg

Pineapple Salsa

Preparation Time: 10 minutes; Cooking Time: 8 minutes; Serve: 2
Ingredients:
- 1 cup pineapple, diced
- 1/3 cup cilantro, chopped
- 1 cup tomatoes, diced
- 1 cup peppers, diced
- 4 tbsp lime juice
- 1/4 cup onion, minced
- Pepper
- Salt

Directions:
1. Add all ingredients into the inner pot of instant pot duo crisp and stir well.
2. Seal the pot with pressure cooking lid and cook on high for 8 minutes.
3. Once done, release pressure using a quick release. Remove lid.
4. Stir and serve.

Nutritional Value (Amount per Serving):
Calories 137; Fat 1 g; Carbohydrates 35.6 g; Sugar 12.7 g; Protein 3.9 g; Cholesterol 0 mg

Banana Buckwheat Porridge

Preparation Time: 10 minutes; Cooking Time: 6 minutes; Serve: 4

Ingredients:
- 1 cup raw buckwheat grouts, rinsed
- 1/4 cup raisins
- 1 banana, sliced
- 3 cups almond milk
- 1/2 tsp vanilla
- 1 tsp cinnamon

Directions:
1. Add all ingredients into the inner pot of instant pot duo crisp and stir well.
2. Seal the pot with pressure cooking lid and cook on high for 6 minutes.
3. Once done, allow to release pressure naturally. Remove lid.
4. Serve and enjoy.

Nutritional Value (Amount per Serving):

Calories 571; Fat 44 g; Carbohydrates 45.6 g; Sugar 15.8 g; Protein 8.5 g; Cholesterol 0 mg

Banana Oatmeal

Preparation Time: 10 minutes; Cooking Time: 5 minutes; Serve: 2

Ingredients:
- 1 cup oatmeal
- 1 banana, sliced
- 1 cup of water
- 1 cup almond milk
- 1 tbsp maple syrup
- 1 1/2 tsp cinnamon

Directions:
1. Spray instant pot inner pot with cooking spray.
2. Add water, oatmeal, and almond milk and stir well.
3. Add maple syrup, cinnamon, and banana and stir well.
4. Seal the pot with pressure cooking lid and cook on high for 5 minutes.
5. Once done, allow to release pressure naturally. Remove lid.
6. Stir and serve.

Nutritional Value (Amount per Serving):

Calories 514; Fat 31.5 g; Carbohydrates 55.9 g; Sugar 17.6 g; Protein 8.8 g; Cholesterol 0 mg

Smooth Mashed Potatoes

Preparation Time: 10 minutes; Cooking Time: 25 minutes; Serve: 4

Ingredients:
- 4 large potatoes, peeled and cubed
- 1 fresh sprig rosemary
- 2 garlic cloves
- 1 cup vegetable broth
- 1/4 cup almond milk
- 2 tbsp olive oil

Directions:
1. Add potatoes, rosemary, garlic, and broth into the inner pot of instant pot duo crisp and stir well.
2. Seal the pot with pressure cooking lid and cook on high for 25 minutes.
3. Once done, release pressure using a quick release. Remove lid.
4. Drain potatoes well and transfer to the large bowl. Remove rosemary sprig.
5. Add oil and almond milk and using potato masher mash the potatoes until smooth.
6. Serve warm and enjoy.

Nutritional Value (Amount per Serving):

Calories 364; Fat 11.4 g; Carbohydrates 60.1 g; Sugar 4.9 g; Protein 7.9 g; Cholesterol 0 mg

Delicious Chickpea Hummus

Preparation Time: 10 minutes; Cooking Time: 45 minutes; Serve: 10

Ingredients:
- 1 cup chickpeas, dried
- 3 garlic cloves, minced
- 3 cups vegetable broth
- 1 tbsp fresh lemon juice
- 2 tbsp olive oil
- 1 tsp salt

Directions:
1. Add broth, chickpeas, and salt into the inner pot of instant pot duo crisp.
2. Seal the pot with pressure cooking lid and high for 45 minutes.
3. Once done, release pressure using a quick release. Remove lid.
4. Drain chickpeas well and transfer to the food processor along with remaining ingredients and process until smooth.
5. Serve and enjoy.

Nutritional Value (Amount per Serving):
Calories 110; Fat 4.4 g; Carbohydrates 12.7 g; Sugar 2.4 g; Protein 5.4 g; Cholesterol 0 mg

Herb Lentil Rice

Preparation Time: 10 minutes; Cooking Time: 25 minutes; Serve: 4

Ingredients:
- 1 1/2 cups brown rice, uncooked
- 1 cup brown lentils, dried
- 3 1/2 cups water
- 1 tsp garlic cloves, minced
- 1/2 cup onion, chopped
- 1 tbsp thyme, dried
- 1 fresh rosemary sprig
- 1 cup potato, peeled and diced
- 1 tbsp olive oil
- Pepper
- Salt

Directions:
1. Add oil into the inner pot of instant pot duo crisp and set pot on sauté mode.
2. Add onion and sauté for 5 minutes. Add garlic and sauté for a minute.
3. Add remaining ingredients and stir well.
4. Seal the pot with pressure cooking lid and cook on high for 20 minutes.
5. Once done, allow to release pressure naturally. Remove lid.
6. Stir well and serve.

Nutritional Value (Amount per Serving):
Calories 352; Fat 5.8 g; Carbohydrates 66.2 g; Sugar 0.8 g; Protein 8.8 g; Cholesterol 0 mg

Easy Cilantro Lime Rice

Preparation Time: 10 minutes; Cooking Time: 12 minutes; Serve: 6

Ingredients:
- 2 cups white rice, long grain
- 2 tbsp olive oil
- 3/4 cup water
- 14 oz vegetable broth
- 3/4 cup fresh cilantro, chopped
- 2 1/2 tbsp fresh lime juice
- 1/2 tsp salt

Directions:
1. Add rice, 2 tablespoon lime juice, oil, water, and broth in the inner pot of instant pot duo crisp and stir well.
2. Seal the pot with pressure cooking lid and cook on high for 12 minutes.
3. Once done, release pressure using a quick release. Remove lid.
4. Fluff the rice using a fork and transfer to the large bowl.
5. Add remaining lime juice, salt, and cilantro and stir well.
6. Serve and enjoy.

Nutritional Value (Amount per Serving):
Calories 281; Fat 5.5 g; Carbohydrates 51.2 g; Sugar 0.6 g; Protein 5.9 g; Cholesterol 0 mg

Spicy Rice

Preparation Time: 10 minutes; Cooking Time: 22 minutes; Serve: 6

Ingredients:

- 2 cups brown rice, uncooked
- 1/2 tsp onion powder
- 2 tbsp tomato paste
- 1 tbsp cumin
- 2 tbsp chili powder
- 1/2 tsp garlic powder
- 2 cups vegetable broth
- 1 tsp salt

Directions:

1. Add water and rice into the inner pot of instant pot duo crisp.
2. Seal the pot with pressure cooking lid and cook on high for 22 minutes.
3. Once done, release pressure using a quick release. Remove lid.
4. Add remaining ingredients and stir well.
5. Serve and enjoy.

Nutritional Value (Amount per Serving):

Calories 259; Fat 2.8 g; Carbohydrates 51.7 g; Sugar 1.2 g; Protein 7.2 g; Cholesterol 0 mg

Refried Pinto Beans

Preparation Time: 10 minutes; Cooking Time: 35 minutes; Serve: 8

Ingredients:

- 2 cups pinto beans, dried and rinsed
- 4 cups vegetable broth
- 1 jalapeno, minced
- 1 tbsp garlic, minced
- 1 onion, chopped
- 1 tsp ground cumin
- 1 1/2 tsp oregano
- 4 cups of water
- 1 tbsp olive oil
- 1/2 tsp pepper
- 1 tsp salt

Directions:

1. Add oil into the inner pot of instant pot duo crisp and set pot on sauté mode.
2. Add jalapeno, garlic, and onion and sauté until softened.
3. Add beans, seasoning, water, and broth. Stir well.
4. Seal the pot with pressure cooking lid and cook on high for 30 minutes.
5. Once done, allow to release pressure naturally. Remove lid.
6. Mash beans using potato mashed until desired consistency get.
7. Serve and enjoy.

Nutritional Value (Amount per Serving):

Calories 211; Fat 3.1 g; Carbohydrates 32.8 g; Sugar 2 g; Protein 13.1 g; Cholesterol 0 mg

Sweetcorn Risotto

Preparation Time: 10 minutes; Cooking Time: 13 minutes; Serve: 4

Ingredients:

- 1 cup Arborio rice
- 1/2 cup sweet corn
- 1 tsp mix herbs
- 3 cups vegetable stock
- 1 tbsp olive oil
- 1 tsp garlic, minced
- 1/2 cup peas
- 1 red pepper, diced
- 1 large onion, chopped
- 1/4 pepper
- 1/2 tsp salt

Directions:

1. Add oil into the inner pot of instant pot duo crisp and set pot on sauté mode.
2. Add onion and garlic and sauté for 5 minutes.
3. Add rice and stir to combine.

4. Add remaining ingredients and stir well.
5. Seal the pot with pressure cooking lid and cook on high for 8 minutes.
6. Once done, release pressure using a quick release. Remove lid.
7. Serve and enjoy.

Nutritional Value (Amount per Serving):
Calories 269; Fat 4.8 g; Carbohydrates 50.8 g; Sugar 5.3 g; Protein 6.2 g; Cholesterol 0 mg

Sweet Carrots

Preparation Time: 10 minutes; Cooking Time: 3 minutes; Serve: 8
Ingredients:
- 2 lbs carrots, peeled and sliced thickly
- 3 tbsp raisins
- 1 tbsp maple syrup
- 1 tbsp butter
- 1 cup of water
- Pepper
- Salt

Directions:
1. Add water, carrots, and raisins in the inner pot of instant pot duo crisp.
2. Seal the pot with pressure cooking lid and cook on high for 3 minutes.
3. Once done, release pressure using a quick release. Remove lid.
4. Drain carrots and transfer to the mixing bowl.
5. Add butter and maple syrup over carrots and toss well. Season with pepper and salt.
6. Serve and enjoy.

Nutritional Value (Amount per Serving):
Calories 76; Fat 1.5 g; Carbohydrates 15.5 g; Sugar 9.1 g; Protein 1.1 g; Cholesterol 4 mg

Spicy Rice

Preparation Time: 10 minutes; Cooking Time: 3 minutes; Serve: 2
Ingredients:
- 1 cup rice, long grain
- 1/4 cup green hot sauce
- 1/2 cup fresh cilantro, chopped
- 1/2 avocado flesh
- 1 1/4 cup vegetable broth
- Pepper
- Salt

Directions:
1. Add broth and rice in the inner pot of instant pot duo crisp and stir well.
2. Seal the pot with pressure cooking lid and cook on high for 3 minutes.
3. Once done, allow to release pressure naturally. Remove lid.
4. Fluff the rice using a fork.
5. Add green sauce, avocado and cilantro in a blender and blend until smooth.
6. Pour blended mixture into the rice and stir well to combine. Season with pepper and salt.
7. Serve and enjoy.

Nutritional Value (Amount per Serving):
Calories 375; Fat 2.6 g; Carbohydrates 75.5 g; Sugar 0.6 g; Protein 10 g; Cholesterol 0 mg

Indian Potato Curry

Preparation Time: 10 minutes; Cooking Time: 7 minutes; Serve: 4
Ingredients:
- 2 medium potatoes, peeled and chopped
- 1/2 tsp garam masala
- 1 Serrano, minced
- 1/2 cup onion masala
- 1 tsp cumin seeds
- 1 1/2 cups water
- 2 cups fresh peas
- 2 tbsp olive oil
- 1/4 tsp pepper

- 1 tsp salt

Directions:
1. Add oil into the inner pot of instant pot duo crisp and set pot on sauté mode.
2. Add Serrano pepper and cumin seeds and sauté for 1-2 minutes.
3. Add remaining ingredients and stir well.
4. Seal the pot with pressure cooking lid and cook on high for 5 minutes.
5. Once done, release pressure using a quick release. Remove lid.
6. Serve and enjoy.

Nutritional Value (Amount per Serving):
Calories 244; Fat 9.5 g; Carbohydrates 33.4 g; Sugar 6.2 g; Protein 7.7 g; Cholesterol 2 mg

Veggie Quinoa

Preparation Time: 10 minutes; Cooking Time: 7 minutes; Serve: 4
Ingredients:
- 1 1/2 cups quinoa, rinsed and drained
- 1 carrot, chopped
- 1 cup green beans, chopped
- 1 potato, cubed
- 1 tomato, chopped
- 1 small onion, chopped
- 2 tsp ginger paste
- 1 garlic clove, minced
- 1/4 cup cilantro, chopped
- 1 1/2 cups water
- 1/4 cup coconut milk
- 1 tsp garam masala
- 1/2 tsp chili powder
- 1/2 tsp black pepper
- 1/4 tsp turmeric
- 1 bay leaf
- 4 cloves
- 1 tsp cumin seeds
- 2-star anise
- 2 tbsp olive oil
- Salt

Directions:
1. Add oil into the inner pot of instant pot duo crisp and set pot on sauté mode.
2. Add cumin seeds, cloves, and star anise and sauté for 30 seconds. Add ginger and garlic and sauté for 1 minute.
3. Add tomatoes, onions, and dry spices and sauté for 1-2 minutes.
4. Add all the vegetables, salt, and coconut milk, water, and quinoa. Stir well.
5. Seal the pot with pressure cooking lid and cook on high for 4 minutes.
6. Once done, allow to release pressure naturally for 10 minutes then release remaining pressure using a quick release. Remove lid.
7. Serve and enjoy.

Nutritional Value (Amount per Serving):
Calories 404; Fat 15.2 g; Carbohydrates 58 g; Sugar 3.2 g; Protein 11.8 g; Cholesterol 0 mg

Healthy Quinoa Black Bean Chili

Preparation Time: 10 minutes; Cooking Time: 12 minutes; Serve: 6
Ingredients:
- 1/2 cup quinoa, rinsed and drained
- 14 oz can black beans, rinsed and drained
- 14 oz can tomato, diced
- 2 tbsp tomato paste
- 4 cups vegetable broth
- 2 celery stalks, diced
- 1 tsp garlic, minced
- 1 onion, chopped
- 1 tsp chili powder
- 1 tsp ground coriander
- 2 tsp ground cumin
- 2 tsp paprika
- 3 sweet potatoes, peeled and diced
- 1 bell pepper, diced
- 1 tsp salt

Directions:

1. Add all ingredients into the inner pot of instant pot duo crisp and stir well.
2. Seal the pot with pressure cooking lid and cook on high for 12 minutes.
3. Once done, release pressure using a quick release. Remove lid.
4. Stir and serve.

Nutritional Value (Amount per Serving):
Calories 267; Fat 2.6 g; Carbohydrates 51.2 g; Sugar 6.2 g; Protein 11.5 g; Cholesterol 0 mg

Delicious Pigeon Pea

Preparation Time: 10 minutes; Cooking Time: 7 minutes; Serve: 4
Ingredients:

- 1 cup split pigeon pea, rinsed and drained
- 1 tbsp ginger, chopped
- 1 green chili, sliced
- 1/4 tsp cumin seeds
- 1 tbsp olive oil
- 2 cups spinach
- 1/2 tsp garam masala
- 3 cups of water
- 1 large tomato, chopped
- 1 tbsp garlic, chopped
- Spices:
- 1/4 tsp turmeric
- 1/2 tsp chili powder
- 1 tsp salt

Directions:
1. Add oil into the inner pot of instant pot duo crisp and set pot on sauté mode.
2. Add cumin seeds, garlic, ginger, and green chili and sauté for 30 seconds.
3. Add tomatoes and spices and sauté for 1 minute.
4. Add lentils and water. Stir well.
5. Seal the pot with pressure cooking lid and cook on high for 3 minutes.
6. Once done, release pressure using a quick release. Remove lid.
7. Set pot on sauté mode. Add spinach and garam masala and stir until spinach is wilted.
8. Serve and enjoy.

Nutritional Value (Amount per Serving):
Calories 97; Fat 4.3 g; Carbohydrates 12.2 g; Sugar 1.6 g; Protein 3.5 g; Cholesterol 0 mg

Flavorful Mushroom Rice

Preparation Time: 10 minutes; Cooking Time: 10 minutes; Serve: 4
Ingredients:

- 2 cups rice, soak for 30 minutes and drained
- 1/2-inch cinnamon stick
- 2 tbsp vegetable oil
- 1/2 tsp caraway seed
- 15 oz mushrooms, sliced
- 2 tbsp cashews
- 1/4 cup coconut milk
- 4 cloves
- 2 cups of water
- 1/2 tsp garam masala
- 1 tsp chili powder
- 1/2 tsp turmeric
- 4 green cardamom
- 2-star anise
- 1 bay leaf
- 3 garlic cloves
- 1 tbsp ginger, minced
- 2 tbsp green chilies
- 1 onion, chopped
- Salt

Directions:
1. Add oil into the inner pot of instant pot duo crisp and set pot on sauté mode.
2. Add cashews and sauté for a minute.
3. Add caraway seeds, green chilies, garlic, ginger, all dry spices and sauté for 1-2 minutes.
4. Add onion and cook for 2 minutes.
5. Add remaining ingredients and stir everything well.

6. Seal the pot with pressure cooking lid and cook on high for 4 minutes.
7. Once done, allow to release pressure naturally for 10 minutes then release remaining pressure using a quick release. Remove lid.
8. Stir and serve.

Nutritional Value (Amount per Serving):
Calories 530; Fat 14.3 g; Carbohydrates 90.5 g; Sugar 4.4 g; Protein 12.6 g; Cholesterol 0 mg

Rice Lentil Porridge

Preparation Time: 10 minutes; Cooking Time: 21 minutes; Serve: 4
Ingredients:

- 1/2 cup yellow lentils, soaked for 15 minutes and drained
- 1 cup rice, soaked for 15 minutes and drained
- 6 cups vegetable stock
- 1 bay leaf
- 1 tsp turmeric
- 1 1/2 tsp cumin seeds
- 2 tbsp olive oil
- 1 1/2 tsp salt

Directions:
1. Add oil into the inner pot of instant pot duo crisp and set pot on sauté mode.
2. Add cumin seeds and bay leaf and sauté for 30 seconds.
3. Add lentils, turmeric, rice, salt, and stock. Stir well.
4. Seal the pot with pressure cooking lid and cook on high for minutes.
5. Once done, allow to release pressure naturally for 10 minutes then release remaining pressure using a quick release. Remove lid.
6. Stir and serve.

Nutritional Value (Amount per Serving):
Calories 320; Fat 7.9 g; Carbohydrates 51.9 g; Sugar 1.2 g; Protein 10.1 g; Cholesterol 0 mg

Wheat Berry Pilaf

Preparation Time: 10 minutes; Cooking Time: 35 minutes; Serve: 6
Ingredients:

- 1 1/2 cups wheat berries, rinsed and drained
- 1/2 cup onion, minced
- 1 tsp coriander seeds
- 2 tsp cumin seeds
- 1 tbsp olive oil
- 3 cups of water
- 1 1/2 tsp turmeric
- 1 tbsp garlic, minced
- Salt

Directions:
1. Add oil into the inner pot of instant pot duo crisp and set pot on sauté mode.
2. Add onion and cook until softened.
3. Add turmeric, garlic, coriander, and cumin and sauté for 2 minutes.
4. Add wheat berries and sauté for 2 minutes.
5. Add water and stir everything well.
6. Seal the pot with pressure cooking lid and cook on high for 30 minutes.
7. Once done, allow to release pressure naturally. Remove lid.
8. Stir well and serve.

Nutritional Value (Amount per Serving):
Calories 84; Fat 2.9 g; Carbohydrates 13.5 g; Sugar 0.5 g; Protein 2.4 g; Cholesterol 0 mg

Spicy Tomato Chutney

Preparation Time: 10 minutes; Cooking Time: 6 minutes; Serve: 4
Ingredients:

- 4 green tomatoes, chopped
- 1/2 tsp mustard seeds

- 1 tbsp brown sugar
- 2 jalapeno pepper, chopped
- 1/2 tsp turmeric
- 1 tbsp olive oil
- 1 tsp salt

Directions:
1. Add oil into the inner pot of instant pot duo crisp and set pot on sauté mode.
2. Once the oil is hot then add mustard seeds and let them pop.
3. Add remaining ingredients and stir well.
4. Seal the pot with pressure cooking lid and cook on high for 5 minutes.
5. Once done, release pressure using a quick release. Remove lid.
6. Mash tomatoes mixture using a potato masher until getting the desired consistency.
7. Serve and enjoy.

Nutritional Value (Amount per Serving):
Calories 66; Fat 3.9 g; Carbohydrates 7.7 g; Sugar 5.7 g; Protein 1.3 g; Cholesterol 0 mg

Roasted Beans

Preparation Time: 10 minutes; Cooking Time: 30 minutes; Serve: 4

Ingredients:
- 1 lb green beans
- 1/2 tsp onion powder
- 2 tbsp olive oil
- 3/4 tsp garlic powder
- 1/2 tsp pepper
- 1/2 tsp salt

Directions:
1. In a large bowl, add all ingredients and toss well.
2. Arrange green beans into the instant pot air fryer basket and place basket in the pot.
3. Seal the pot with air fryer lid and select bake mode and cook at 400 F for 25-30 minutes.
4. Serve and enjoy.

Nutritional Value (Amount per Serving):
Calories 99; Fat 7.2 g; Carbohydrates 8.9 g; Sugar 1.8 g; Protein 2.2 g; Cholesterol 0 mg

Parmesan Zucchini & Eggplant

Preparation Time: 10 minutes; Cooking Time: 35 minutes; Serve: 6

Ingredients:
- 1 eggplant, sliced
- 1 tbsp olive oil
- 1 tbsp garlic, minced
- 1 cup cherry tomatoes, halved
- 3 medium zucchinis, sliced
- 1/4 cup basil, chopped
- 3 oz Parmesan cheese, grated
- 1/4 cup parsley, chopped
- 1/4 tsp pepper
- 1/4 tsp salt

Directions:
1. Line instant pot air fryer basket with parchment paper or foil.
2. In a mixing bowl, add cherry tomatoes, eggplant, zucchini, olive oil, garlic, cheese, basil, pepper, and salt toss well.
3. Transfer vegetable mixture into the air fryer basket and place basket in the pot.
4. Seal the pot with air fryer basket and select bake mode and cook at 350 F for 35 minutes.
5. Garnish with parsley and serve.

Nutritional Value (Amount per Serving):
Calories 109; Fat 5.8 g; Carbohydrates 10.2 g; Sugar 4.8 g; Protein 7 g; Cholesterol 10 mg

Roasted Vegetables

Preparation Time: 10 minutes; Cooking Time: 30 minutes; Serve: 4

Ingredients:
- 8 oz carrots, cut into wedges
- 2 shallots, quartered

- 8 oz baby potatoes, wash and cut in half
- 8 oz Brussels sprouts, halved
- 2 tbsp balsamic vinegar
- 1 tbsp honey
- 3 tbsp olive oil
- 1/2 tsp pepper
- 3/4 tsp salt

Directions:
1. Spray baking instant pot air fryer basket with cooking spray.
2. In a large bowl, add shallots, potatoes, carrots, Brussels sprouts, olive oil, honey, vinegar, pepper and salt. Toss well.
3. Transfer vegetables into the air fryer basket and place basket in the pot.
4. Seal the pot with air fryer lid and select roast mode and cook at 400 F for 30 minutes.
5. Serve and enjoy.

Nutritional Value (Amount per Serving):
Calories 192; Fat 10.8 g; Carbohydrates 23.2 g; Sugar 8.4 g; Protein 4 g; Cholesterol 0 mg

Healthy Pumpkin Porridge

Preparation Time: 10 minutes; Cooking Time: 3 minutes; Serve: 2
Ingredients:
- 1/2 cup pumpkin puree
- 3/4 tsp pumpkin pie spice
- 1/2 cup almond milk
- 1 1/4 cups water
- 1 tbsp brown sugar
- 1 cup quick oats

Directions:
1. Add all ingredients into the inner pot of instant pot duo crisp and stir well.
2. Seal the pot with pressure cooking lid and cook on high for 3 minutes.
3. Once done, allow to release pressure naturally. Remove lid.
4. Stir and serve warm.

Nutritional Value (Amount per Serving):
Calories 333; Fat 17.2 g; Carbohydrates 40.8 g; Sugar 8.9 g; Protein 7.5 g; Cholesterol 0 mg

Easy Apple Cinnamon Oatmeal

Preparation Time: 10 minutes; Cooking Time: 3 minutes; Serve: 2
Ingredients:
- 1 cup quick oats
- 3 cups of water
- 3/4 tsp cinnamon
- 2 medium apples, chopped

Directions:
1. Add water and oats into the inner pot of instant pot duo crisp.
2. Seal the pot with pressure cooking lid and cook on high for 3 minutes.
3. Once done, allow to release pressure naturally. Remove lid.
4. Just before serving add apple and cinnamon.
5. Stir and serve.

Nutritional Value (Amount per Serving):
Calories 273; Fat 3.1 g; Carbohydrates 59.2 g; Sugar 23.6 g; Protein 6 g; Cholesterol 0 mg

Spinach Risotto

Preparation Time: 10 minutes; Cooking Time: 10 minutes; Serve: 4
Ingredients:
- 1 1/2 cups Arborio rice
- 8 oz mushrooms, sliced
- 1 1/2 cups butternut squash, peeled and diced
- 1/2 cup dry white wine
- 3 1/2 cups vegetable broth
- 1 bell pepper, diced
- 1 tbsp garlic, minced
- 1 onion, chopped
- 3 cups spinach, chopped

- 1/4 tsp oregano
- 1/2 tsp coriander
- 1 tbsp olive oil
- 1 tsp pepper
- 1 tsp salt

Directions:
1. Add oil into the inner pot of instant pot duo crisp and set pot on sauté mode.
2. Add squash, bell pepper, garlic, and onion and sauté for 5 minutes.
3. Add remaining ingredients except spinach and stir well.
4. Seal the pot with pressure cooking lid and cook on high for 5 minutes.
5. Once done, release pressure using a quick release. Remove lid.
6. Add spinach and stir well and let it sit for 5 minutes.
7. Stir well and serve.

Nutritional Value (Amount per Serving):
Calories 411; Fat 5.5 g; Carbohydrates 73 g; Sugar 5.8 g; Protein 12.7 g; Cholesterol 0 mg

Chickpea Stew

Preparation Time: 10 minutes; Cooking Time: 25 minutes; Serve: 6
Ingredients:
- 28 oz cans chickpeas, rinsed and drained
- 1/2 tsp ground cumin
- 1 tsp smoked paprika
- 2 large onion, chopped
- 2 tbsp olive oil
- 24 oz can tomato
- 1/4 cup dates, pitted and chopped
- 1/4 tsp allspice
- 1/2 tsp sea salt

Directions:
1. Add oil into the inner pot of instant pot duo crisp and set pot on sauté mode.
2. Add onion, allspice, cumin, paprika and salt and sauté for 5 minutes.
3. Add remaining ingredients and stir well.
4. Seal the pot with pressure cooking lid and cook on high for 20 minutes.
5. Once done, allow to release pressure naturally. Remove lid.
6. Stir and serve.

Nutritional Value (Amount per Serving):
Calories 264; Fat 6.4 g; Carbohydrates 46.2 g; Sugar 10.7 g; Protein 8.4 g; Cholesterol 0 mg

Quick Veggie Pasta

Preparation Time: 10 minutes; Cooking Time: 4 minutes; Serve: 4
Ingredients:
- 1/2 lb pasta, uncooked
- 1/4 green onion, sliced
- 1/4 tsp red chili flakes
- 1 tsp ground ginger
- 1 tbsp garlic, minced
- 3 tbsp coconut amino
- 2 cups vegetable broth
- 1 1/2 cups baby spinach, chopped
- 1 cup frozen peas
- 8 oz mushrooms, sliced
- 2 carrots, peeled and chopped
- 1/4 tsp pepper
- 1 tsp salt

Directions:
1. Add all ingredients except spinach into the inner pot of instant pot duo crisp and stir well.
2. Seal the pot with pressure cooking lid and cook on high for 4 minutes.
3. Once done, allow to release pressure naturally. Remove lid.
4. Add spinach and stir well and let it sit for 5 minutes.
5. Serve and enjoy.

Nutritional Value (Amount per Serving):
Calories 258; Fat 2.3 g; Carbohydrates 45.9 g; Sugar 4.8 g; Protein 13.4 g; Cholesterol 41 mg

Baked Beans

Preparation Time: 10 minutes; Cooking Time: 40 minutes; Serve: 4
Ingredients:

- 1 cup navy beans, dry, soaked overnight and drained
- 2 tbsp tomato paste
- 1/2 tbsp vinegar
- 1/2 tbsp Worcestershire sauce
- 1/2 tsp mustard
- 1 onion, chopped
- 1 tbsp olive oil
- 1/2 cup water
- 1/2 cup vegetable stock
- 1 1/2 tbsp molasses
- 2 tbsp brown sugar
- 1/2 tsp pepper
- 1/2 tsp sea salt

Directions:

1. Add oil into the inner pot of instant pot duo crisp and set pot on sauté mode.
2. Add onion and sauté for 3 minutes.
3. Add remaining ingredients and stir to combine.
4. Seal the pot with pressure cooking lid and cook on high for 40 minutes.
5. Once done, release pressure using a quick release. Remove lid.
6. Stir well and serve.

Nutritional Value (Amount per Serving):
Calories 267; Fat 4.5 g; Carbohydrates 46.5 g; Sugar 13.2 g; Protein 12.5 g; Cholesterol 0 mg

Easy Lentil Tacos

Preparation Time: 10 minutes; Cooking Time: 15 minutes; Serve: 4
Ingredients:

- 2 cups brown lentils
- 1 tsp chili powder
- 1/2 tsp onion powder
- 1/2 cup tomato paste
- 4 cups vegetable broth
- 1/2 tsp ground cumin
- 1/2 tsp garlic powder
- 1 tsp salt

Directions:

1. Add all ingredients into the inner pot of instant pot duo crisp and stir well.
2. Seal the pot with pressure cooking lid and cook on high for 15 minutes.
3. Once done, release pressure using a quick release. Remove lid.
4. Stir well and serve.

Nutritional Value (Amount per Serving):
Calories 108; Fat 1.9 g; Carbohydrates 13 g; Sugar 5.5 g; Protein 9 g; Cholesterol 0 mg

Rice Black Bean Burritos

Preparation Time: 10 minutes; Cooking Time: 24 minutes; Serve: 4
Ingredients:

- 1 cup black beans, dry, soaked overnight and drained
- 2 cups brown rice
- 1 tsp paprika
- 1 tbsp ground cumin
- 1 onion, chopped
- 1 tbsp chili powder
- 4 1/2 vegetable broth
- 1 cup tomato puree
- 1 tsp olive oil
- 1 tsp garlic, minced

Directions:

1. Add oil into the inner pot of instant pot duo crisp and set pot on sauté mode.
2. Add garlic and onion and sauté for 2 minutes.
3. Add 2 cups broth and rice. Stir well.
4. Seal the pot with pressure cooking lid and cook on high for 12 minutes.

5. Once done, release pressure using a quick release. Remove lid.
6. Add beans, remaining broth, chili powder, cumin, tomato puree, and paprika. Stir well.
7. Seal the pot again with pressure cooking lid and cook on high for 10 minutes.
8. Once done, allow to release pressure naturally. Remove lid.
9. Serve in a tortilla.

Nutritional Value (Amount per Serving):
Calories 618; Fat 5.3 g; Carbohydrates 124.3 g; Sugar 5.5 g; Protein 20.7 g; Cholesterol 0 mg

Veggie Risotto

Preparation Time: 10 minutes; Cooking Time: 13 minutes; Serve: 4
Ingredients:

- 1 cup Arborio rice
- 1/2 cup peas
- 1 red pepper, diced
- 1 onion, chopped
- 1 tsp dried mix herbs
- 3 cups vegetable stock
- 1 tbsp olive oil
- 1 tsp garlic, minced
- 1/2 cup corn
- 1/4 pepper
- 1/2 tsp salt

Directions:
1. Add oil into the inner pot of instant pot duo crisp and set pot on sauté mode.
2. Add onion and garlic and sauté for 5 minutes.
3. Add rice and stir well. Add remaining ingredients and stir well.
4. Seal the pot with pressure cooking lid and cook on high for 8 minutes.
5. Once done, release pressure using a quick release. Remove lid.
6. Stir and serve.

Nutritional Value (Amount per Serving):
Calories 288; Fat 4.2 g; Carbohydrates 56 g; Sugar 5.4 g; Protein 6.7 g; Cholesterol 0 mg

Tasty Pumpkin Risotto

Preparation Time: 10 minutes; Cooking Time: 15 minutes; Serve: 8
Ingredients:

- 3 cups pumpkin, diced
- 1 cup cream cheese
- 1 tsp sage, dried
- 3 tbsp olive oil
- 4 cups vegetable broth
- 2 tbsp white wine
- 1 onion, chopped
- 1 tsp garlic, minced

Directions:
1. Add oil, garlic, and onion into the inner pot of instant pot duo crisp and set pot on sauté mode. Sauté onion until soften.
2. Add pumpkin and sauté for a minute.
3. Add white wine, sage, rice, and broth and stir well.
4. Seal the pot with pressure cooking lid and cook on high for 10 minutes.
5. Once done, allow to release pressure naturally. Remove lid.
6. Add cream cheese and stir well.
7. Serve and enjoy.

Nutritional Value (Amount per Serving):
Calories 377; Fat 16.6 g; Carbohydrates 48 g; Sugar 4.1 g; Protein 9 g; Cholesterol 32 mg

Roasted Broccoli with Cashews

Preparation Time: 10 minutes; Cooking Time: 15 minutes; Serve: 2
Ingredients:

- 3 cups broccoli florets
- 1/2 tbsp coconut amino

- 1/4 cup cashews, roasted
- 1 tbsp olive oil
- 1/2 tsp salt

Directions:

1. In a bowl, add broccoli, salt, and oil. Toss well.
2. Place broccoli into the instant pot air fryer basket and place basket into the pot.
3. Seal the pot with air fryer lid and select bake mode and cook at 375 F for 15 minutes.
4. In a large bowl, add roasted broccoli, cashews and coconut amino and toss well.
5. Serve and enjoy.

Nutritional Value (Amount per Serving):

Calories 209; Fat 15.4 g; Carbohydrates 15.4 g; Sugar 3.2 g; Protein 6.4 g; Cholesterol 0 mg

Chapter 5: Poultry

Crispy Chicken Wings

Preparation Time: 10 minutes; Cooking Time: 23 minutes; Serve: 4

Ingredients:
- 12 chicken wings
- 1/4 cup butter, melted
- 1/2 cup chicken stock
- Pepper
- Salt

Directions:
1. Pour the stock into the instant pot duo crisp then place metal rack in the pot.
2. Arrange chicken wings on top of the rack.
3. Seal the pot with pressure cooking lid and cook on high pressure for 8 minutes.
4. Once done, release pressure using a quick release. Remove lid.
5. Transfer chicken wings to a plate and dump leftover stock from the pot.
6. Add chicken wings into the air fryer basket. Drizzle with melted butter and season with pepper and salt.
7. Seal the pot with air fryer lid and select air fry mode and set a timer for 10 minutes.
8. After 10 minutes open the lid and mix chicken wings and continue to air fry for 5 minutes more or until desired crispness get.
9. Serve and enjoy.

Nutritional Value (Amount per Serving):
Calories 901; Fat 42.7 g; Carbohydrates 0.1 g; Sugar 0.1 g; Protein 121.7 g; Cholesterol 404 mg

Hot Sauce Chicken Wings

Preparation Time: 10 minutes; Cooking Time: 30 minutes; Serve: 4

Ingredients:
- 12 chicken wings
- 1/4 tsp garlic powder
- 1/4 tsp cayenne pepper
- 1 tbsp vinegar
- 1/4 tsp Worcestershire sauce
- 1/2 cup hot sauce
- 1/4 cup butter
- 1 cup chicken stock
- Pepper
- Salt

Directions:
1. Pour chicken stock into the instant pot duo crisp.
2. Add chicken wings into the air fryer basket and place basket in the pot.
3. Seal the pot with pressure cooking lid and cook on high pressure for 10 minutes.
4. Meanwhile, in small saucepan, mix together butter, garlic powder, cayenne pepper, vinegar, Worcestershire sauce, and hot sauce and heat over medium-high heat until butter is melted.
5. Remove saucepan from heat and set aside.
6. Once chicken wings are done then release pressure using a quick release. Remove lid.
7. Remove air fryer basket from pot then dump leftover liquid from the pot.
8. Spray chicken wings with cooking spray and toss well. Season with pepper and salt.
9. Again place air fryer basket in the pot.
10. Seal the pot with air fryer lid and air fry chicken wings for 20 minutes at 400 F. Toss chicken wings after every 5 minutes.
11. Transfer chicken wings into the large mixing bowl. Pour prepared sauce over chicken wings and toss until wings are well coated.
12. Serve and enjoy.

Nutritional Value (Amount per Serving):
Calories 675; Fat 33.8 g; Carbohydrates 1 g; Sugar 0.7 g; Protein 86.6 g; Cholesterol 295 mg

Delicious Whole Chicken

Preparation Time: 10 minutes; Cooking Time: 38 minutes; Serve: 4

Ingredients:

- 3 lbs whole chicken, wash and pat dry
- 1 1/2 cups chicken stock
- 2 tbsp Montreal steak seasoning
- 1/2 tsp Italian seasoning
- 3/4 tsp paprika
- 1/2 tsp onion powder
- 1/2 tsp garlic powder
- 2 tbsp olive oil
- Pepper
- Salt

Directions:

1. Mix together olive oil, Montreal steak seasoning, Italian seasoning, paprika, onion powder, garlic powder, pepper, and salt and rub all over the chicken.
2. Pour the stock into the instant pot duo crisp.
3. Place chicken in air fryer basket and place basket in the pot.
4. Seal the pot with pressure cooking lid and cook on high pressure for 18 minutes.
5. Once done, allow to release pressure naturally. Remove lid.
6. Remove the air fryer basket from pot. Dump leftover liquid from the pot.
7. Again, place air fryer basket in the pot.
8. Seal the pot with air fryer lid and air fry chicken for 10 minutes at 400 F.
9. Flip chicken and air fry for 10 minutes more.
10. Serve and enjoy.

Nutritional Value (Amount per Serving):

Calories 725; Fat 32.6 g; Carbohydrates 1.1 g; Sugar 0.6 g; Protein 98.8 g; Cholesterol 303 mg

Cheesy Chicken Rice Casserole

Preparation Time: 10 minutes; Cooking Time: 20 minutes; Serve: 4

Ingredients:

- 1 1/2 lbs chicken breasts, skinless, boneless, and cut into cubes
- 2 cups cheddar cheese, shredded
- 2 tbsp butter, melted
- 1 cup crackers, crushed
- 1 1/2 cups broccoli florets, steamed
- 10.5 oz can cream of chicken soup
- 1 1/2 cups rice
- 1 1/2 cups chicken stock
- 2 tbsp butter
- 3 garlic cloves, chopped
- Pepper
- Salt

Directions:

1. Add butter in instant pot duo crisp and select sauté mode.
2. Once butter is melted then add chicken and cook for 4-5 minutes. Add garlic and cook for 1 minute.
3. Add rice and stock and stir well.
4. Add chicken soup and do not stir. Seal the pot with pressure cooking lid and cook on pressure cook mode for 12 minutes.
5. Once done, release pressure using a quick release. Remove lid.
6. Stir chicken rice mixture well. Add 1 cup cheese and broccoli and stir well.
7. Now sprinkle remaining cheese on top of chicken mixture.
8. Mix together melted butter and crushed crackers and sprinkle on top of the cheese layer.
9. Seal the pot with air fryer lid and select broil mode and broil until cheese is melted.
10. Serve and enjoy.

Nutritional Value (Amount per Serving):

Calories 1044; Fat 49 g; Carbohydrates 74.3 g; Sugar 1.9 g; Protein 72.6 g; Cholesterol 240 mg

Chili Chicken Wings

Preparation Time: 10 minutes; Cooking Time: 15 minutes; Serve: 2

Ingredients:

- 1 lb chicken wings
- 1 tsp parsley
- 1/4 tsp nutmeg
- 1 tsp garlic, minced
- 1 tsp chili powder
- 2 tbsp honey
- 1 tbsp olive oil
- Pepper
- Salt

Directions:

1. Add chicken wings into the mixing bowl. Pour remaining ingredients over chicken and toss well.
2. Pour 1 cup of water into the instant pot duo crisp.
3. Add chicken wings into the air fryer basket and place in the pot.
4. Seal the pot with pressure cooking lid and cook on high pressure for 10 minutes.
5. Once done, release pressure using a quick release. Remove lid.
6. Remove the air fryer basket from pot. Dump all leftover liquid from pot.
7. Return air fryer basket to the instant pot.
8. Seal the pot with air fryer lid and air fry chicken wings for 4-5 minutes.
9. Serve and enjoy.

Nutritional Value (Amount per Serving):

Calories 563; Fat 24.1 g; Carbohydrates 18.7 g; Sugar 17.4 g; Protein 66 g; Cholesterol 202 mg

Apple Cider Chicken

Preparation Time: 10 minutes; Cooking Time: 20 minutes; Serve: 6

Ingredients:

- 3 lbs whole chicken, wash and pat dry
- 1/4 tsp red pepper flakes
- 1 1/2 tbsp coconut amino
- 2 tbsp honey
- 1 cup apple cider
- 1 tbsp olive oil
- Pepper
- Salt

Directions:

1. Season chicken with pepper and salt.
2. Add oil into the instant pot duo crisp and set pot on sauté mode.
3. Once the oil is hot then add chicken into the pot and sear chicken until lightly golden brown.
4. Remove chicken from pot and set aside.
5. In a small bowl, whisk together honey, red pepper flakes, coconut amino, and apple cider and pour into the instant pot.
6. Return chicken to the instant pot.
7. Seal the pot with pressure cooking lid and cook on high pressure for 18 minutes.
8. Once done, allow to release pressure naturally for 10 minutes then release remaining pressure using a quick release. Remove lid.
9. Pour apple cider sauce over chicken.
10. Slice and serve.

Nutritional Value (Amount per Serving):

Calories 496; Fat 19.2 g; Carbohydrates 11.4 g; Sugar 10.3 g; Protein 65.7 g; Cholesterol 202 mg

Creamy Coconut Chicken

Preparation Time: 10 minutes; Cooking Time: 6 hours 10 minutes; Serve: 4

Ingredients:

- 1 1/2 lbs chicken thighs, boneless
- 2 bell peppers, sliced
- 1/2 tsp cayenne pepper
- 3/4 tsp garlic powder
- 1 tsp ground coriander
- 1 tsp ground cumin
- 1 1/2 tsp paprika
- 1 tbsp chili powder
- 1/2 cup coconut milk
- 1 tbsp water
- 1/4 cup fresh lime juice
- 1 cup chicken broth
- 1 tsp sea salt

Directions:
1. Spray pan with cooking spray and heat over medium-high heat.
2. In a small bowl, mix together all spices.
3. Rub spice mixture over chicken and place chicken on the hot pan and cook for 2 minutes on each side.
4. Transfer seared chicken to the inner pot of instant pot duo crisp.
5. Add bell peppers, water, broth, and salt over chicken.
6. Seal the pot with pressure cooking lid and select slow cook mode and cook on low pressure for 6 hours.
7. Shred chicken using a fork. Add coconut milk and lime juice and stir well.
8. Serve and enjoy.

Nutritional Value (Amount per Serving):
Calories 439; Fat 20.8 g; Carbohydrates 9.2 g; Sugar 4.6 g; Protein 52.3 g; Cholesterol 151 mg

Tasty Asian Chicken

Preparation Time: 10 minutes; Cooking Time: 3 hours 5 minutes; Serve: 4
Ingredients:
- 1 lb chicken thighs, boneless and skinless
- 1 tsp cardamom
- 1 tsp cumin
- 1 tsp coriander
- 1 tsp ginger, minced
- 1 tbsp garlic, minced
- 1 fresh lime juice
- 5 oz tomato paste
- 14 oz coconut milk
- 1/4 cayenne pepper
- 2 tsp olive oil
- 1 onion, diced
- 1/2 tsp salt

Directions:
1. Add oil into the instant pot duo crisp and set pot on sauté mode.
2. Add onion and sauté for 3-5 minutes.
3. Add ginger, garlic, and spices and sauté for 1 minute.
4. Add tomato paste and coconut milk and stir well. Add chicken and stir well.
5. Seal the pot with pressure cooking lid and select slow cook mode and cook on high pressure for 3 hours.
6. Shred chicken using a fork. Add lime juice and stir well.
7. Serve and enjoy.

Nutritional Value (Amount per Serving):
Calories 516; Fat 34.8 g; Carbohydrates 17.5 g; Sugar 9.1 g; Protein 37.3 g; Cholesterol 101 mg

Easy Chicken Chilli

Preparation Time: 10 minutes; Cooking Time: 4 hours; Serve: 6
Ingredients:
- 2 1/2 lbs chicken breast, boneless and skinless
- 1/4 cup fresh cilantro, chopped
- 2 poblano peppers, diced
- 1 1/2 jalapeno peppers, diced
- 1 tbsp garlic, minced
- 1 medium onion, minced
- 6 cups chicken broth

- 1 tsp oregano
- 2 tsp cumin
- Pepper
- Salt

Directions:
1. Add 2 cups broth, poblanos, jalapeno, garlic, oregano, cumin, cilantro, and onion in blender and blend until smooth.
2. Add chicken, blended broth mixture, and remaining broth into the inner pot of instant pot duo crisp. Stir well.
3. Seal the pot with pressure cooking lid and select slow cook mode and cook on low for 4 hours.
4. Shred chicken using fork.
5. Serve and enjoy.

Nutritional Value (Amount per Serving):
Calories 274; Fat 6.4 g; Carbohydrates 5.3 g; Sugar 2.4 g; Protein 45.7 g; Cholesterol 121 mg

Italian Spinach Tomato Chicken

Preparation Time: 10 minutes; Cooking Time: 4 hours; Serve: 6
Ingredients:
- 2 lbs chicken breast, skinless and boneless
- 1 tbsp garlic, minced
- 28 oz can tomato, diced
- 1 onion, sliced
- 6 cups fresh spinach
- 1 tbsp Italian seasoning
- 3 tbsp balsamic vinegar
- Pepper
- Salt

Directions:
1. Season chicken with pepper and salt and place into the inner pot of instant pot duo crisp.
2. Add remaining ingredients except spinach and stir well.
3. Seal the pot with pressure cooking lid and select slow cook mode and cook on low for 4 hours.
4. Shred chicken using a fork. Add spinach and stir until spinach is wilted.
5. Serve and enjoy.

Nutritional Value (Amount per Serving):
Calories 226; Fat 4.6 g; Carbohydrates 10.4 g; Sugar 5.7 g; Protein 34.4 g; Cholesterol 98 mg

Simple Salsa Chicken

Preparation Time: 10 minutes; Cooking Time: 4 hours; Serve: 6
Ingredients:
- 1 1/2 lbs chicken breast, skinless and boneless
- 2 lb chicken thighs, skinless and boneless
- 2 cups salsa
- Pepper
- Salt

Directions:
1. Add all ingredients into the inner pot of instant pot duo crisp and stir well.
2. Seal the pot with pressure cooking lid and select slow cook mode and cook on low for 4 hours.
3. Shred chicken using a fork.
4. Stir well and serve.

Nutritional Value (Amount per Serving):
Calories 440; Fat 14.2 g; Carbohydrates 5.4 g; Sugar 2.7 g; Protein 69.1 g; Cholesterol 207 mg

Delicious Chicken Tacos

Preparation Time: 10 minutes; Cooking Time: 4 hours; Serve: 6

Ingredients:
- 2 1/2 lbs chicken breasts, skinless and boneless
- 20 oz can fire-roasted tomatoes, crushed
- 3/4 tsp garlic powder
- 1 tsp oregano
- 3 tbsp adobo sauce
- 1 medium onion, minced
- 1/2 tsp cumin
- 1/2 tsp coriander
- Pepper
- Salt

Directions:
1. Season chicken with pepper and salt and place in inner pot of instant pot duo crisp.
2. Add remaining ingredients over chicken.
3. Seal the pot with pressure cooking lid and select slow cook mode and cook on low for 4 hours.
4. Shred chicken using a fork.
5. Stir well and serve.

Nutritional Value (Amount per Serving):
Calories 402; Fat 14.1 g; Carbohydrates 9.3 g; Sugar 5.2 g; Protein 55.8 g; Cholesterol 168 mg

Basil Chicken Curry

Preparation Time: 10 minutes; Cooking Time: 30 minutes; Serve: 6
Ingredients:
- 6 chicken thighs, skinless and boneless
- 1 tbsp fresh ginger, grated
- 1 tbsp garlic, chopped
- 1 jalapeno, chopped
- 1/4 cup fresh basil leaves
- 1 fresh lime juice
- 1 tbsp curry powder
- 1 onion, sliced
- 14.5 oz can coconut milk
- 1 tsp salt

Directions:
1. Add all ingredients except basil and lime juice into the inner pot of instant pot duo crisp and stir well.
2. Seal the pot with pressure cooking lid and cook on high pressure for 30 minutes.
3. Once done, allow to release pressure naturally. Remove lid.
4. Shred the chicken using a fork.
5. Add lime juice and basil and stir well.
6. Serve and enjoy.

Nutritional Value (Amount per Serving):
Calories 315; Fat 21.2 g; Carbohydrates 6.1 g; Sugar 1.1 g; Protein 26.6 g; Cholesterol 76 mg

Tender Chicken Breasts

Preparation Time: 10 minutes; Cooking Time: 15 minutes; Serve: 3
Ingredients:
- 3 chicken breasts, skinless and boneless
- 1 tbsp olive oil
- 1 cup of water
- 1/4 tsp dried basil
- 1/8 tsp dried oregano
- 1/4 tsp pepper
- 1/4 tsp garlic salt

Directions:
1. Add oil into the instant pot duo crisp and set pot on sauté mode.
2. Season chicken with basil, oregano, pepper, and garlic salt and place into the pot.
3. Sear chicken for 3 minutes then turns to the other side and sear for 3 minutes more.
4. Remove chicken from pot.
5. Pour 1 cup of water into the pot then place steamer rack in the pot.
6. Place chicken on top of the steamer rack.

7. Seal the pot with pressure cooking lid and cook on high pressure for 5 minutes.
8. Once done, allow to release pressure naturally. Remove lid.
9. Remove chicken from pot and place on a plate. Dump leftover liquid from the pot.
10. Place chicken into the air fryer basket then place basket in the pot.
11. Seal the pot with air fryer lid and select broil mode and cook for 5 minutes.
12. Serve and enjoy.

Nutritional Value (Amount per Serving):
Calories 203; Fat 11 g; Carbohydrates 0.3 g; Sugar 0.1 g; Protein 24.7 g; Cholesterol 76 mg

Easy Taco Chicken Wings

Preparation Time: 10 minutes; Cooking Time: 20 minutes; Serve: 6
Ingredients:
- 1 1/2 lbs chicken wings
- 4 tbsp taco seasoning
- 1/4 tsp pepper
- 1 1/2 tsp salt

Directions:
1. Add chicken wings into the mixing bowl. Sprinkle remaining ingredients over chicken wings and toss well.
2. Pour 1 cup water into the inner pot of instant pot duo crisp then place steamer rack into the pot.
3. Arrange chicken wings on top of the steamer rack.
4. Seal the pot with pressure cooking lid and cook on high pressure for 10 minutes.
5. Once done, allow to release pressure naturally. Remove lid.
6. Remove chicken wings from the pot. Dump leftover liquid from the pot.
7. Add chicken wings into the air fryer basket then place a basket in the pot.
8. Seal the pot with air fryer lid and select broil mode and cook for 10 minutes.
9. Serve and enjoy.

Nutritional Value (Amount per Serving):
Calories 463; Fat 22.1 g; Carbohydrates 17.9 g; Sugar 0 g; Protein 46.6 g; Cholesterol 139 mg

Vegetable Chicken Curry

Preparation Time: 10 minutes; Cooking Time: 15 minutes; Serve: 4
Ingredients:
- 1 1/4 lbs chicken thighs, skinless, boneless and cut into pieces
- 1/4 cup fresh cilantro, chopped
- 1 sweet potato, peeled and diced
- 1 onion, sliced
- 2 medium zucchinis, diced
- 1 tbsp olive oil
- 14 oz coconut milk
- 2 tbsp green curry paste
- 1 Tsp sea salt

Directions:
1. Add oil into the inner pot of instant pot duo crisp and set the pot on sauté mode.
2. Add onion and zucchini and sauté for 5 minutes.
3. Add remaining ingredients and stir everything well.
4. Seal the pot with pressure cooking lid and cook on high pressure for 10 minutes.
5. Once done, release pressure using a quick release. Remove lid.
6. Serve and enjoy.

Nutritional Value (Amount per Serving):
Calories 603; Fat 39.4 g; Carbohydrates 19.5 g; Sugar 8 g; Protein 45.4 g; Cholesterol 126 mg

Potato Chicken Curry

Preparation Time: 10 minutes; Cooking Time: 30 minutes; Serve: 8
Ingredients:

- 4 lbs chicken thighs
- 4 cups potatoes, peeled and diced
- 2 tbsp olive oil
- 2 tbsp curry powder
- 1 tsp onion powder
- 1 tsp garlic powder
- 1 cup of water
- 2 cups of coconut milk
- 1 tsp kosher salt

Directions:
1. In a mixing bowl, mix together chicken, olive oil, 1 tbsp curry powder, onion powder, garlic powder, and salt and let it sit for 1 hour.
2. Add marinated chicken into the inner pot of instant pot duo crisp.
3. Set pot on sauté mode and cook chicken for 5 minutes.
4. Add potatoes, remaining curry powder, and coconut milk and stir well.
5. Seal the pot with pressure cooking lid and cook on high pressure for 25 minutes.
6. Once done, release pressure using a quick release. Remove lid.
7. Stir well and serve.

Nutritional Value (Amount per Serving):
Calories 658; Fat 34.9 g; Carbohydrates 16.5 g; Sugar 3.1 g; Protein 68.5 g; Cholesterol 202 mg

Hot Buffalo Chicken

Preparation Time: 10 minutes; Cooking Time: 12 minutes; Serve: 6
Ingredients:
- 2 lbs chicken breasts
- 1/2 cup buffalo wing sauce
- 1/2 cup onion, chopped
- 1/2 cup celery, diced
- 1/2 cup chicken broth

Directions:
1. Add all ingredients into the inner pot of instant pot duo crisp and stir well.
2. Seal the pot with pressure cooking lid and cook on high pressure for 12 minutes.
3. Once done, release pressure using a quick release. Remove lid.
4. Remove chicken from pot and shred using a fork.
5. Return shredded chicken to the pot and stir well and serve.

Nutritional Value (Amount per Serving):
Calories 296; Fat 11.3 g; Carbohydrates 1.3 g; Sugar 0.6 g; Protein 44.3 g; Cholesterol 135 mg

Yummy Mexican Chicken

Preparation Time: 10 minutes; Cooking Time: 15 minutes; Serve: 6
Ingredients:
- 2 lbs chicken breasts
- 2 tsp cumin
- 2 tsp garlic powder
- 4 oz jalapenos, diced
- 10.5 oz tomatoes, diced
- 1/2 cup green bell pepper
- 1/2 cup red bell pepper
- 1 onion, diced
- 1 fresh lime juice
- 2/3 cup chicken broth
- 1/2 tsp chili powder
- 1 tbsp olive oil
- 1/4 tsp salt

Directions:
1. Add oil into the inner pot of instant pot duo crisp and set pot on sauté mode.
2. Add onion, bell peppers and salt and sauté for 3 minutes.
3. Add remaining ingredients and stir well.
4. Seal the pot with pressure cooking lid and cook on high pressure for 12 minutes.
5. Once done, release pressure using a quick release. Remove lid.
6. Remove chicken from pot and shred using a fork.
7. Return shredded chicken to the pot and stir well.

8. Serve and enjoy.

Nutritional Value (Amount per Serving):

Calories 347; Fat 14.2 g; Carbohydrates 7.8 g; Sugar 4 g; Protein 45.7 g; Cholesterol 135 mg

Balsamic Chicken

Preparation Time: 10 minutes; Cooking Time: 17 minutes; Serve: 6

Ingredients:

- 2 lbs chicken breasts
- 1/3 cup balsamic vinegar
- 1 onion, chopped
- 1/2 cup chicken broth
- 1 tbsp Dijon mustard
- 1/2 tsp dried thyme
- 1 tsp garlic, chopped

Directions:

1. Mix together Dijon, chicken broth, and vinegar and pour into the inner pot of instant pot duo crisp.
2. Add chicken, thyme, garlic, and onion and stir well.
3. Seal the pot with pressure cooking lid and cook on high pressure for 12 minutes.
4. Once done, release pressure using a quick release. Remove lid.
5. Remove chicken from pot and shred using a fork. Pour the leftover liquid of pot over shredded chicken.
6. Line air fryer basket with foil.
7. Add shredded chicken to the air fryer basket and place basket in the pot.
8. Seal the pot with air fryer lid and select broil mode and cook for 5 minutes.
9. Serve and enjoy.

Nutritional Value (Amount per Serving):

Calories 303; Fat 11.4 g; Carbohydrates 2.3 g; Sugar 0.9 g; Protein 44.5 g; Cholesterol 135 mg

Italian Chicken Wings

Preparation Time: 10 minutes; Cooking Time: 15 minutes; Serve: 4

Ingredients:

- 12 chicken wings
- 1 tbsp chicken seasoning
- 3 tbsp olive oil
- 1 tbsp garlic powder
- 1 tbsp basil
- 1/2 tbsp oregano
- 3 tbsp tarragon
- Pepper
- Salt

Directions:

1. Add all ingredients into the mixing bowl and toss well.
2. Pour 1 cup water into the inner pot of instant pot duo crisp then place steamer rack in the pot.
3. Arrange chicken wings on top of the steamer rack.
4. Seal the pot with pressure cooking lid and cook on high pressure for 10 minutes.
5. Once done, release pressure using a quick release. Remove lid.
6. Remove chicken wings from the pot. Dump leftover liquid from the pot.
7. Add chicken wings into the air fryer basket then place a basket in the pot.
8. Seal the pot with air fryer lid and select broil mode and cook for 5 minutes.
9. Serve and enjoy.

Nutritional Value (Amount per Serving):

Calories 588; Fat 29.6 g; Carbohydrates 2.6 g; Sugar 0.5 g; Protein 74.6 g; Cholesterol 227 mg

Yummy Hawaiian Chicken

Preparation Time: 10 minutes; Cooking Time: 12 minutes; Serve: 6

Ingredients:
- 2 lbs chicken breasts, skinless, boneless, and cut into chunks
- 2 tbsp cornstarch
- 1 cup chicken broth
- 20 oz can pineapple tidbits
- 1 tbsp garlic, crushed
- 2 tbsp brown sugar
- 6 tbsp soy sauce
- 1/2 tsp ground ginger
- 1/2 tsp salt

Directions:
1. Add all ingredients except cornstarch into the inner pot of instant pot duo crisp and stir well.
2. Seal the pot with pressure cooking lid and cook on high pressure for 10 minutes.
3. Once done, release pressure using a quick release. Remove lid.
4. In a small bowl, whisk together 1/4 cup water and cornstarch and pour into the pot.
5. Set pot on sauté mode. Cook chicken on sauce mode until sauce thickens.
6. Serve over rice and enjoy.

Nutritional Value (Amount per Serving):
Calories 377; Fat 11.5 g; Carbohydrates 18.7 g; Sugar 12.1 g; Protein 46 g; Cholesterol 135 mg

Spicy Chicken Wings

Preparation Time: 10 minutes; Cooking Time: 20 minutes; Serve: 4

Ingredients:
- 2 lbs frozen chicken wings
- 2 tbsp apple cider vinegar
- 2 tbsp butter, melted
- 1/2 cup hot pepper sauce
- 1/2 cup water
- 1/2 tsp paprika
- 1 oz ranch seasoning

Directions:
1. Add water, vinegar, butter, and hot pepper sauce into the instant pot duo crisp.
2. Add chicken wings and stir well.
3. Seal the pot with pressure cooking lid and cook on high for 5 minutes.
4. Once done, release pressure using a quick release. Remove lid.
5. Sprinkle paprika and ranch seasoning over the chicken.
6. Seal the pot with air fryer lid and select air fry mode and cook at 375 F for 15 minutes.
7. Toss wings in sauce and serve.

Nutritional Value (Amount per Serving):
Calories 521; Fat 38.2 g; Carbohydrates 0.2 g; Sugar 0.1 g; Protein 36.6 g; Cholesterol 167 mg

Cheesy Chicken Wings

Preparation Time: 10 minutes; Cooking Time: 18 minutes; Serve: 4

Ingredients:
- 2 lbs chicken wings
- 1/2 cup chicken stock
- 1 tsp season salt
- For sauce:
- 1/2 cup parmesan cheese, grated
- 1 tbsp garlic, crushed
- 1 stick butter, melted
- 1/2 tsp black pepper
- 1/2 tsp dried parsley flakes
- 1 tsp garlic powder

Directions:
1. Season chicken wings with seasoned salt.
2. Add chicken wings to the inner pot of instant pot duo crisp along with the chicken stock.
3. Seal the pot with pressure cooking lid and cook on high for 8 minutes.
4. Meanwhile, mix together butter, pepper, parmesan cheese, parsley flakes, garlic powder, and garlic. Set aside.
5. Once chicken wings done then release pressures using a quick release. Remove lid.

6. Remove chicken wings from the pot and clean the pot.
7. Spray instant pot air fryer basket with cooking spray and place in the pot.
8. Toss chicken wings with melted butter and add into the air fryer basket.
9. Seal the pot with air fryer lid and select broil mode and cook for 10 minutes.
10. Serve and enjoy.

Nutritional Value (Amount per Serving):
Calories 652; Fat 40.6 g; Carbohydrates 1.6 g; Sugar 0.3 g; Protein 67.3 g; Cholesterol 265 mg

Chicken Rice

Preparation Time: 10 minutes; Cooking Time: 12 minutes; Serve: 6
Ingredients:
- 2 lbs chicken thighs, skinless, boneless, and cut into pieces
- 18 oz enchilada sauce
- 15 oz frozen mixed vegetables
- 1 oz taco seasoning
- 2 cups rice, uncooked
- 1 cup chicken stock

Directions:
1. Spray instant pot duo crisp inner pot with cooking spray and set the pot on sauté mode.
2. Season chicken with taco seasoning and place in the pot.
3. Sear chicken until brown from all the sides, about 10 minutes.
4. Add rice, stock, enchilada sauce, and vegetables and stir well.
5. Seal the pot with pressure cooking lid and cook on high for 2 minutes.
6. Once done, allow to release pressure naturally for 10 minutes then release remaining pressure using a quick release. Remove lid.
7. Stir well and serve.

Nutritional Value (Amount per Serving):
Calories 787; Fat 15.2 g; Carbohydrates 114.6 g; Sugar 2.9 g; Protein 60.2 g; Cholesterol 136 mg

Spicy Chicken Breast

Preparation Time: 10 minutes; Cooking Time: 35 minutes; Serve: 2
Ingredients:
- 2 chicken breasts, bone-in, and skin-on
- 1 tbsp ground fennel
- 1 tbsp chili powder
- 1 tbsp olive oil
- 1 tsp ground cumin
- 1 tsp garlic powder
- 1 tsp onion powder
- 1 tbsp paprika
- 1/2 tsp black pepper
- 1 tsp sea salt

Directions:
1. In a small bowl, mix together all dried spices.
2. Brush chicken with olive oil and rub with spice mixture.
3. Place chicken in the instant pot air fryer basket and place basket in the pot.
4. Seal the pot with air fryer lid and select air fry mode and cook at 375 F for 35 minutes.
5. Serve and enjoy.

Nutritional Value (Amount per Serving):
Calories 108; Fat 8.9 g; Carbohydrates 8.3 g; Sugar 1.4 g; Protein 2.3 g; Cholesterol 1 mg

Tasty Butter Chicken

Preparation Time: 10 minutes; Cooking Time: 8 minutes; Serve: 6
Ingredients:
- 3 lbs chicken breasts, boneless, skinless, and cut into cubes
- 1/2 cup butter, cut into cubes
- 2 tbsp tomato paste
- 1 tsp turmeric powder
- 2 tbsp garam masala

- 1 tbsp ginger paste
- 1 tbsp garlic paste
- 1 onion, diced
- 1/4 cup fresh cilantro, chopped
- 1/2 cup heavy cream
- 1 1/4 cup tomato sauce
- 2/3 cup chicken stock
- 1 1/2 tsp olive oil
- 1 tsp kosher salt

Directions:
1. Add 3 tbsp butter and oil in the inner pot of instant pot duo crisp and set pot on sauté mode.
2. Add garlic paste and onion and sauté for a minute.
3. Add chicken, tomato sauce, stock, tomato paste, turmeric, garam masala, ginger paste, and salt and stir to combine.
4. Seal the pot with pressure cooking lid and cook on high for 5 minutes.
5. Once done, release pressure using a quick release. Remove lid.
6. Set pot on sauté mode. Add remaining butter and heavy cream and cook for 2 minutes.
7. Stir well and serve.

Nutritional Value (Amount per Serving):
Calories 643; Fat 37.3 g; Carbohydrates 7.2 g; Sugar 3.8 g; Protein 67.4 g; Cholesterol 256 mg

Chicken Pasta

Preparation Time: 10 minutes; Cooking Time: 15 minutes; Serve: 4
Ingredients:
- 1 lb chicken breasts, boneless and skinless, cut into bite-size pieces
- 1 tbsp garlic, minced
- 2 bell peppers, seeded and diced
- 2 tbsp olive oil
- 1 onion, diced
- 1 cup chicken stock
- 3 tbsp fajita seasoning
- 8 oz penne pasta, dry
- 7 oz can tomato

Directions:
1. Add olive oil in the inner pot of instant pot duo crisp and set pot on sauté mode.
2. Add chicken and half fajita seasoning in the pot and sauté chicken for 3-5 minutes.
3. Add garlic, bell pepper, onions, and remaining fajitas seasoning and sauté for 2 minutes.
4. Add tomatoes, stock, and pasta and stir well.
5. Seal the pot with pressure cooking lid and cook on high for 6 minutes.
6. Once done, release pressure using a quick release. Remove lid.
7. Set pot on sauté mode and cook for 1-2 minutes.
8. Serve and enjoy.

Nutritional Value (Amount per Serving):
Calories 509; Fat 17 g; Carbohydrates 46.2 g; Sugar 6.1 g; Protein 40.9 g; Cholesterol 142 mg

Easy Cheesy Chicken

Preparation Time: 10 minutes; Cooking Time: 17 minutes; Serve: 6
Ingredients:
- 1 1/2 lbs chicken tenders
- 25 oz tomato sauce
- 2 tbsp butter
- 1/2 cup olive oil
- 1/2 tsp garlic powder
- 1/2 cup parmesan cheese, grated
- 2 cups mozzarella cheese, shredded

Directions:
1. Add olive oil into the inner pot of instant pot duo crisp and set pot on sauté mode.
2. Add chicken and sauté until lightly brown from both the sides.
3. Add garlic powder, tomato sauce, butter, and parmesan cheese on top of chicken.
4. Seal the pot with pressure cooking lid and cook on high for 15 minutes.

5. Once done, release pressure using a quick release. Remove lid.
6. Sprinkle mozzarella cheese on top of chicken. Cover pot with air fryer lid and select broil mode and cook for 1-2 minutes.
7. Serve and enjoy.

Nutritional Value (Amount per Serving):
Calories 457; Fat 31.4 g; Carbohydrates 6.9 g; Sugar 5.1 g; Protein 37.9 g; Cholesterol 118 mg

Creamy Italian Chicken

Preparation Time: 10 minutes; Cooking Time: 10 minutes; Serve: 8
Ingredients:
- 2 lbs chicken breasts, skinless and boneless
- 1 cup chicken stock
- 1/4 cup butter
- 14 oz can cream of chicken soup
- 8 oz cream cheese
- 1 tbsp Italian seasoning

Directions:
1. Add the chicken stock into the inner pot of instant pot duo crisp.
2. Add cream of chicken soup, Italian seasoning, and butter into the pot and stir well.
3. Seal the pot with pressure cooking lid and cook on high for 10 minutes.
4. Once done, release pressure using a quick release. Remove lid.
5. Add cream cheese and stir until cheese is melted
6. Serve and enjoy.

Nutritional Value (Amount per Serving):
Calories 416; Fat 27.5 g; Carbohydrates 4.6 g; Sugar 0.6 g; Protein 36.3 g; Cholesterol 153 mg

Paprika Chicken

Preparation Time: 10 minutes; Cooking Time: 30 minutes; Serve: 4
Ingredients:
- 4 chicken breasts, skinless and boneless, cut into chunks
- 2 tsp garlic, minced
- 2 tbsp smoked paprika
- 3 tbsp olive oil
- 2 tbsp lemon juice
- Pepper
- Salt

Directions:
1. In a small bowl, mix together garlic, lemon juice, paprika, oil, pepper, and salt.
2. Rub chicken with garlic mixture.
3. Add chicken into the instant pot air fryer basket and place basket in the pot.
4. Seal the pot with air fryer lid and select bake mode and cook at 350 F for 30 minutes.
5. Serve and enjoy.

Nutritional Value (Amount per Serving):
Calories 381; Fat 21.8 g; Carbohydrates 2.6 g; Sugar 0.5 g; Protein 42.9 g; Cholesterol 130 mg

Garlic Lemon Chicken

Preparation Time: 10 minutes; Cooking Time: 40 minutes; Serve: 4
Ingredients:
- 2 lbs chicken drumsticks
- 4 tbsp butter
- 2 tbsp parsley, chopped
- 1 fresh lemon juice
- 10 garlic cloves, minced
- 2 tbsp olive oil
- Pepper
- Salt

Directions:
1. Add butter, parsley, lemon juice, garlic, oil, pepper, and salt into the mixing bowl and mix well.

2. Add chicken to the bowl and toss until well coated.
3. Transfer chicken into the instant pot air fryer basket and place basket in the pot.
4. Seal the pot with air fryer lid and select bake mode and cook at 400 F for 40 minutes.
5. Serve and enjoy.

Nutritional Value (Amount per Serving):
Calories 560; Fat 31.6 g; Carbohydrates 2.9 g; Sugar 0.4 g; Protein 63.1 g; Cholesterol 230 mg

Flavorful Herb Chicken

Preparation Time: 10 minutes; Cooking Time: 4 hours; Serve: 6
Ingredients:
- 6 chicken breasts, skinless and boneless
- 1 onion, sliced
- 14 oz can tomatoes, diced
- 1 tsp dried basil
- 1 tsp dried rosemary
- 1 tbsp olive oil
- 1/2 cup balsamic vinegar
- 1/2 tsp thyme
- 1 tsp dried oregano
- 4 garlic cloves
- Pepper
- Salt

Directions:
1. Add all ingredients into the inner pot of instant pot duo crisp and stir well.
2. Seal the pot with pressure cooking lid and select slow cook mode and cook on high for 4 hours.
3. Stir well and serve.

Nutritional Value (Amount per Serving):
Calories 328; Fat 13.3 g; Carbohydrates 6.3 g; Sugar 3.1 g; Protein 43.2 g; Cholesterol 130 mg

Chicken Fajitas

Preparation Time: 10 minutes; Cooking Time: 10 minutes; Serve: 6
Ingredients:
- 4 chicken breasts, skinless and boneless
- 1/2 cup bell pepper, sliced
- 1/2 cup water
- 1 packet fajita seasoning
- 1 onion, sliced
- 1/4 tsp garlic powder

Directions:
1. Add all ingredients into the inner pot of instant pot duo crisp and stir well.
2. Seal the pot with pressure cooking lid and cook on high for 10 minutes.
3. Once done, release pressure using a quick release. Remove lid.
4. Shred chicken using a fork and stir well.
5. Serve and enjoy.

Nutritional Value (Amount per Serving):
Calories 198; Fat 7.3 g; Carbohydrates 3.1 g; Sugar 1.3 g; Protein 28.5 g; Cholesterol 87 mg

Jamaican Chicken

Preparation Time: 10 minutes; Cooking Time: 15 minutes; Serve: 6
Ingredients:
- 6 chicken drumsticks
- 1 tbsp jerk seasoning
- 3 tbsp soy sauce
- 1/4 cup red wine vinegar
- 1/4 cup brown sugar
- 1/2 cup ketchup
- 1 tsp salt

Directions:
1. Add all ingredients except chicken into the inner pot of instant pot duo crisp and stir well.
2. Add chicken and stir to coat.
3. Seal the pot with pressure cooking lid and cook on high for 10 minutes.

4. Once done, release pressure using a quick release. Remove lid.
5. Remove chicken from pot. Set pot on sauté mode and cook sauce for 5 minutes.
6. Pour sauce over chicken and serve.

Nutritional Value (Amount per Serving):
Calories 126; Fat 2.7 g; Carbohydrates 11.7 g; Sugar 10.6 g; Protein 13.5 g; Cholesterol 40 mg

Flavorful Lemon Chicken

Preparation Time: 10 minutes; Cooking Time: 4 hours 5 minutes; Serve: 4
Ingredients:

- 20 oz chicken breasts, skinless, boneless, and cut into pieces
- 1 tsp dried parsley
- 2 tbsp olive oil
- 2 tbsp butter
- 3 tbsp flour
- 1/4 cup chicken broth
- 1/2 cup fresh lemon juice
- 1/8 tsp dried thymeFla
- 1/4 tsp dried basil
- 1/2 tsp dried oregano
- 1 tsp salt

Directions:
1. In a bowl, toss chicken with flour.
2. Heat butter and oil in a pan over medium-high heat.
3. Add chicken to the pan and sear until brown.
4. Transfer chicken into the inner pot of instant pot duo crisp.
5. Add remaining ingredients on top of chicken.
6. Seal the pot with pressure cooking lid and select slow cook mode and cook on low for 4 hours.
7. Serve and enjoy.

Nutritional Value (Amount per Serving):
Calories 412; Fat 23.7 g; Carbohydrates 5.3 g; Sugar 0.7 g; Protein 42.3 g; Cholesterol 141 mg

Dijon Chicken

Preparation Time: 10 minutes; Cooking Time: 50 minutes; Serve: 4
Ingredients:

- 1 1/2 lbs chicken thighs, skinless and boneless
- 2 tbsp Dijon mustard
- 1/4 cup French mustard
- 4 tbsp maple syrup
- 2 tsp olive oil

Directions:
1. In a large bowl, mix together maple syrup, olive oil, Dijon mustard, and French mustard.
2. Add chicken to the bowl and mix until chicken is well coated.
3. Transfer chicken into the instant pot air fryer basket and place basket in the pot.
4. Seal the pot with air fryer lid and select bake mode and cook at 375 F for 45-50 minutes.
5. Serve and enjoy.

Nutritional Value (Amount per Serving):
Calories 401; Fat 15.3 g; Carbohydrates 13.8 g; Sugar 12 g; Protein 49.6 g; Cholesterol 151 mg

Mango Chicken

Preparation Time: 10 minutes; Cooking Time: 15 minutes; Serve: 2
Ingredients:

- 2 chicken breasts, skinless and boneless
- 1 ripe mango, peeled and diced
- 1/2 tbsp turmeric
- 1/2 cup chicken broth
- 2 garlic cloves, minced
- 1/2 tsp ginger, grated
- 1 fresh lime juice
- 1/2 tsp pepper
- 1/2 tsp salt

Directions:
1. Add chicken into the inner pot of instant pot duo crisp and top with mango.
2. Add lime juice, broth, turmeric, pepper, and salt.
3. Seal the pot with pressure cooking lid and cook on high for 15 minutes.
4. Once done, allow to release pressure naturally. Remove lid.
5. Shred chicken using a fork and stir well.
6. Serve and enjoy.

Nutritional Value (Amount per Serving):
Calories 407; Fat 12.1 g; Carbohydrates 30 g; Sugar 23.6 g; Protein 45.3 g; Cholesterol 130 mg

Honey Cashew Butter Chicken

Preparation Time: 10 minutes; Cooking Time: 7 minutes; Serve: 3
Ingredients:
- 1 lb chicken breast, cut into chunks
- 2 tbsp rice vinegar
- 2 tbsp honey
- 2 tbsp coconut aminos
- 1/4 cup cashew butter
- 2 garlic cloves, minced
- 1/4 cup chicken broth
- 1/2 tbsp sriracha

Directions:
1. Add chicken into the inner pot of instant pot duo crisp.
2. In a small bowl, mix together cashew butter, garlic, broth, sriracha, vinegar, honey, and coconut aminos and pour over chicken.
3. Seal the pot with pressure cooking lid and cook on high for 7 minutes.
4. Once done, release pressure using a quick release. Remove lid.
5. Stir well and serve.

Nutritional Value (Amount per Serving):
Calories 366; Fat 2.1 g; Carbohydrates 20.7 g; Sugar 11.6 g; Protein 36.4 g; Cholesterol 97 mg

Sweet & Tangy Tamarind Chicken

Preparation Time: 10 minutes; Cooking Time: 15 minutes; Serve: 4
Ingredients:
- 2 lbs chicken breasts, skinless, boneless, and cut into pieces
- 1 tbsp ketchup
- 1 tbsp vinegar
- 2 tbsp ginger, grated
- 1 garlic clove, minced
- 3 tbsp olive oil
- 1 tbsp arrowroot powder
- 1/2 cup tamarind paste
- 2 tbsp brown sugar
- 1 tsp salt

Directions:
1. Add oil into the inner pot of instant pot duo crisp and set the pot on sauté mode.
2. Add ginger and garlic and sauté for 30 seconds.
3. Add chicken and sauté for 3-4 minutes.
4. In a small bowl, mix together the tamarind paste, brown sugar, ketchup, vinegar, and salt and pour over chicken and stir well.
5. Seal the pot with pressure cooking lid and cook on high for 8 minutes.
6. Once done, release pressure using a quick release. Remove lid.
7. In a small bowl, whisk arrowroot powder with 2 tbsp water and pour it into the pot.
8. Set pot on sauté mode and cook chicken for 1-2 minutes.
9. Serve and enjoy.

Nutritional Value (Amount per Serving):
Calories 598; Fat 27.6 g; Carbohydrates 18.9 g; Sugar 14 g; Protein 66.4 g; Cholesterol 202 mg

Chapter 6: Fish & Seafood

Salmon with Carrots

Preparation Time: 10 minutes; Cooking Time: 20 minutes; Serve: 4

Ingredients:
- 1 lb salmon, cut into four pieces
- 2 tbsp olive oil
- 2 cups baby carrots
- Pepper
- Salt

Directions:
1. Spray instant pot air fryer basket with cooking spray.
2. Place salmon pieces into the air fryer basket.
3. In a bowl, toss baby carrots with oil, pepper, and salt. Arrange carrot around the salmon.
4. Place air fryer basket in the pot.
5. Seal the pot with air fryer lid and select bake mode and cook at 400 F for 20 minutes.
6. Serve and enjoy.

Nutritional Value (Amount per Serving):
Calories 225; Fat 14.1 g; Carbohydrates 3.5 g; Sugar 2 g; Protein 22.3 g; Cholesterol 50 mg

Rosemary Salmon

Preparation Time: 10 minutes; Cooking Time: 15 minutes; Serve: 4

Ingredients:
- 1 lbs salmon, cut into 4 pieces
- 1/2 tbsp dried rosemary
- 1 tbsp dried chives
- 1 tbsp olive oil
- Pepper
- Salt

Directions:
1. Line instant pot air fryer basket with parchment paper.
2. Place salmon pieces skin side down on parchment paper into the air fryer basket.
3. Mix together olive oil, chives, and rosemary. Brush salmon with oil mixture.
4. Place air fryer basket in the pot.
5. Seal the pot with air fryer lid and select bake mode and cook at 400 F for 15 minutes.
6. Serve and enjoy.

Nutritional Value (Amount per Serving):
Calories 182; Fat 10.6 g; Carbohydrates 0.3 g; Sugar 0 g; Protein 22 g; Cholesterol 50 mg

Broiled Tilapia

Preparation Time: 10 minutes; Cooking Time: 5 minutes; Serve: 4

Ingredients:
- 24 oz tilapia fish fillets
- 1/8 tsp cayenne pepper
- 1/4 tsp cinnamon
- 1/4 tsp paprika
- 1 tbsp olive oil
- 2 lemons, sliced
- 1 tsp dry mustard powder
- 1/2 tsp basil
- 1/2 tsp salt

Directions:
1. Line instant pot air fryer basket with parchment paper.
2. In a small bowl, mix together all dry spices.
3. Place fish fillets on parchment paper in air fryer basket and brush with oil.
4. Sprinkle spice mixture on fish fillets.
5. Arrange lemon slices on top of fish fillets.
6. Place air fryer basket in the pot.
7. Seal the pot with air fryer lid and select broil mode and cook for 5 minutes.

8. Serve and enjoy.

Nutritional Value (Amount per Serving):

Calories 412; Fat 21.8 g; Carbohydrates 35.5 g; Sugar 1.7 g; Protein 18.4 g; Cholesterol 38 mg

Salmon Patties

Preparation Time: 10 minutes; Cooking Time: 50 minutes; Serve: 5

Ingredients:

- 12 oz salmon
- 1 egg, lightly beaten
- 2 tbsp dill, chopped
- 1/2 cup potato, boiled and mashed
- 2 tbsp capers, drained
- 1 tbsp fresh lemon juice
- 1/4 tsp salt

Directions:

1. Place salmon on center of foil piece and season with salt. Wrap foil around the salmon.
2. Place salmon packet into the instant pot air fryer basket and place basket in the pot.
3. Seal the pot with air fryer lid and select bake mode and cook at 350 F for 15 minutes.
4. Remove salmon from the pot and transfer to a bowl.
5. Shred cooked salmon. Add remaining ingredients and mix until well combined.
6. Make small patties from the salmon mixture.
7. Line instant pot air fryer basket with parchment paper.
8. Place salmon patties on parchment paper in the air fryer basket. Place basket in the pot.
9. Seal the pot with air fryer lid and select bake mode and cook at 350 F for 25 minutes. Turn halfway through.
10. Serve and enjoy.

Nutritional Value (Amount per Serving):

Calories 113; Fat 5.2 g; Carbohydrates 2.3 g; Sugar 0.2 g; Protein 14.8 g; Cholesterol 63 mg

Tuna Patties

Preparation Time: 10 minutes; Cooking Time: 35 minutes; Serve: 4

Ingredients:

- 28 oz can tuna
- 1 egg, lightly beaten
- 14 oz can pineapple, crushed and drained
- 1/4 tsp red chili flakes
- 1/4 tsp ground ginger
- 1 tsp garlic cloves, minced
- 1 tbsp soy sauce
- 4 tbsp almond flour
- 1/2 cup cilantro, chopped
- 1/2 tbsp fresh lime juice
- Pepper
- Salt

Directions:

1. In a bowl, add all ingredients and mix well until well combined.
2. Make small patties from mixture.
3. Line instant pot air fryer basket with parchment paper.
4. Place patties on parchment paper in the air fryer basket. Place basket in the pot.
5. Seal the pot with air fryer lid and select bake mode and cook at 400 F for 35 minutes. Turn patties after 25 minutes.
6. Serve and enjoy.

Nutritional Value (Amount per Serving):

Calories 353; Fat 6.2 g; Carbohydrates 18.3 g; Sugar 14.6 g; Protein 54.3 g; Cholesterol 100 mg

Creamy Indian Shrimp

Preparation Time: 10 minutes; Cooking Time: 4 minutes; Serve: 4

Ingredients:

- 1 lb shrimp, shelled and deveined
- 7.5 oz can coconut milk
- 1 tsp garam masala
- 1/2 tsp chili powder
- 1/2 tsp turmeric
- 1/2 tbsp garlic, minced
- 1/2 tbsp ginger, minced
- 1 tsp salt

Directions:
1. Spray baking dish with cooking spray.
2. Add all ingredients into the baking dish and stir everything well. Cover dish with foil.
3. Pour 2 cup water into the inner pot of instant pot duo crisp then place steamer rack in the pot.
4. Place baking dish on top of the steamer rack.
5. Seal the pot with pressure cooking lid and cook on low for 4 minutes.
6. Once done, release pressure using a quick release. Remove lid.
7. Serve and enjoy.

Nutritional Value (Amount per Serving):
Calories 245; Fat 13.4 g; Carbohydrates 4.4 g; Sugar 0.1 g; Protein 27.1 g; Cholesterol 239 mg

Lemon Salmon

Preparation Time: 10 minutes; Cooking Time: 20 minutes; Serve: 4
Ingredients:
- 1 lb wild salmon
- 2 tbsp fresh lemon juice
- 1/2 tsp dill weeds
- 1 tsp garlic, minced
- 1 tbsp olive oil
- 1/2 tsp parsley
- 1/2 tsp tarragon

Directions:
1. Add olive oil, garlic, lemon juice and herbs in a bowl and mix well.
2. Line instant pot air fryer basket with parchment paper.
3. Place salmon on parchment paper in the air fryer basket. Brush salmon with herb mixture.
4. Place basket in the pot.
5. Seal the pot with air fryer lid and select bake mode and cook at 300 F for 20 minutes.
6. Serve and enjoy.

Nutritional Value (Amount per Serving):
Calories 184; Fat 10.6 g; Carbohydrates 0.5 g; Sugar 0.2 g; Protein 22.2 g; Cholesterol 50 mg

Crispy Fish Fillet

Preparation Time: 10 minutes; Cooking Time: 15 minutes; Serve: 4
Ingredients:
- 15 oz sole fillet
- 3 tsp lemon juice
- 2 tbsp Dijon mustard
- 1/4 cup breadcrumbs
- 2 tsp Worcestershire sauce

Directions:
1. Line instant pot air fryer basket with parchment paper.
2. Place a fish fillet on parchment paper in the air fryer basket. Spray fish fillets with cooking spray.
3. In a small bowl, mix together lemon juice, Worcestershire sauce and mustard. Brush fish fillet with lemon mixture.
4. Sprinkle breadcrumbs on top of fish fillets.
5. Place basket in the pot.
6. Seal the pot with air fryer lid and select bake mode and cook at 400 F for 12-15 minutes.
7. Serve and enjoy.

Nutritional Value (Amount per Serving):

Calories 160; Fat 2.3 g; Carbohydrates 5.9 g; Sugar 1.1 g; Protein 27 g; Cholesterol 72 mg

Baked Shrimp

Preparation Time: 10 minutes; Cooking Time: 8 minutes; Serve: 4

Ingredients:

- 1 lb shrimp, peeled and deveined
- 2 tsp Italian seasoning
- 2 tsp parsley, dried
- 1 tbsp honey
- 2 tbsp lemon juice
- 2 tsp soy sauce
- 1 tsp olive oil

Directions:

1. Spray instant pot air fryer basket with cooking spray.
2. In a large bowl, mix together soy sauce, olive oil, Italian seasoning, parsley, honey and lemon juice.
3. Add shrimp and toss well.
4. Add shrimp in instant pot air fryer basket and place basket in the pot.
5. Seal the pot with air fryer lid and select bake mode and cook at 400 F for 8 minutes.
6. Serve and enjoy.

Nutritional Value (Amount per Serving):

Calories 171; Fat 3.9 g; Carbohydrates 6.7 g; Sugar 4.7 g; Protein 26.1 g; Cholesterol 240 mg

Crispy Crust Fish Fillets

Preparation Time: 10 minutes; Cooking Time: 12 minutes; Serve: 4

Ingredients:

- 1 egg, beaten
- 1 cup breadcrumbs
- 4 fish fillets
- 4 tbsp olive oil
- Pepper
- Salt

Directions:

1. In a shallow dish, mix together breadcrumbs, oil, pepper, and salt.
2. In another dish add beaten egg.
3. Line instant pot air fryer basket with parchment paper.
4. Dip fish fillet in egg then coat with breadcrumbs and place on parchment paper in the air fryer basket.
5. Place basket in the pot.
6. Seal the pot with air fryer lid and select air fry mode and cook at 350 F for 12 minutes.
7. Serve and enjoy.

Nutritional Value (Amount per Serving):

Calories 454; Fat 27.7 g; Carbohydrates 35 g; Sugar 1.8 g; Protein 18.3 g; Cholesterol 72 mg

Crispy Fish Strips

Preparation Time: 10 minutes; Cooking Time: 12 minutes; Serve: 4

Ingredients:

- 1 lb catfish fillets, cut into strips
- 1 egg white, lightly beaten
- 1/2 cup almond meal
- 1 tsp lemon pepper

Directions:

1. In a shallow dish, mix together almond meal and lemon pepper.
2. In another dish add beaten egg white.
3. Line instant pot air fryer basket with parchment paper.
4. Dip fish strips in egg white then coat with almond meal and place on parchment paper in the air fryer basket.
5. Place basket in the pot.

6. Seal the pot with air fryer lid and select air fry mode and cook at 400 F for 12 minutes.
7. Serve and enjoy.

Nutritional Value (Amount per Serving):

Calories 227; Fat 14.6 g; Carbohydrates 3 g; Sugar 0.6 g; Protein 21.1 g; Cholesterol 53 mg

Fish Sticks

Preparation Time: 10 minutes; Cooking Time: 10 minutes; Serve: 4

Ingredients:

- 1 large egg, beaten
- 1 lb tilapia fillets, cut into strips
- 1 cup breadcrumbs
- 2 tsp Old Bay Seasoning
- 1 tbsp olive oil

Directions:

1. In a shallow dish, mix together breadcrumbs, old bay seasoning, and oil.
2. In another dish add beaten egg.
3. Line instant pot air fryer basket with parchment paper.
4. Dip fish sticks in egg then coat with breadcrumbs and place on parchment paper in the air fryer basket.
5. Place basket in the pot.
6. Seal the pot with air fryer lid and select air fry mode and cook at 400 F for 10 minutes.
7. Serve and enjoy.

Nutritional Value (Amount per Serving):

Calories 248; Fat 7.2 g; Carbohydrates 19.5 g; Sugar 1.8 g; Protein 26.3 g; Cholesterol 102 mg

Fish Cakes

Preparation Time: 10 minutes; Cooking Time: 15 minutes; Serve: 4

Ingredients:

- 2 cups white fish
- 1 tsp Worcestershire sauce
- 1 1/2 tsp chili powder
- 1 tsp milk
- 1 tsp butter
- 1 small onion, diced
- 1/4 cup breadcrumbs
- 1 cup potatoes, mashed
- 1 tsp mix herbs
- 1 tsp allspice
- 1 tsp coriander
- Pepper
- Salt

Directions:

1. Add all ingredients into the mixing bowl and mix until combined.
2. Make small patties from mixture and place in the refrigerator for 2 hours.
3. Line instant pot air fryer basket with parchment paper.
4. Place patties on parchment paper in air fryer basket.
5. Place basket in the pot.
6. Seal the pot with air fryer lid and select air fry mode and cook at 400 F for 15 minutes.
7. Serve and enjoy.

Nutritional Value (Amount per Serving):

Calories 145; Fat 8.1 g; Carbohydrates 13.4 g; Sugar 2.1 g; Protein 5.2 g; Cholesterol 3 mg

Lemon Pepper Tilapia

Preparation Time: 10 minutes; Cooking Time: 7 minutes; Serve: 4

Ingredients:

- 1 lb tilapia fillets
- 1/2 tsp lemon pepper
- Salt

Directions:

1. Line instant pot air fryer basket with parchment paper.
2. Place tilapia fillets on parchment paper in air fryer basket.
3. Place basket in the pot.
4. Seal the pot with air fryer lid and select broil mode and cook for 7 minutes.
5. Serve and enjoy.

Nutritional Value (Amount per Serving):
Calories 94; Fat 1 g; Carbohydrates 0.2 g; Sugar 0 g; Protein 21.1 g; Cholesterol 55 mg

Cajun Salmon

Preparation Time: 10 minutes; Cooking Time: 8 minutes; Serve: 2
Ingredients:
- 1/2 lb salmon fillet
- 1/2 tsp paprika
- 1/4 tsp sage
- 1/4 tsp oregano
- 1/4 tsp thyme
- 1/2 tsp cayenne pepper
- 1 tsp garlic powder
- Pepper
- Salt

Directions:
1. Rub seasoning all over the salmon.
2. Line instant pot air fryer basket with parchment paper.
3. Place seasoned salmon fillet on parchment paper in air fryer basket.
4. Place basket in the pot.
5. Seal the pot with air fryer lid and select air fry mode and cook 350 F for 8 minutes.
6. Serve and enjoy.

Nutritional Value (Amount per Serving):
Calories 159; Fat 7.2 g; Carbohydrates 1.9 g; Sugar 0.5 g; Protein 22.4 g; Cholesterol 50 mg

Salmon Patties

Preparation Time: 10 minutes; Cooking Time: 15 minutes; Serve: 4
Ingredients:
- 1 egg, lightly beaten
- 14 oz can salmon, drained and shred using a fork
- 1 small onion, minced
- 1/2 tsp garlic powder
- 2 tbsp mayonnaise
- 4 tbsp flour
- 4 tbsp cup cornmeal
- Pepper
- Salt

Directions:
1. Line instant pot air fryer basket with parchment paper.
2. In a bowl, mix together salmon, garlic powder, mayonnaise, flour, cornmeal, egg, onion, pepper, and salt until well combined.
3. Make small patties from mixture and place on parchment paper in the air fryer basket.
4. Place basket in the pot.
5. Seal the pot with air fryer lid and select air fry mode and cook at 350 F for 15 minutes.
6. Serve and enjoy.

Nutritional Value (Amount per Serving):
Calories 247; Fat 9.9 g; Carbohydrates 15.6 g; Sugar 1.5 g; Protein 22.8 g; Cholesterol 97 mg

Spicy Tilapia

Preparation Time: 10 minutes; Cooking Time: 10 minutes; Serve: 4
Ingredients:
- 1 lb tilapia fillets
- 2 tsp paprika
- 1 tbsp olive oil
- 1/2 cup parmesan cheese, grated

- 1 tbsp parsley, chopped
- Pepper
- Salt

Directions:
1. Line instant pot air fryer basket with parchment paper.
2. In a shallow dish, mix together paprika, grated cheese, pepper, salt, and parsley.
3. Drizzle tilapia fillets with olive oil and coat with paprika and cheese mixture.
4. Place coated tilapia fillet on parchment paper in the air fryer basket.
5. Place basket in the pot.
6. Seal the pot with air fryer lid and select air fry mode and cook at 400 F for 10 minutes.
7. Serve and enjoy.

Nutritional Value (Amount per Serving):
   Calories 138; Fat 5.4 g; Carbohydrates 0.8 g; Sugar 0.1 g; Protein 22.4 g; Cholesterol 58 mg

Air Fried Shrimp

Preparation Time: 10 minutes; Cooking Time: 5 minutes; Serve: 4
Ingredients:
- 1 1/4 lbs shrimp, peeled and deveined
- 1 tbsp olive oil
- 1/2 tsp paprika
- 1/2 tsp old bay seasoning
- 1/4 tsp cayenne pepper
- 1/4 tsp salt

Directions:
1. Add all ingredients into the mixing bowl and toss well.
2. Place seasoned shrimp in instant pot air fryer basket and place basket in the pot.
3. Seal the pot with air fryer lid and select air fry mode and cook at 400 F for 5 minutes.
4. Serve and enjoy.

Nutritional Value (Amount per Serving):
   Calories 200; Fat 6 g; Carbohydrates 2.4 g; Sugar 0 g; Protein 32.3 g; Cholesterol 299 mg

Parmesan Salmon

Preparation Time: 10 minutes; Cooking Time: 15 minutes; Serve: 4
Ingredients:
- 4 salmon fillets
- 1/4 cup parmesan cheese, grated
- 1/2 cup walnuts
- 1 tsp olive oil
- 1 tbsp lemon rind

Directions:
1. Line instant pot air fryer basket with parchment paper.
2. Place salmon fillets on parchment paper in air fryer basket.
3. Add walnuts into the food processor and process until finely ground.
4. Mix together ground walnuts, cheese, oil, and lemon rind.
5. Spoon walnut mixture over the salmon fillets and press gently.
6. Place air fryer basket in the pot.
7. Seal the pot with air fryer lid and select bake mode and cook at 400 F for 15 minutes.
8. Serve and enjoy.

Nutritional Value (Amount per Serving):
   Calories 349; Fat 21.8 g; Carbohydrates 1.9 g; Sugar 0.3 g; Protein 38.9 g; Cholesterol 80 mg

Delicious Pesto Salmon

Preparation Time: 10 minutes; Cooking Time: 20 minutes; Serve: 2
Ingredients:
- 2 salmon fillets
- 1/4 cup parmesan cheese, grated
- For pesto:
- 1/4 cup olive oil

- 1 1/2 cups fresh basil leaves
- 3 garlic cloves, peeled and chopped
- 1/4 cup parmesan cheese, grated
- 1/4 cup pine nuts
- 1/4 tsp black pepper
- 1/2 tsp salt

Directions:
1. Add all pesto ingredients into the blender and blend until smooth.
2. Line instant pot air fryer basket with parchment paper.
3. Place salmon fillet on parchment paper in the air fryer basket. Spread 2 tablespoons of the pesto on each salmon fillet.
4. Sprinkle cheese on top of the pesto.
5. Place basket in the pot.
6. Seal the pot with air fryer lid and select bake mode and cook at 400 F for 20 minutes.
7. Serve and enjoy.

Nutritional Value (Amount per Serving):
Calories 589; Fat 48.7 g; Carbohydrates 4.5 g; Sugar 0.7 g; Protein 38.9 g; Cholesterol 81 mg

Crisp & Delicious Catfish

Preparation Time: 10 minutes; Cooking Time: 20 minutes; Serve: 2
Ingredients:
- 2 catfish fillets
- 1/4 cup cornmeal
- 1/2 tsp garlic powder
- 1/2 tsp onion powder
- 1/2 tsp salt

Directions:
1. Add cornmeal, garlic powder, onion powder, and salt into a zip-lock bag.
2. Add fish fillets to the zip-lock bag. Seal bag and shake gently to coat fish fillet.
3. Line instant pot air fryer basket with parchment paper.
4. Place coated fish fillets on parchment paper in the air fryer basket. Place basket in the pot.
5. Seal the pot with air fryer lid and select air fry mode and cook at 400 F for 20 minutes. Turn fish fillets halfway through.
6. Serve and enjoy.

Nutritional Value (Amount per Serving):
Calories 276; Fat 12.7 g; Carbohydrates 12.7 g; Sugar 0.5 g; Protein 26.3 g; Cholesterol 75 mg

Easy Paprika Salmon

Preparation Time: 10 minutes; Cooking Time: 7 minutes; Serve: 2
Ingredients:
- 2 salmon fillets, remove any bones
- 2 tsp paprika
- 2 tsp olive oil
- Pepper
- Salt

Directions:
1. Brush each salmon fillet with oil, paprika, pepper, and salt.
2. Line instant pot air fryer basket with parchment paper.
3. Place salmon fillets on parchment paper in the air fryer basket. Place basket in the pot.
4. Seal the pot with air fryer lid and select air fry mode and cook at 390 F for 7 minutes.
5. Serve and enjoy.

Nutritional Value (Amount per Serving):
Calories 282; Fat 15.9 g; Carbohydrates 1.2 g; Sugar 0.2 g; Protein 34.9 g; Cholesterol 78 mg

Ranch Fish Fillets

Preparation Time: 10 minutes; Cooking Time: 12 minutes; Serve: 2
Ingredients:

- 2 fish fillets
- 1 egg, lightly beaten
- 1 1/4 tbsp olive oil
- 1/4 cup breadcrumbs
- 1/2 packet ranch dressing mix

Directions:
1. In a shallow dish, mix together breadcrumbs, ranch dressing mix, and oil.
2. Dip fish fillet in egg then coats with breadcrumb mixture and place on parchment paper in the air fryer basket. Place basket in the pot.
3. Seal the pot with air fryer lid and select air fry mode and cook at 400 F for 12 minutes.
4. Serve and enjoy.

Nutritional Value (Amount per Serving):
Calories 373; Fat 22.9 g; Carbohydrates 25.7 g; Sugar 1.2 g; Protein 18 g; Cholesterol 113 mg

Crispy Coconut Shrimp

Preparation Time: 10 minutes; Cooking Time: 10 minutes; Serve: 2
Ingredients:
- 1 cup egg white, lightly beaten
- 12 large shrimp
- 1 tbsp cornstarch
- 1 cup shredded coconut
- 1 cup flour
- 1 cup breadcrumbs

Directions:
1. Line instant pot air fryer basket with parchment paper.
2. In a shallow dish, mix together coconut and breadcrumbs.
3. In another dish, mix together flour and cornstarch.
4. Add egg white in a small bowl.
5. Dip shrimp in egg white then roll in flour mixture and coat with breadcrumb mixture.
6. Place coated shrimp in instant pot air fryer basket. Place basket in the pot.
7. Seal the pot with air fryer lid and select air fry mode and cook at 350 F for 10 minutes.
8. Serve and enjoy.

Nutritional Value (Amount per Serving):
Calories 700; Fat 17.6 g; Carbohydrates 97.7 g; Sugar 6.9 g; Protein 35.8 g; Cholesterol 69 mg

Healthy Shrimp Pasta

Preparation Time: 10 minutes; Cooking Time: 4 minutes; Serve: 6
Ingredients:
- 1 lb jumbo shrimp, peeled and deveined
- 1/2 cup green onion, chopped
- 1 tbsp sriracha sauce
- 1 1/2 cups yogurt
- 1 tbsp vinegar
- 1 lime juice
- 1/4 cup Fresno pepper, diced
- 1/4 cup honey
- 1 tsp coconut oil
- 1 tsp garlic, minced
- 4 cups of water
- 13 oz spaghetti noodles, break in half
- 1/4 tsp pepper

Directions:
1. Add oil into the inner pot of instant pot duo crisp and set pot on sauté mode.
2. Add Fresno peppers and garlic and sauté for 30 seconds.
3. Add noodles then pour water over noodles.
4. Add shrimp, lime juice, honey, vinegar, and pepper on top of noodles.
5. Seal the pot with pressure cooking lid and cook on high for 3 minutes.
6. Once done, release pressure using a quick release. Remove lid.
7. Add sriracha, yogurt, and green onions and stir well.
8. Serve and enjoy.

Nutritional Value (Amount per Serving):

Calories 348; Fat 4.6 g; Carbohydrates 51.5 g; Sugar 17.9 g; Protein 24.2 g; Cholesterol 205 mg

Delicious Cod Nuggets

Preparation Time: 10 minutes; Cooking Time: 15 minutes; Serve: 4

Ingredients:

- 1 lb cod fillet, cut into chunks
- 1/2 cup all-purpose flour
- 1 tbsp olive oil
- 1 cup cracker crumbs
- 1 egg, lightly beaten
- Pepper
- Salt

Directions:

1. Line instant pot air fryer basket with parchment paper.
2. Add crackers crumb and oil in food processor and process until it forms crumbly.
3. Season fish chunks with pepper and salt.
4. Coat fish chunks with flour then dip in egg and coat with cracker crumbs.
5. Place coated fish chunks on parchment paper in the air fryer basket. Place basket in the pot.
6. Seal the pot with air fryer lid and select air fry mode and cook at 350 F for 15 minutes.
7. Serve and enjoy.

Nutritional Value (Amount per Serving):

Calories 272; Fat 9.7 g; Carbohydrates 21.5 g; Sugar 0.4 g; Protein 24.4 g; Cholesterol 97 mg

Balsamic Salmon

Preparation Time: 10 minutes; Cooking Time: 8 minutes; Serve: 2

Ingredients:

- 2 salmon fillets
- 2 tbsp balsamic vinegar
- 2 tbsp honey
- 1 cup of water
- Pepper
- Salt

Directions:

1. Season salmon with pepper and salt.
2. In a small bowl, mix together vinegar and honey.
3. Brush salmon with vinegar and honey mixture.
4. Pour water into the inner pot of instant pot duo crisp then place steamer rack into the pot.
5. Place salmon skin-side down on the steamer rack.
6. Seal the pot with pressure cooking lid and cook on high for 3 minutes.
7. Once done, release pressure using a quick release. Remove lid.
8. Seal the pot with air fryer lid and select air fry mode and cook at 400 F for 5 minutes.
9. Serve and enjoy.

Nutritional Value (Amount per Serving):

Calories 303; Fat 11 g; Carbohydrates 17.5 g; Sugar 17.3 g; Protein 34.6 g; Cholesterol 78 mg

Garlic Shrimp

Preparation Time: 10 minutes; Cooking Time: 8 minutes; Serve: 4

Ingredients:

- 1 lb shrimp, peeled and deveined
- 2 tsp olive oil
- For sauce:
- 1/4 cup honey
- 1/4 cup soy sauce
- 1 tbsp ginger, minced
- 1 tbsp garlic, minced

Directions:

1. In a mixing bowl, mix together all sauce ingredients. Add shrimp into the bowl and toss well.

2. Add oil, shrimp with sauce mixture into the inner pot of instant pot duo crisp and cook on sauté mode for 3 minutes.
3. Seal the pot with pressure cooking lid and cook on high for 5 minutes.
4. Once done, release pressure using a quick release. Remove lid.
5. Stir well and serve.

Nutritional Value (Amount per Serving):
Calories 235; Fat 4.4 g; Carbohydrates 22 g; Sugar 17.7 g; Protein 27.1 g; Cholesterol 239 mg

Tuna Noodles

Preparation Time: 10 minutes; Cooking Time: 4 minutes; Serve: 4
Ingredients:

- 1 can tuna, drained
- 15 oz egg noodles
- 3 cups of water
- 3/4 cup frozen peas
- 4 oz cheddar cheese, shredded
- 28 oz can cream of mushroom soup

Directions:
1. Add noodles and water into the inner pot of instant pot duo crisp and stir well.
2. Add cream of mushroom soup, peas, and tuna on top of noodles.
3. Seal the pot with pressure cooking lid and cook on high for 4 minutes.
4. Once done, release pressure using a quick release. Remove lid.
5. Add cheese and stir well and serve.

Nutritional Value (Amount per Serving):
Calories 470; Fat 18.6 g; Carbohydrates 47.5 g; Sugar 6.2 g; Protein 27.7 g; Cholesterol 80 mg

Shrimp Scampi

Preparation Time: 10 minutes; Cooking Time: 4 minutes; Serve: 6
Ingredients:

- 1 lb frozen shrimp
- 2 cups pasta, uncooked
- 1/2 tsp paprika
- 1/2 tsp red pepper flakes
- 1 tbsp garlic, minced
- 1/2 cup parmesan cheese
- 1/2 cup half and half
- 1 cup chicken broth
- 2 tbsp butter, melted
- Pepper
- Salt

Directions:
1. Add butter into the inner pot of instant pot duo crisp and set pot on sauté mode.
2. Add garlic, and red pepper flakes and cook for 2 minutes.
3. Add shrimp, pepper, noodles, paprika, broth, and salt. Stir well.
4. Seal the pot with pressure cooking lid and cook on high for 2 minutes.
5. Once done, release pressure using a quick release. Remove lid.
6. Add cheese and half and half and stir until cheese is melted.
7. Serve and enjoy.

Nutritional Value (Amount per Serving):
Calories 280; Fat 9.3 g; Carbohydrates 25.8 g; Sugar 0.2 g; Protein 22.6 g; Cholesterol 164 mg

Steam Shrimp

Preparation Time: 10 minutes; Cooking Time: 6 minutes; Serve: 4
Ingredients:

- 2 lbs shrimp, cleaned
- 1 1/2 tsp old bay seasoning
- 1 tsp Cajun seasoning
- Pepper
- Salt

Directions:

1. Add all ingredients into the inner pot of instant pot duo crisp and stir well.
2. Seal the pot with pressure cooking lid and select steam mode and cook for 6 minutes.
3. Once done, release pressure using a quick release. Remove lid.
4. Stir well and serve.

Nutritional Value (Amount per Serving):
Calories 270; Fat 3.8 g; Carbohydrates 3.5 g; Sugar 0 g; Protein 51.7 g; Cholesterol 478 mg

Lemon Garlic Shrimp

Preparation Time: 10 minutes; Cooking Time: 5 minutes; Serve: 4
Ingredients:
- 20 jumbo shrimp
- 1 fresh lemon juice
- 1/4 tsp red pepper flakes
- 1/4 cup fresh parsley, chopped
- 1/4 cup butter
- 1 tbsp garlic, minced
- 1 1/2 cups fish broth
- 1 cup white rice
- Pepper
- Salt

Directions:
1. Add all ingredients into the inner pot of instant pot duo crisp and stir well.
2. Seal the pot with pressure cooking lid and cook on high for 5 minutes.
3. Once done, release pressure using a quick release. Remove lid.
4. Stir and serve.

Nutritional Value (Amount per Serving):
Calories 505; Fat 13.1 g; Carbohydrates 39.4 g; Sugar 5.8 g; Protein 56.4 g; Cholesterol 611 mg

Delicious Shrimp Paella

Preparation Time: 10 minutes; Cooking Time: 5 minutes; Serve: 4
Ingredients:
- 1 lb jumbo shrimp, frozen
- 1/2 cup white wine
- 1 cup fish broth
- 1 red pepper, chopped
- 4 garlic cloves, chopped
- 1 onion, chopped
- 1/4 butter
- 1 cup of rice
- 1/4 cup cilantro, chopped
- 1/4 tsp red pepper flakes
- 1 tsp turmeric
- 1 tsp paprika
- 1/4 tsp pepper
- 1/2 tsp salt

Directions:
1. Add butter into the inner pot of instant pot duo crisp and set pot on sauté mode.
2. Add garlic and onion and cook for a minute.
3. Add remaining ingredients and stir well.
4. Seal the pot with pressure cooking lid and cook on high for 5 minutes.
5. Once done, release pressure using a quick release. Remove lid.
6. Serve and enjoy.

Nutritional Value (Amount per Serving):
Calories 310; Fat 1.3 g; Carbohydrates 44.4 g; Sugar 5.1 g; Protein 24.6 g; Cholesterol 235 mg

Parmesan Shrimp Risotto

Preparation Time: 10 minutes; Cooking Time: 6 minutes; Serve: 6
Ingredients:
- 1 lb jumbo shrimp, deveined and uncooked
- 1 lb Arborio rice
- 1 tbsp butter
- 1 tbsp olive oil
- 1/2 onion, diced
- 1 tbsp garlic, minced
- 1/2 cup peas

- 1 3/4 cups parmesan cheese, grated
- 8 cups chicken broth

Directions:
1. Add butter and oil into the inner pot of instant pot duo crisp and set pot on sauté mode.
2. Add onion and garlic and cook for 2-3 minutes.
3. Add shrimp and cook until just opaque. Remove shrimp from pot and set aside.
4. Add broth and rice. Stir well.
5. Seal the pot with pressure cooking lid and cook on high for 6 minutes.
6. Once done, allow to release pressure naturally. Remove lid.
7. Stir in parmesan cheese, peas, and shrimp.
8. Serve and enjoy.

Nutritional Value (Amount per Serving):
Calories 464; Fat 8.3 g; Carbohydrates 66.3 g; Sugar 3.4 g; Protein 28.6 g; Cholesterol 166 mg

Asian Pineapple Shrimp

Preparation Time: 10 minutes; Cooking Time: 2 minutes; Serve: 4
Ingredients:
- 1 1/2 cups pineapple chunks
- 2 tbsp soy sauce
- 1/4 cup dry white wine
- 1/2 cup pineapple juice
- 12 oz quinoa, rinsed and drained
- 1 bell pepper, sliced
- 2 scallions, chopped
- 1 lb shrimp, frozen
- 3/4 tbsp chili paste
- 2 tbsp Thai sweet chili paste

Directions:
1. Add all ingredients except scallion and pineapple chunks into the inner pot of instant pot duo crisp and stir well.
2. Seal the pot with pressure cooking lid and cook on high for 2 minutes.
3. Once done, allow to release pressure naturally. Remove lid.
4. Add pineapple chunks and scallion and stir well.
5. Serve and enjoy.

Nutritional Value (Amount per Serving):
Calories 548; Fat 7.7 g; Carbohydrates 76.9 g; Sugar 14.9 g; Protein 39.4 g; Cholesterol 240 mg

Shrimp Macaroni

Preparation Time: 10 minutes; Cooking Time: 8 minutes; Serve: 6
Ingredients:
- 1 lb frozen shrimp, cooked
- 1 cup shredded gouda cheese
- 2 cups cheddar cheese, shredded
- 1 1/2 cups elbow macaroni, uncooked
- 1/4 tsp ground nutmeg
- 1/4 tsp white pepper
- 2 tbsp parsley, chopped
- 2 tbsp chives, minced
- 1 1/2 tbsp hot sauce
- 1 cup blue cheese, crumbled
- 1/2 tsp onion powder
- 1 tsp ground mustard
- 1 tbsp butter
- 1 cup half and half
- 2 cups of milk

Directions:
1. Add milk, butter, mustard, onion powder, white pepper, half and half, and ground nutmeg into the inner pot of instant pot duo crisp and stir well.
2. Seal the pot with pressure cooking lid and cook on high for 3 minutes.
3. Once done, allow to release pressure naturally. Remove lid.
4. Add remaining ingredients and stir well and cook on sauté mode for 5 minutes.
5. Serve and enjoy.

Nutritional Value (Amount per Serving):

Calories 590; Fat 38.1 g; Carbohydrates 17.7 g; Sugar 5.2 g; Protein 43.7 g; Cholesterol 234 mg

Asiago Shrimp Risotto

Preparation Time: 10 minutes; Cooking Time: 14 minutes; Serve: 4

Ingredients:

- 1 lb shrimp, thawed, peeled and deveined
- 4 1/2 cups chicken stock
- 2 tbsp dry white wine
- 1 1/2 cups arborio rice
- 1/4 cup fresh parsley, chopped
- 1 cup asiago cheese, grated
- 1 tsp garlic, minced
- 1 small onion, chopped
- 4 tbsp butter
- Pepper
- Salt

Directions:

1. Add 2 tablespoon of butter into the inner pot of instant pot duo crisp and set pot on sauté mode.
2. Add garlic and onion and cook 3-5 minutes.
3. Add rice and stir for a minute.
4. Add 3 cups chicken stock, wine, pepper, and salt. Stir well.
5. Seal the pot with pressure cooking lid and cook on high for 10 minutes.
6. Once done, release pressure using a quick release. Remove lid.
7. Add shrimp and remaining stock. Stir well.
8. Stir in remaining butter and cheese. Cook on sauté mode for 5 minutes.
9. Serve and enjoy.

Nutritional Value (Amount per Serving):

Calories 545; Fat 16.5 g; Carbohydrates 61.5 g; Sugar 1.7 g; Protein 33.5 g; Cholesterol 276 mg

Steam Clams

Preparation Time: 10 minutes; Cooking Time: 4 minutes; Serve: 4

Ingredients:

- 5 lbs clams, wash
- 10 garlic cloves, minced
- 1 stick butter
- 1 cup white wine
- 1/2 cup fresh parsley, chopped
- 1 lb baby potatoes
- 2 tsp sea salt

Directions:

1. Add butter into the inner pot of instant pot duo crisp and set pot on sauté mode.
2. Add potatoes, garlic and cook for a minute.
3. Add white wine and cook for 3 minutes. Add clams and stir well.
4. Seal the pot with pressure cooking lid and cook on high for 1 minute.
5. Transfer clams and potatoes to bowl and set aside.
6. Add parsley and remaining butter to the pot and set the pot on sauté mode and cook for 5 minutes. Stir well and pour over clams.
7. Serve and enjoy.

Nutritional Value (Amount per Serving):

Calories 603; Fat 24.3 g; Carbohydrates 80.8 g; Sugar 19.4 g; Protein 7.3 g; Cholesterol 61 mg

Shrimp Creole

Preparation Time: 10 minutes; Cooking Time: 14 minutes; Serve: 6

Ingredients:

- 2 lbs shrimp, peeled and deveined
- 14 oz can tomato, diced
- 1 tsp sweet paprika
- 1 bell pepper, stemmed, cored and chopped
- 2 celery stalks, chopped

- 1 large onion, chopped
- 2 tbsp vegetable oil
- 1/4 cup fresh parsley, chopped
- 2 cups chicken broth
- 1/2 tsp garlic powder
- 1/2 tsp onion powder
- 1 tsp dried thyme
- 4 scallions, sliced
- 1 tbsp Worcestershire sauce
- 2 tbsp can tomato paste
- 1/2 cup dry white wine
- 1/4 tsp black pepper

Directions:
1. Add oil into the inner pot of instant pot duo crisp and set pot on sauté mode.
2. Add celery, onion, and black pepper and cook for 4 minutes.
3. Add thyme, paprika, garlic powder, onion powder, pepper, and oregano. Stir well.
4. Add tomatoes, broth, tomato paste, wine, and Worcestershire sauce and stir well.
5. Seal the pot with pressure cooking lid and cook on high for 10 minutes.
6. Once done, release pressure using a quick release. Remove lid.
7. Add scallions, parsley, and shrimp. Stir well.
8. Serve and enjoy.

Nutritional Value (Amount per Serving):
Calories 294; Fat 7.8 g; Carbohydrates 13.6 g; Sugar 6.4 g; Protein 37.8 g; Cholesterol 318 mg

Honey Shrimp

Preparation Time: 10 minutes; Cooking Time: 4 minutes; Serve: 4
Ingredients:
- 1 lb shrimp, peeled and deveined
- 2 tsp olive oil
- For sauce:
- 1 tbsp garlic, minced
- 1/4 cup honey
- 1/4 cup soy sauce
- 1 tbsp ginger, minced

Directions:
1. In a bowl, whisk together soy sauce, ginger, garlic, and honey.
2. Add shrimp into the large zip-lock bag then pour soy sauce mixture over shrimp and shake well.
3. Add oil into the inner pot of instant pot duo crisp and set pot on sauté mode.
4. Add marinated shrimp into the pot and stir well.
5. Seal the pot with pressure cooking lid and cook on high for 4 minutes.
6. Once done, release pressure using a quick release. Remove lid.
7. Stir and serve.

Nutritional Value (Amount per Serving):
Calories 235; Fat 4.4 g; Carbohydrates 22 g; Sugar 17.7 g; Protein 27.1 g; Cholesterol 239 mg

Asparagus Salmon

Preparation Time: 10 minutes; Cooking Time: 3 minutes; Serve: 2
Ingredients:
- 1 lb salmon
- 8 oz asparagus spears
- 1 tbsp fresh lemon juice
- 1 tbsp olive oil
- 1/2 cup cherry tomatoes, cut in half
- 1 sprig fresh rosemary
- Pepper
- Salt

Directions:
1. Pour one cup of water into the instant pot duo crisp then place steamer rack in the pot.
2. Place salmon on top of the steamer rack then arrange rosemary and asparagus on top of salmon.
3. Seal the pot with pressure cooking lid and cook on high for 3 minutes.
4. Once done, release pressure using a quick release. Remove lid.

5. Transfer salmon and asparagus on a plate.
6. Add cherry tomatoes on top of salmon.
7. Season with pepper and salt.
8. Drizzle with oil and lemon juice.
9. Serve and enjoy.

Nutritional Value (Amount per Serving):
Calories 394; Fat 21.3 g; Carbohydrates 6.5 g; Sugar 3.5 g; Protein 47 g; Cholesterol 100 mg

Sweet & Sour Fish Chunks

Preparation Time: 10 minutes; Cooking Time: 9 minutes; Serve: 2
Ingredients:
- 1 lb fish chunks
- 1/2 tbsp sugar
- 1 tbsp olive oil
- 1 tbsp vinegar
- 1 tbsp soy sauce
- Pepper
- Salt

Directions:
1. Add oil into the inner pot of instant pot duo crisp and set the pot on sauté mode.
2. Add fish chunks and sauté for 3 minutes.
3. Add remaining ingredients and stir well.
4. Seal the pot with pressure cooking lid and cook on high for 6 minutes.
5. Once done, allow to release pressure naturally. Remove lid.
6. Stir and serve.

Nutritional Value (Amount per Serving):
Calories 259; Fat 9 g; Carbohydrates 7.8 g; Sugar 7.2 g; Protein 41 g; Cholesterol 0 mg

Salmon with Lime Jalapeno Sauce

Preparation Time: 10 minutes; Cooking Time: 5 minutes; Serve: 2
Ingredients:
- 2 salmon fillets
- 1 cup of water
- Pepper
- Sea salt

For sauce:
- 1 jalapeno pepper, seed remove and diced
- 1/2 tsp paprika
- 1 tbsp parsley, chopped
- 1 tbsp hot water
- 1/2 tsp cumin
- 1 tbsp olive oil
- 1 tbsp honey
- 1 garlic clove, minced
- 1 lime juice

Directions:
1. In a small bowl, mix together all sauce ingredients and set aside.
2. Pour water into the inner pot instant pot duo crisp then place steamer rack into the pot.
3. Season salmon with pepper and salt and place on top of the steamer rack.
4. Seal the pot with pressure cooking lid and cook on high for 5 minutes.
5. Once done, release pressure using a quick release. Remove lid.
6. Transfer salmon on plate and drizzle with chili lime sauce.
7. Serve and enjoy.

Nutritional Value (Amount per Serving):
Calories 336; Fat 18.3 g; Carbohydrates 10.2 g; Sugar 9 g; Protein 35 g; Cholesterol 78 mg

Jambalaya

Preparation Time: 10 minutes; Cooking Time: 10 minutes; Serve: 6
Ingredients:

- 12 oz shrimp, cooked
- 1 3/4 cup chicken stock
- 14.5 oz can tomato, diced
- 2 tsp Cajun seasoning
- 3 garlic cloves, minced
- 2 celery ribs, chopped
- 1 green pepper, chopped
- 1 lb chicken thighs, cut into pieces
- 12 oz sausage, sliced
- 1/2 tsp thyme
- 1 1/2 cup rice
- 1/4 cup scallions, sliced
- 2 tsp olive oil
- 1/2 tsp salt

Directions:
1. Add oil into the inner pot of instant pot duo crisp and set the pot on sauté mode.
2. Add sausage to the pot and sauté for 5 minutes.
3. Remove sausage from pot and set aside.
4. Add chicken and sauté for 3-5 minutes.
5. Add onion, rice, garlic, celery, and green pepper to the pot. Stir and cook for 2 minutes.
6. Add stock, thyme, Cajun seasoning, tomatoes, and salt. Stir well.
7. Seal the pot with pressure cooking lid and cook on high for 8 minutes.
8. Once done, allow to release pressure naturally for 5 minutes then release remaining pressure using a quick release. Remove lid.
9. Set pot on sauté mode.
10. Add sausage and cooked shrimp and sauté for 5 minutes.
11. Garnish with scallions and serve.

Nutritional Value (Amount per Serving):
Calories 613; Fat 24.8 g; Carbohydrates 43.7 g; Sugar 3.4 g; Protein 50.4 g; Cholesterol 234 mg

Shrimp & Beans

Preparation Time: 10 minutes; Cooking Time: 5 minutes; Serve: 4
Ingredients:
- 1 lb frozen shrimp
- 14 oz can black beans, rinsed and drained
- 1 cup of rice
- 1/4 cup butter
- 1 1/2 cups chicken broth
- 2 tbsp garlic, minced
- Pepper
- Salt

Directions:
1. Add butter into the inner pot of instant pot duo crisp and set pot on sauté mode.
2. Add rice and sauté until brown.
3. Add remaining ingredients and stir well.
4. Seal the pot with pressure cooking lid and cook on high for 5 minutes.
5. Once done, allow to release pressure naturally. Remove lid.
6. Stir and serve.

Nutritional Value (Amount per Serving):
Calories 503; Fat 14.8 g; Carbohydrates 57.3 g; Sugar 1.1 g; Protein 34 g; Cholesterol 201 mg

Shrimp Vegetable Risotto

Preparation Time: 10 minutes; Cooking Time: 5 minutes; Serve: 6
Ingredients:
- 1 cup of rice
- 2 tbsp butter
- 1 cup of water
- 1/4 cup frozen vegetables
- 1 tbsp lemon juice
- 1/4 cup parmesan cheese, shredded
- 1 lb frozen shrimp
- Pepper
- Salt

Directions:

1. Add butter into the inner pot of instant pot duo crisp and set the pot on sauté mode.
2. Add rice, lemon juice, water, pepper, and salt. Stir well.
3. Add remaining ingredients into the pot and stir well.
4. Seal the pot with pressure cooking lid and cook on high for 5 minutes.
5. Once done, release pressure using a quick release. Remove lid.
6. Stir and serve.

Nutritional Value (Amount per Serving):
Calories 236; Fat 5.7 g; Carbohydrates 26.4 g; Sugar 0.3 g; Protein 18.3 g; Cholesterol 125 mg

Prawn jambalaya

Preparation Time: 10 minutes; Cooking Time: 14 minutes; Serve: 6
Ingredients:
- 1 lb prawns
- 1 lb chicken breasts, diced
- 2 tbsp olive oil
- 1 lb sausage, cooked and sliced
- 2 cups onion, diced
- 1 cup tomatoes, crushed
- 3 1/2 cups chicken stock
- 1 1/2 cups rice
- 2 tbsp garlic, minced
- 1 tbsp Worcestershire sauce
- 1 tbsp Creole seasoning
- 2 cups bell pepper, diced

Directions:
1. Add all ingredients except prawns and sausage into the inner pot of instant pot duo crisp and stir well.
2. Seal the pot with pressure cooking lid and cook on high for 12 minutes.
3. Release pressure using a quick release method than open the lid.
4. Add prawns and sausage and stir well.
5. Seal the pot with pressure cooking lid and cook on high for 2 minutes.
6. Once done, release pressure using a quick release. Remove lid.
7. Stir and serve.

Nutritional Value (Amount per Serving):
Calories 744; Fat 33.8 g; Carbohydrates 47.7 g; Sugar 5.4 g; Protein 58.7 g; Cholesterol 290 mg

Flavorful Poached Salmon

Preparation Time: 10 minutes; Cooking Time: 4 minutes; Serve: 4
Ingredients:
- 15 oz salmon fillet
- 2 black peppercorns
- 1 lemon zest
- 3 scallions, chopped
- 1/4 cup fresh dill
- 1/2 tsp fennel seeds
- 2 cups chicken broth
- 1/2 cup dry white wine
- 1 bay leaf
- 1 tsp white wine vinegar
- Pepper
- Salt

Directions:
1. Place steamer rack in the instant pot.
2. Season salmon fillet with pepper and salt and place on the steamer rack.
3. Cover fish with vinegar, wine, and broth then add remaining ingredients.
4. Seal the pot with pressure cooking lid and cook on high for 4 minutes.
5. Once done, release pressure using a quick release. Remove lid.
6. Serve and enjoy.

Nutritional Value (Amount per Serving):
Calories 201; Fat 7.5 g; Carbohydrates 5.4 g; Sugar 1.2 g; Protein 24.1 g; Cholesterol 47 mg

Sea Bass Curry

Preparation Time: 10 minutes; Cooking Time: 3 minutes; Serve: 4

Ingredients:

- 1 lb sea bass, cut into 1-inch cubes
- 1 tsp fish sauce
- 1/4 cup fresh cilantro, chopped
- 1/2 tsp white pepper
- 1 tsp ground ginger
- 1 tsp ground turmeric
- 1 tbsp red curry paste
- 1 lime juice
- 1 tsp garlic, minced
- 2 tsp sriracha
- 1 tsp honey
- 1 tsp coconut amino
- 14 oz coconut milk
- 1/2 tsp sea salt

Directions:

1. Place bass cubes into the inner pot of instant pot duo crisp.
2. Mix together the remaining ingredients and pour over the bass.
3. Seal the pot with pressure cooking lid and cook on high for 3 minutes.
4. Once done, release pressure using a quick release. Remove lid.
5. Serve and enjoy.

Nutritional Value (Amount per Serving):

Calories 402; Fat 27.8 g; Carbohydrates 10.5 g; Sugar 5.1 g; Protein 29.4 g; Cholesterol 60 mg

Parmesan Shrimp Alfredo

Preparation Time: 10 minutes; Cooking Time: 12 minutes; Serve: 4

Ingredients:

- 1 bag frozen shrimp, cooked
- 1 cup half and half
- 2 tsp flour
- 1 cup parmesan cheese, grated
- 2 cups chicken broth
- 1 tbsp olive oil
- 1/4 cup onion, diced
- 1 box pasta
- Pepper
- Salt

Directions:

1. Add olive oil into the inner pot of instant pot duo crisp and set pot on sauté mode.
2. Add onion into the pot and sauté for 3-5 minutes.
3. Add broth, shrimp, and pasta and stir well.
4. Seal the pot with pressure cooking lid and cook on high for 7 minutes.
5. Once done, release pressure using a quick release. Remove lid.
6. Set instant pot on sauté mode. Add cheese, flour, and half and half and cook until thickened.
7. Season with pepper and salt.
8. Stir and serve.

Nutritional Value (Amount per Serving):

Calories 280; Fat 13.9 g; Carbohydrates 22.8 g; Sugar 0.8 g; Protein 16.1 g; Cholesterol 93 mg

Chapter 7: Appetizers

Crispy French Fries

Preparation Time: 10 minutes; Cooking Time: 20 minutes; Serve: 4
Ingredients:

- 2 large potatoes, scrub and cut into fries shape
- 1/2 tsp garlic powder
- 1 tbsp olive oil
- 1/4 tsp pepper
- 1/2 tsp salt

Directions:

1. Soak potato fries in water for 15 minutes. Drain well and pat dry.
2. Add potato fries into the mixing bowl. Add garlic powder, oil, pepper, and salt and toss well.
3. Transfer potato fries into the air fryer basket then place the basket into the instant pot.
4. Seal the pot with air fryer lid and air fry potato fries for 10 minutes at 375 F.
5. Toss potato fries well and air fry for 10 minutes more.
6. Serve immediately and enjoy.

Nutritional Value (Amount per Serving):
Calories 159; Fat 3.7 g; Carbohydrates 29.3 g; Sugar 2.2 g; Protein 3.2 g; Cholesterol 0 mg

Sweet Potato Fries

Preparation Time: 10 minutes; Cooking Time: 10 minutes; Serve: 2
Ingredients:

- 2 sweet potatoes, clean and cut into fries shape
- 2 tsp olive oil
- 1 cup breadcrumbs
- 1 tsp chili powder
- 1/2 tsp onion powder
- 1/2 tsp garlic powder
- 1 tsp salt

Directions:

1. In a small bowl, mix together breadcrumbs, garlic powder, onion powder, chili powder, and salt.
2. Add sweet potato fries into the mixing bowl.
3. Pour oil over sweet potato fries and toss well to coat.
4. Sprinkle breadcrumb mixture over sweet potato fries and toss until well coated.
5. Spray instant pot duo crisp air fryer basket with cooking spray.
6. Add coated sweet potato fries into the air fryer basket then place a basket in the pot.
7. Seal the pot with air fryer lid and air fry sweet potato fries for 10 minutes at 400 F.
8. Serve and enjoy.

Nutritional Value (Amount per Serving):
Calories 439; Fat 8 g; Carbohydrates 82.4 g; Sugar 4.6 g; Protein 9.9 g; Cholesterol 0 mg

Quick Buffalo Chicken Dip

Preparation Time: 10 minutes; Cooking Time: 10 minutes; Serve: 12
Ingredients:

- 2 chicken breasts, skinless and boneless
- 1/2 cup cheddar cheese, shredded
- 1 celery stalk, chopped
- 4 oz ranch dressing
- 4 oz cream cheese
- 1/4 cup water
- 1/2 cup buffalo chicken sauce
- Pepper
- Salt

Directions:

1. Add chicken, water, and buffalo chicken sauce into the inner pot of instant pot duo crisp and stir well.

2. Seal the pot with pressure cooking lid and cook on high pressure for 7 minutes.
3. Once done, allow to release pressure naturally. Remove lid.
4. Shred the chicken using a fork.
5. Add remaining ingredients and stir well. Set pot on sauté mode and cook until cheese is melted.
6. Serve and enjoy.

Nutritional Value (Amount per Serving):
Calories 119; Fat 7.9 g; Carbohydrates 0.9 g; Sugar 0.3 g; Protein 10.6 g; Cholesterol 42 mg

Chicken Meatballs

Preparation Time: 10 minutes; Cooking Time: 18 minutes; Serve: 4
Ingredients:
- 1 large egg
- 4 tbsp cheddar cheese, grated
- 1 lb ground chicken
- 1/2 cup almond flour
- 3 tbsp hot sauce
- 2 tbsp ranch dressing

Directions:
1. Spray instant pot air fryer basket with cooking spray and place basket in the pot.
2. Add all ingredients to the bowl and mix until well combined.
3. Make small meatballs from mixture and place in the air fryer basket.
4. Seal the pot with air fryer lid and select bake mode and cook at 400 F for 15-18 minutes.
5. Serve and enjoy.

Nutritional Value (Amount per Serving):
Calories 330; Fat 17.1 g; Carbohydrates 3.7 g; Sugar 0.5 g; Protein 38.1 g; Cholesterol 150 mg

Jalapeno Poppers

Preparation Time: 10 minutes; Cooking Time: 20 minutes; Serve: 24
Ingredients:
- 12 large jalapeno peppers, cut in half and remove seeds
- 4 oz cheddar cheese, shredded
- 4.5 oz cream cheese
- 2 oz feta cheese, crumbled
- 1 tsp onion powder
- 1/4 cup cilantro, chopped

Directions:
1. Add all ingredients except jalapeno peppers into the bowl and mix to combine.
2. Stuff cheese mixture into each jalapeno half.
3. Line instant pot duo crisp air fryer basket with parchment paper or foil.
4. Arrange half jalapeno peppers into the air fryer basket then place a basket in the pot.
5. Seal the pot with air fryer lid and select bake mode and cook at 400 F for 20 minutes.
6. Cook the remaining half peppers using the same temperature and time.
7. Serve and enjoy.

Nutritional Value (Amount per Serving):
Calories 63; Fat 4.6 g; Carbohydrates 3.6 g; Sugar 1.6 g; Protein 2.6 g; Cholesterol 13 mg

Zucchini Bites

Preparation Time: 10 minutes; Cooking Time: 15 minutes; Serve: 4
Ingredients:
- 1 egg
- 2 cups zucchini, grated
- 1/4 cup cilantro, chopped
- 1/2 cup parmesan cheese, grated
- Pepper
- Salt

Directions:
1. Line instant pot duo crisp air fryer basket with parchment paper or foil.

2. In a bowl, mix together zucchini, cilantro, cheese, egg, pepper, and salt.
3. Pour mixture into the four cupcake liners and place it into the air fryer basket then place a basket in the pot.
4. Seal the pot with air fryer lid and select bake mode and cook at 400 F for 15 minutes.
5. Serve and enjoy.

Nutritional Value (Amount per Serving):
Calories 36; Fat 2 g; Carbohydrates 2.2 g; Sugar 1.1 g; Protein 3.2 g; Cholesterol 43 mg

Sweet Pepper Poppers

Preparation Time: 10 minutes; Cooking Time: 18 minutes; Serve: 10
Ingredients:

- 1 lb mini sweet peppers, halved
- 1/4 cup onion, grated
- 1/2 cup feta cheese, crumbled
- 8 oz cream cheese
- 8 oz gouda cheese, grated
- 2 tbsp cilantro, chopped
- 1 tsp garlic, minced

Directions:
1. Line instant pot duo crisp air fryer basket with parchment paper or foil.
2. Add all ingredients except peppers into the bowl and mix to combine.
3. Stuff each pepper halves with cheese mixture.
4. Arrange half stuff peppers into the air fryer basket and place basket in the pot.
5. Seal the pot with air fryer lid and select bake mode and cook at 400 F for 15-18 minutes.
6. Cook the remaining half peppers using the same temperature and time.
7. Serve and enjoy.

Nutritional Value (Amount per Serving):
Calories 185; Fat 15.8 g; Carbohydrates 2.7 g; Sugar 1.6 g; Protein 8.6 g; Cholesterol 57 mg

Turkey Jerky

Preparation Time: 10 minutes; Cooking Time: 6 hours; Serve: 4
Ingredients:

- 1 lb turkey tenderloins, trimmed fat and sliced 1/4-inch thick
- 2 tsp Worcestershire sauce
- 1/4 cup soy sauce
- 1/2 cup water
- 1/2 tsp garlic powder
- 1/2 tsp onion powder
- 1/2 tsp liquid smoke
- 1/4 tsp black pepper
- 1 1/2 tbsp brown sugar

Directions:
1. In a mixing bowl, mix together onion powder, Worcestershire sauce, soy sauce, water, liquid smoke, pepper, sugar, and garlic powder. Stir well.
2. Add meat slices and mix until well coated.
3. Cover mixing bowl and place in the refrigerator for overnight.
4. Spray the dehydrating tray with cooking spray and place in instant pot duo crisp air fryer basket.
5. Arrange marinated meat slices on dehydrating tray.
6. Place air fryer basket into the pot.
7. Seal the pot with air fryer lid and select dehydrate mode and cook at 145 F for 6 hours.
8. Store or serve.

Nutritional Value (Amount per Serving):
Calories 147; Fat 1.5 g; Carbohydrates 5.6 g; Sugar 4.3 g; Protein 29.2 g; Cholesterol 45 mg

Lime Apple Chips

Preparation Time: 10 minutes; Cooking Time: 8 hours; Serve: 4

Ingredients:
- 4 green apples, cored and sliced 1/8-inch thick
- 1/2 fresh lime juice

Directions:
1. Add apple slices and lime juice in a bowl and mix well and let it sit for 5 minutes.
2. Spray the dehydrating tray with cooking spray and place in instant pot duo crisp air fryer basket.
3. Arrange apple slices on dehydrating tray.
4. Place air fryer basket into the pot.
5. Seal the pot with air fryer lid and select dehydrate mode and cook at 145 F for 8 hours.
6. Store in an air-tight container.

Nutritional Value (Amount per Serving):
Calories 117; Fat 0.4 g; Carbohydrates 31.3 g; Sugar 23.3 g; Protein 0.6 g; Cholesterol 0 mg

Cinnamon Sweet Potato Chips

Preparation Time: 10 minutes; Cooking Time: 12 hours; Serve: 2
Ingredients:
- 2 sweet potatoes, peel and sliced thinly
- 1 tsp olive oil
- 1/8 tsp ground cinnamon
- Seal salt

Directions:
1. Add sweet potato slices in a bowl.
2. Add cinnamon, oil, and salt and toss well.
3. Spray the dehydrating tray with cooking spray and place in instant pot duo crisp air fryer basket.
4. Arrange sweet potato slices on dehydrating tray.
5. Place air fryer basket into the pot.
6. Seal the pot with air fryer lid and select dehydrate mode and cook at 125 F for 12 hours.
7. Store in an air-tight container.

Nutritional Value (Amount per Serving):
Calories 197; Fat 2.6 g; Carbohydrates 41.9 g; Sugar 0.8 g; Protein 2.3 g; Cholesterol 0 mg

Tasty Eggplant Slices

Preparation Time: 10 minutes; Cooking Time: 4 hours; Serve: 4
Ingredients:
- 1 eggplant, cut into 1/4-inch thick slices
- 1/4 tsp garlic powder
- 1 tsp paprika
- 1/4 tsp onion powder

Directions:
1. Add all ingredients into the mixing bowl and toss until well coated.
2. Spray the dehydrating tray with cooking spray and place in instant pot duo crisp air fryer basket.
3. Arrange eggplant slices on the dehydrating tray.
4. Place air fryer basket into the pot.
5. Seal the pot with air fryer lid and select dehydrate mode and cook at 145 F for 4 hours.
6. Serve or store.

Nutritional Value (Amount per Serving):
Calories 31; Fat 0.3 g; Carbohydrates 7.3 g; Sugar 3.6 g; Protein 1.3 g; Cholesterol 0 mg

Cauliflower Popcorn

Preparation Time: 10 minutes; Cooking Time: 40 minutes; Serve: 4

Ingredients:

- 1 large cauliflower head, cut into florets
- 2 tbsp coconut oil, melted
- 2 tbsp butter, melted
- Salt

Directions:

1. Add cauliflower florets into the bowl.
2. Pour melted coconut oil and butter over cauliflower florets. Season with salt and toss well.
3. Add cauliflower florets into the instant pot air fryer basket and place basket in the pot.
4. Seal the pot with air fryer lid and select bake mode and cook at 400 F for 40 minutes. Stir after every 15 minutes.
5. Serve and enjoy.

Nutritional Value (Amount per Serving):

Calories 162; Fat 12.8 g; Carbohydrates 11.1 g; Sugar 5 g; Protein 4.2 g; Cholesterol 15 mg

Avocado Fries

Preparation Time: 10 minutes; Cooking Time: 25 minutes; Serve: 4
Ingredients:

- 2 eggs, beaten
- 2 avocado, chopped into wedges
- 1/4 cup sunflower seeds, crushed
- 1/2 cup almond flour
- 1/2 tsp onion powder
- 1 tsp salt

Directions:

1. In a bowl, add beaten eggs.
2. In another bowl, add almond flour, sunflower seed, onion powder, and salt.
3. Dip avocado slices in egg mixture then coat with almond flour mixture and place into the instant pot air fryer basket.
4. Place basket in the pot. Seal the pot with air fryer lid and select bake mode and cook at 400 F for 25 minutes.
5. Serve and enjoy.

Nutritional Value (Amount per Serving):

Calories 338; Fat 29.9 g; Carbohydrates 12.6 g; Sugar 0.9 g; Protein 8.3 g; Cholesterol 82 mg

Onion Rings

Preparation Time: 10 minutes; Cooking Time: 25 minutes; Serve: 4
Ingredients:

- 2 eggs
- 2 large onion, cut into rings
- 2 tbsp thyme, sliced
- 1 1/2 cups almond flour
- 1/2 tsp black pepper
- 1/2 tsp garlic powder
- 1/2 tsp salt

Directions:

1. In a bowl, whisk eggs.
2. In another bowl, combine together almond flour, thyme, salt, garlic powder and black pepper.
3. Dip onion rings in egg mixture then coat with almond flour mixture and place into the instant pot air fryer basket.
4. Place basket in the pot. Seal the pot with air fryer lid and select bake mode and cook at 400 F for 25 minutes.
5. Serve and enjoy.

Nutritional Value (Amount per Serving):

Calories 319; Fat 22.3 g; Carbohydrates 17.5 g; Sugar 3.5 g; Protein 12.8 g; Cholesterol 82 mg

Brussels sprouts Chips

Preparation Time: 10 minutes; Cooking Time: 10 minutes; Serve: 2

Ingredients:

- 10 Brussels sprouts split leaves
- 1 tbsp olive oil
- Pepper
- Salt

Directions:

1. Add all ingredients to the bowl and toss well.
2. Place Brussels sprouts into the instant pot air fryer basket.
3. Place basket in the pot. Seal the pot with air fryer lid and select bake mode and cook at 350 F for 10 minutes.
4. Serve and enjoy.

Nutritional Value (Amount per Serving):

Calories 250; Fat 8.5 g; Carbohydrates 40 g; Sugar 9.5 g; Protein 15 g; Cholesterol 0 mg

Asian Beef Jerky

Preparation Time: 10 minutes; Cooking Time: 6 hours; Serve: 4

Ingredients:

- 1 lb flank steak, trimmed fat and sliced into thin strips
- 1/2 tsp onion powder
- 1/2 tsp black pepper
- 1/2 tbsp brown sugar
- 1/4 cup soy sauce
- 1/4 cup Worcestershire sauce
- 1/2 tsp red pepper flakes
- 1/2 tsp liquid smoke
- 1/2 tsp garlic powder

Directions:

1. Add red pepper flakes, black pepper, brown sugar, soy sauce, liquid smoke, garlic powder, onion powder, and Worcestershire sauce in a large zip-lock bag and mix well.
2. Add sliced meat in the bag.
3. Seal bag and shake until meat is well coated.
4. Place in refrigerator overnight.
5. Spray the dehydrating tray with cooking spray and place in instant pot duo crisp air fryer basket.
6. Arrange marinated meat slices on dehydrating tray.
7. Place air fryer basket into the pot.
8. Seal the pot with air fryer lid and select dehydrate mode and cook at 160 F for 6 hours.
9. Store in an air-tight container.

Nutritional Value (Amount per Serving):

Calories 251; Fat 9.5 g; Carbohydrates 6.1 g; Sugar 4.6 g; Protein 32.7 g; Cholesterol 62 mg

Simple Zucchini Chips

Preparation Time: 10 minutes; Cooking Time: 15 minutes; Serve: 3

Ingredients:

- 4 small zucchinis, sliced
- 1/2 cup parmesan cheese, grated
- Pepper
- Salt

Directions:

1. Arrange sliced zucchinis into the instant pot air fryer basket and sprinkle with parmesan cheese. Season with pepper and salt.
2. Place basket in the pot. Seal the pot with air fryer lid and select bake mode and cook at 400 F for 15 minutes.
3. Serve hot and enjoy.

Nutritional Value (Amount per Serving):

Calories 40; Fat 1.3 g; Carbohydrates 5.5 g; Sugar 2.7 g; Protein 3.4 g; Cholesterol 3 mg

Radish Chips

Preparation Time: 10 minutes; Cooking Time: 15 minutes; Serve: 4
Ingredients:
- 15 oz fresh radishes, sliced
- 2 tbsp olive oil
- 1/2 tsp pepper
- 1/2 tsp sea salt

Directions:
1. Add all ingredients to the bowl and toss well.
2. Arrange sliced radishes into the instant pot air fryer basket.
3. Place basket in the pot. Seal the pot with air fryer lid and select bake mode and cook at 400 F for 15 minutes.
4. Serve and enjoy.

Nutritional Value (Amount per Serving):
Calories 78; Fat 7.1 g; Carbohydrates 3.8 g; Sugar 2 g; Protein 0.8 g; Cholesterol 0 mg

Roasted Red Pepper Hummus

Preparation Time: 10 minutes; Cooking Time: 40 minutes; Serve: 4
Ingredients:
- 1 cup chickpeas, dry and rinsed
- 2 tbsp olive oil
- 1/4 tsp cumin
- 2 garlic cloves
- 2 1/2 tbsp tahini
- 3 tbsp fresh lemon juice
- 1/2 cup roasted red peppers
- 3 cups chicken broth
- 1/2 tsp salt

Directions:
1. Add chickpeas and broth into the inner pot of instant pot duo crisp and stir well.
2. Seal the pot with pressure cooking lid and cook on high for 40 minutes.
3. Once done, allow to release pressure naturally. Remove lid.
4. Drain chickpeas well and reserved half cup broth.
5. Transfer chickpeas, reserved broth, and remaining ingredients into the food processor and process until smooth.
6. Serve and enjoy.

Nutritional Value (Amount per Serving):
Calories 338; Fat 16.3 g; Carbohydrates 35.2 g; Sugar 7.2 g; Protein 15.3 g; Cholesterol 0 mg

Spicy Spinach Dip

Preparation Time: 10 minutes; Cooking Time: 8 minutes; Serve: 8
Ingredients:
- 1 lb fresh spinach
- 1 tbsp hot sauce
- 1 tsp cumin
- 1 tsp chili powder
- 1 tsp onion powder
- 1/2 cup olives, sliced
- 2 jalapeno pepper, minced
- 1 cup cheddar cheese, shredded
- 1 cup mozzarella cheese, shredded
- 4 oz cream cheese, cubed
- 1/4 cup half and half
- 1/4 cup sour cream
- 1 tbsp olive oil
- 2 large tomatoes, chopped
- 4 garlic cloves, minced
- 1/4 tsp pepper
- 1/2 tsp salt

Directions:
1. Add oil into the instant pot duo crisp and set pot on sauté mode.
2. Add tomatoes, spinach, and garlic and sauté until spinach is cooked.

3. Turn off the sauté mode. Add remaining ingredients and stir well.
4. Seal the pot with pressure cooking lid and cook on high pressure for 4 minutes.
5. Once done, release pressure using a quick release. Remove lid.
6. Serve and enjoy.

Nutritional Value (Amount per Serving):
Calories 194; Fat 15.8 g; Carbohydrates 7 g; Sugar 1.9 g; Protein 8.4 g; Cholesterol 38 mg

Teriyaki Beef Jerky

Preparation Time: 10 minutes; Cooking Time: 6 hours; Serve: 4

Ingredients:
- 3/4 lbs beef bottom round thin meat
- 2 1/2 tbsp soy sauce
- 3 tbsp Worcestershire sauce
- 1/2 tsp liquid smoke
- 1/4 cup teriyaki sauce
- 1/2 tsp onion powder
- 1/2 tsp garlic, minced
- 1/2 tsp red pepper flakes

Directions:
1. Cut meat into the thin slices.
2. Add teriyaki sauce, soy sauce, Worcestershire sauce, onion powder, garlic, red pepper flakes, and liquid smoke in the large bowl.
3. Add meat slices in the bowl and mix until coated.
4. Cover bowl and place in the refrigerator for overnight.
5. Spray the dehydrating tray with cooking spray and place in instant pot duo crisp air fryer basket.
6. Arrange marinated meat slices on dehydrating tray. Place air fryer basket into the pot.
7. Seal the pot with air fryer lid and select dehydrate mode and cook at 160 F for 6 hours.
8. Store or serve.

Nutritional Value (Amount per Serving):
Calories 172; Fat 13.7 g; Carbohydrates 6.3 g; Sugar 5.1 g; Protein 17.7 g; Cholesterol 61 mg

Baba Ghanoush

Preparation Time: 10 minutes; Cooking Time: 13 minutes; Serve: 6

Ingredients:
- 1 eggplant, pierce with a fork
- 2 tbsp sesame seeds
- 2 tbsp sesame oil
- 2 tsp lemon juice
- 1/2 tsp ground cumin
- 1 garlic clove, minced
- 1/2 onion, chopped
- 1 tsp sea salt

Directions:
1. Pour 1 cup of water into the inner pot of instant pot duo crisp. Place steamer rack in the pot.
2. Place eggplant on top of the steamer rack.
3. Seal the pot with pressure cooking lid and cook on high pressure for 8 minutes.
4. Once done, release pressure using a quick release. Remove lid.
5. Remove eggplant from pot and clean the pot. Peel and slice cooked eggplant.
6. Add oil into the pot and set a pot on sauté mode.
7. Add onion and eggplant and sauté for 3-5 minutes.
8. Add remaining ingredients and stir everything well to combine.
9. Turn off the instant pot. Blend eggplant mixture using blender until smooth.
10. Serve and enjoy.

Nutritional Value (Amount per Serving):
Calories 82; Fat 6.2 g; Carbohydrates 6.3 g; Sugar 2.7 g; Protein 1.5 g; Cholesterol 0 mg

Creamy Eggplant Dip

Preparation Time: 10 minutes; Cooking Time: 8 minutes; Serve: 8
Ingredients:

- 2 eggplants, cut into wedges
- 1 tsp dried oregano
- 1 tbsp garlic, crushed
- 1/2 lemon juice
- 2 tbsp olive oil
- 1 cup of water
- 1/2 tsp Italian seasoning
- 1/4 tsp pepper
- 1 tsp salt

Directions:

1. Pour 1 cup of water into the inner pot of instant pot duo crisp. Place steamer rack in the pot.
2. Arrange eggplant on top of the steamer rack.
3. Seal the pot with a lid and cook on high for 8 minutes.
4. Once done, release pressure using a quick release. Remove lid.
5. Remove eggplant wedges from pot and peel.
6. Transfer eggplant and remaining ingredients into the blender and blend until smooth.
7. Serve and enjoy.

Nutritional Value (Amount per Serving):
Calories 68; Fat 3.9 g; Carbohydrates 8.7 g; Sugar 4.2 g; Protein 1.5 g; Cholesterol 0 mg

Instant Pot Salsa

Preparation Time: 10 minutes; Cooking Time: 10 minutes; Serve: 10
Ingredients:

- 4 cups tomatoes, peel, core, and dice
- 6 oz can tomato paste
- 15 oz can tomato sauce
- 1/2 cup apple cider vinegar
- 1 tbsp cayenne pepper sauce
- 1 tbsp cumin
- 1 tbsp garlic, minced
- 2 jalapeno pepper, diced
- 2 bell peppers, diced
- 1 onion, diced
- 2 tbsp kosher salt

Directions:

1. Add all ingredients into the inner pot of instant pot duo crisp and stir well.
2. Seal the pot with a lid and cook on high for 10 minutes.
3. Once done, allow to release pressure naturally. Remove lid.
4. Allow to cool completely then store or serve.

Nutritional Value (Amount per Serving):
Calories 58; Fat 0.6 g; Carbohydrates 12.3 g; Sugar 7.7 g; Protein 2.5 g; Cholesterol 0 mg

Tomatillo Salsa

Preparation Time: 10 minutes; Cooking Time: 15 minutes; Serve: 12
Ingredients:

- 2 lbs tomatillos, husk removed
- 2 cups of water
- 2 garlic cloves, peeled
- 35 dried arbol chilies, stems removed
- 1 tbsp olive oil
- Salt

Directions:

1. Add oil into the inner pot of instant pot duo crisp and set pot on sauté mode.
2. Add garlic and chilies to the pot and sauté for 2-3 minutes.
3. Add remaining ingredients and stir well.
4. Seal the pot with pressure cooking lid and cook on high for 12 minutes.
5. Once done, release pressure using a quick release. Remove lid.

6. Blend tomatillo mixture using blender until smooth.
7. Season with salt and serve.

Nutritional Value (Amount per Serving):
Calories 40; Fat 2 g; Carbohydrates 5.6 g; Sugar 0.6 g; Protein 0.9 g; Cholesterol 0 mg

Lamb Jerky

Preparation Time: 10 minutes; Cooking Time: 6 hours; Serve: 4

Ingredients:

- 1 lb boneless lamb, trimmed fat and slice into thin strips
- 1/2 tsp onion powder
- 1 1/2 tbsp Worcestershire sauce
- 2 1/2 tbsp soy sauce
- 1/4 tsp black pepper
- 1/2 tbsp oregano
- 1/2 tsp garlic powder

Directions:

1. Add soy sauce, garlic powder, oregano, Worcestershire sauce, onion powder, and black pepper in the large bowl and mix well.
2. Add meat slices in the bowl and mix until coated.
3. Cover bowl and place in the refrigerator for overnight.
4. Spray the dehydrating tray with cooking spray and place in instant pot duo crisp air fryer basket.
5. Arrange marinated meat slices on dehydrating tray.
6. Place air fryer basket into the pot.
7. Seal the pot with air fryer lid and select dehydrate mode and cook at 145 F for 6 hours.
8. Serve and enjoy.

Nutritional Value (Amount per Serving):
Calories 226; Fat 8.4 g; Carbohydrates 2.8 g; Sugar 1.5 g; Protein 32.6 g; Cholesterol 102 mg

Buffalo Chicken Dip

Preparation Time: 10 minutes; Cooking Time: 12 minutes; Serve: 10

Ingredients:

- 2 lbs chicken breast, skinless, boneless and halves
- 1/4 cup hot sauce
- 8 oz cream cheese
- 1 cup chicken broth

Directions:

1. Add chicken and broth into the inner pot of instant pot duo crisp.
2. Seal the pot with pressure cooking lid and cook on high for 10 minutes.
3. Once done, allow to release pressure naturally for 10 minutes then release remaining pressure using a quick release. Remove lid.
4. Remove chicken from pot and shred using a fork.
5. Clean the instant pot.
6. Add shredded chicken, hot sauce, and cream cheese into the instant pot and cook on sauté mode until cheese is melted.
7. Serve and enjoy.

Nutritional Value (Amount per Serving):
Calories 187; Fat 10.3 g; Carbohydrates 0.8 g; Sugar 0.2 g; Protein 21.5 g; Cholesterol 83 mg

Jalapeno Chicken Dip

Preparation Time: 10 minutes; Cooking Time: 14 minutes; Serve: 10

Ingredients:

- 1 lb chicken breast, skinless and boneless
- 1/2 cup water
- 1/2 cup breadcrumbs

- 1/2 cup sour cream
- 8 oz cheddar cheese, shredded
- 2 jalapeno pepper, sliced
- 8 oz cream cheese

Directions:
1. Add chicken, water, cream cheese, and jalapenos into the inner pot of instant pot duo crisp.
2. Seal the pot with pressure cooking lid and cook on high for 12 minutes.
3. Once done, release pressure using a quick release. Remove lid.
4. Remove chicken from pot and shred using a fork. Return shredded chicken to the pot.
5. Add sour cream and cheddar cheese and stir well.
6. Sprinkle breadcrumbs on top. Seal the pot with air fryer lid and select broil mode and cook for 2 minutes.
7. Serve and enjoy.

Nutritional Value (Amount per Serving):
Calories 269; Fat 19.3 g; Carbohydrates 5.4 g; Sugar 0.6 g; Protein 18.1 g; Cholesterol 83 mg

Cauliflower Chicken Dip

Preparation Time: 10 minutes; Cooking Time: 5 minutes; Serve: 8
Ingredients:
- 1 medium cauliflower head, chopped
- 2 cups cheddar cheese, shredded
- 4 oz cream cheese, cubed
- 1 tsp paprika
- 1/4 cup ranch dressing
- 1/2 cup buffalo sauce
- 2 cups cooked chicken, shredded
- Pepper
- Salt

Directions:
1. Add cauliflower, ranch dressing, buffalo sauce, seasonings, and chicken into the inner pot of instant pot duo crisp. Mix well.
2. Seal the pot with pressure cooking lid and cook on high pressure for 5 minutes.
3. Once done, release pressure using a quick release. Remove lid.
4. Add cream cheese and cheddar cheese and stir until combined.
5. Serve and enjoy.

Nutritional Value (Amount per Serving):
Calories 238; Fat 15.5 g; Carbohydrates 5.2 g; Sugar 2.1 g; Protein 19.8 g; Cholesterol 72 mg

Ranch Mushrooms

Preparation Time: 10 minutes; Cooking Time: 11 minutes; Serve: 4
Ingredients:
- 16 oz mushrooms, rinsed
- 1 cup chicken broth
- 1 oz dry ranch dressing mix
- 1/4 cup parmesan cheese
- 1 tbsp garlic, minced
- 1/4 cup butter

Directions:
1. Add butter into the inner pot of instant pot duo crisp and set pot on sauté mode.
2. Add garlic and sauté for 1 minute.
3. Add mushrooms and sauté for 5 minutes.
4. Add remaining ingredients and stir well.
5. Seal the pot with pressure cooking lid and cook on high for 5 minutes.
6. Once done, release pressure using a quick release. Remove lid.
7. Stir well and serve.

Nutritional Value (Amount per Serving):
Calories 147; Fat 12.6 g; Carbohydrates 5.1 g; Sugar 2.3 g; Protein 5.7 g; Cholesterol 32 mg

Spicy Mexican Jerky

Preparation Time: 10 minutes; Cooking Time: 5 hours; Serve: 4

Ingredients:

- 1 lb pork lean meat, sliced thinly
- 1/4 tsp garlic powder
- 1 tsp chili powder
- 1 tsp paprika
- 1/2 tsp oregano
- 1/4 tsp black pepper
- 1 tsp salt

Directions:

1. Add paprika, chili powder, black pepper, oregano, garlic powder, and salt in a bowl and mix well.
2. Add sliced meat in a bowl and mix well.
3. Cover bowl and place in the refrigerator for overnight.
4. Spray the dehydrating tray with cooking spray and place in instant pot duo crisp air fryer basket.
5. Arrange marinated meat slices on dehydrating tray.
6. Place air fryer basket into the pot.
7. Seal the pot with air fryer lid and select dehydrate mode and cook at 160 F for 5 hours.
8. Store or serve.

Nutritional Value (Amount per Serving):

Calories 55; Fat 3.8 g; Carbohydrates 1.4 g; Sugar 0.4 g; Protein 4.1 g; Cholesterol 0 mg

Quick Chicken Dip

Preparation Time: 10 minutes; Cooking Time: 7 minutes; Serve: 12

Ingredients:

- 2 chicken breasts, skinless and boneless
- 1/2 cup cheddar cheese, shredded
- 1 celery stalk, chopped
- 4 oz blue cheese dressing
- 4 oz cream cheese
- 1/4 cup water
- 1/2 cup buffalo chicken sauce
- Pepper
- Salt

Directions:

1. Add chicken, water, and buffalo chicken sauce into the inner pot of instant pot duo crisp and stir well.
2. Seal the pot with pressure cooking lid and cook on high pressure for 7 minutes.
3. Once done, allow to release pressure naturally. Remove lid.
4. Remove chicken from pot and shred using a fork. Return shredded chicken to the pot.
5. Set pot on sauté mode. Add remaining ingredients and cook until cheese is melted.
6. Serve and enjoy.

Nutritional Value (Amount per Serving):

Calories 164; Fat 12.9 g; Carbohydrates 1.1 g; Sugar 0.3 g; Protein 10.9 g; Cholesterol 43 mg

Parmesan Corn

Preparation Time: 10 minutes; Cooking Time: 5 minutes; Serve: 4

Ingredients:

- 4 ears of corn, remove husks
- 1 tbsp parmesan cheese, grated
- 1 tbsp ranch seasoning mix
- 4 tbsp butter, melted

Directions:

1. Pour 1 1/2 cups of water into the inner pot of instant pot duo crisp. Place steamer rack in the pot.
2. Arrange corn on top of the steamer rack.

3. Seal the pot with pressure cooking lid and cook on high for 5 minutes.
4. Once done, release pressure using a quick release. Remove lid.
5. In a small bowl, mix together butter, cheese, and ranch seasoning and set aside.
6. Remove corn from pot and brush with butter mixture.
7. Serve and enjoy.

Nutritional Value (Amount per Serving):
Calories 261; Fat 14.8 g; Carbohydrates 29.3 g; Sugar 5 g; Protein 7.4 g; Cholesterol 36 mg

Perfect Herb Garlic Potatoes

Preparation Time: 10 minutes; Cooking Time: 7 minutes; Serve: 6
Ingredients:
- 2 lbs baby potatoes, wash, pat dry, and halves
- 1/2 cup vegetable broth
- 3 tbsp butter, melted
- 1/2 tsp oregano
- 1/2 tsp rosemary
- 1/2 tsp thyme
- 1 tsp garlic, minced
- 1 tsp sea salt

Directions:
1. Add all ingredients into the inner pot of instant pot duo crisp and stir well.
2. Seal the pot with pressure cooking lid and cook on high for 7 minutes.
3. Once done, release pressure using a quick release. Remove lid.
4. Stir well and serve.

Nutritional Value (Amount per Serving):
Calories 143; Fat 6.1 g; Carbohydrates 19.2 g; Sugar 0.1 g; Protein 4.4 g; Cholesterol 15 mg

Easy Salmon Jerky

Preparation Time: 10 minutes; Cooking Time: 4 hours; Serve: 4
Ingredients:
- 3/4 lbs salmon, cut into 1/4-inch slices
- 3/4 tbsp fresh lemon juice
- 1/2 tbsp molasses
- 1/4 cup soy sauce
- 1/4 tsp liquid smoke
- 1/2 tsp black pepper

Directions:
1. In a bowl, mix together lemon juice, molasses, liquid smoke, black pepper, and soy sauce.
2. Add sliced salmon into the bowl and mix well.
3. Cover bowl and place in the refrigerator for overnight.
4. Remove salmon slices from marinade and pat dry with paper towel.
5. Spray the dehydrating tray with cooking spray and place in instant pot duo crisp air fryer basket.
6. Arrange salmon slices on the dehydrating tray.
7. Place air fryer basket into the pot.
8. Seal the pot with air fryer lid and select dehydrate mode and cook at 145 F for 4 hours.
9. Serve and enjoy.

Nutritional Value (Amount per Serving):
Calories 130; Fat 5.3 g; Carbohydrates 3.3 g; Sugar 1.7 g; Protein 17.6 g; Cholesterol 38 mg

Tasty Ranch Potatoes

Preparation Time: 10 minutes; Cooking Time: 10 minutes; Serve: 6
Ingredients:
- 3 lbs baby potatoes, wash and cut in half
- 1 packet ranch dressing mix
- 4 oz cheddar cheese, shredded
- 1 tsp garlic powder
- 2 tsp dried parsley

- 6 bacon slices, chopped
- 1/4 cup water
- Pepper
- Salt

Directions:
1. Add all ingredients except cheese and ranch dressing into the inner pot of instant pot duo crisp and stir well.
2. Seal the pot with pressure cooking lid and cook on high for 10 minutes.
3. Once done, release pressure using a quick release. Remove lid.
4. Add cheese and ranch dressing mix and stir to combine.
5. Serve and enjoy.

Nutritional Value (Amount per Serving):
Calories 314; Fat 14.5 g; Carbohydrates 29.4 g; Sugar 0.3 g; Protein 17.7 g; Cholesterol 41 mg

Sweet Potato Hummus

Preparation Time: 10 minutes; Cooking Time: 5 minutes; Serve: 10
Ingredients:
- 1 sweet potato, peeled and cut into cubes
- 1 tsp ground cumin
- 1/4 cup tahini
- 14.5 oz can chickpeas, drained
- 1 lemon juice
- 1 tbsp garlic, minced
- 2 tbsp olive oil
- 1/2 tsp salt

Directions:
1. Add oil into the inner pot of instant pot duo crisp and set pot on sauté mode.
2. Add sweet potatoes and sauté for 2 minutes.
3. Add garlic and sauté for 30 seconds. Add lemon juice and stir well.
4. Seal the pot with pressure cooking lid and select pressure cook and set timer for 2 minutes.
5. Once done, release pressure using a quick release. Remove lid.
6. Transfer sweet potato mixture into the food processor along with remaining ingredients and process until smooth.
7. Serve and enjoy.

Nutritional Value (Amount per Serving):
Calories 122; Fat 6.6 g; Carbohydrates 13.4 g; Sugar 0.9 g; Protein 3.4 g; Cholesterol 0 mg

Southwest Corn Dip

Preparation Time: 10 minutes; Cooking Time: 15 minutes; Serve: 8
Ingredients:
- 1 1/2 cups frozen corn
- 1 cup cheddar cheese, shredded
- 8 oz cream cheese
- 1 tsp cumin
- 2 tsp chili powder
- 4 oz can green chilies, diced
- 14 oz can tomatoes, diced
- 1 garlic clove, minced
- 1 jalapeno pepper, chopped
- 1/2 onion, diced
- 4 bacon slices, chopped
- 2 tbsp olive oil
- 1/2 tsp salt

Directions:
1. Add oil into the inner pot of instant pot duo crisp and set pot on sauté mode.
2. Add bacon and cook until crisp. Remove bacon from pot and set aside.
3. Add onion, jalapeno, garlic, and corn and sauté for 4-5 minutes.
4. Add remaining ingredients except for cheddar cheese and bacon and stir well.
5. Seal the pot with pressure cooking lid and cook on high for 5 minutes.
6. Once done, release pressure using a quick release. Remove lid.
7. Set pot on sauté mode. Add bacon and cheese and cook until cheese is melted.

8. Serve and enjoy.

Nutritional Value (Amount per Serving):
Calories 282; Fat 22.6 g; Carbohydrates 11 g; Sugar 3.5 g; Protein 10.9 g; Cholesterol 56 mg

Lemon Chicken Jerky

Preparation Time: 10 minutes; Cooking Time: 6 hours; Serve: 4

Ingredients:
- 1 lb chicken tenders, boneless, skinless and cut into 1/4-inch strips
- 1/2 tsp garlic powder
- 1 tsp lemon juice
- 1/2 cup soy sauce
- 1/4 tsp ground ginger
- 1/4 tsp black pepper

Directions:
1. Mix all ingredients except chicken into the zip-lock bag.
2. Add chicken to the bag.
3. Seal bag and mix until chicken is coated.
4. Place in refrigerator for 60 minutes.
5. Spray the dehydrating tray with cooking spray and place in instant pot duo crisp air fryer basket.
6. Arrange meat slices on dehydrating tray.
7. Place air fryer basket into the pot.
8. Seal the pot with air fryer lid and select dehydrate mode and cook at 145 F for 6 hours.
9. Serve and enjoy.

Nutritional Value (Amount per Serving):
Calories 235; Fat 8.4 g; Carbohydrates 2.9 g; Sugar 0.7 g; Protein 34.9 g; Cholesterol 101 mg

Jalapeno Cheese Dip

Preparation Time: 10 minutes; Cooking Time: 7 minutes; Serve: 8

Ingredients:
- 15 oz Colby cheese, shredded
- 1 cup can tomatoes
- 15 oz cheddar cheese, shredded
- 2 cups of soy milk
- 1/4 cup flour
- 1/4 cup butter
- 1/4 cup lemon juice
- 1 cup pickled jalapenos
- Pepper
- Salt

Directions:
1. Add butter into the inner pot of instant pot duo crisp and set pot on sauté mode.
2. Add milk and flour and stir constantly to avoid lumps.
3. Add cheese and stir well.
4. Add tomatoes and jalapenos and stir well.
5. Seal the pot with pressure cooking lid and cook on high for 7 minutes.
6. Once done, allow to release pressure naturally. Remove lid.
7. Stir well and serve.

Nutritional Value (Amount per Serving):
Calories 531; Fat 41.7 g; Carbohydrates 10.7 g; Sugar 4.2 g; Protein 28.7 g; Cholesterol 122 mg

Chapter 8: Broths & Sauces

Delicious Applesauce

Preparation Time: 10 minutes; Cooking Time: 8 minutes; Serve: 8
Ingredients:

- 10 medium apples, peeled, cored and chopped
- 1/2 tsp cinnamon
- 1 tbsp fresh lemon juice
- 1 cup of water

Directions:
1. Add water, cinnamon, and lemon juice into the instant pot and stir well.
2. Add chopped apples and mix well.
3. Seal the pot with pressure cooking lid and cook on high pressure for 8 minutes.
4. Once done, release pressure using a quick release. Remove lid.
5. Using masher mash the apple mixture. Pour into the bowl.
6. Allow to cool completely then store in the fridge.

Nutritional Value (Amount per Serving):
Calories 146; Fat 0.5 g; Carbohydrates 38.7 g; Sugar 29 g; Protein 0.8 g; Cholesterol 0 mg

Homemade Spaghetti Sauce

Preparation Time: 10 minutes; Cooking Time: 20 minutes; Serve: 8
Ingredients:

- 28 oz can whole tomatoes, peeled
- 1/2 tsp oregano
- 1 tbsp basil
- 1 tbsp onion, minced
- 14.5 oz can tomatoes, diced
- 1 medium onion, diced
- 5 oz tomato paste
- 6 oz water
- 8 oz tomato sauce
- 10 oz spicy sausage
- Salt

Directions:
1. Spray instant pot duo crisp from inside with cooking spray.
2. Set pot on sauté mode. Add sausage and onion and sauté until sausage is cooked.
3. Add remaining ingredients and stir everything well.
4. Seal the pot with pressure cooking lid and cook on pressure cook mode for 20 minutes.
5. Once done, release pressure using a quick release. Remove lid.
6. Stir well and serve.

Nutritional Value (Amount per Serving):
Calories 180; Fat 9.8 g; Carbohydrates 13.9 g; Sugar 8.7 g; Protein 9.4 g; Cholesterol 13.9 mg

Cranberry Sauce

Preparation Time: 10 minutes; Cooking Time: 8 minutes; Serve: 10
Ingredients:

- 15 oz fresh cranberries
- 2 tbsp Swerve
- 1 tsp cinnamon
- 2 cinnamon sticks
- 1 cup of orange juice
- 1/4 cup honey

Directions:
1. Add all ingredients into the instant pot duo crisp and stir well.
2. Seal the pot with pressure cooking lid and cook on high pressure for 8 minutes.
3. Once done, allow to release pressure naturally. Remove lid.
4. Pour sauce in a bowl and let it cool completely.
5. Store in refrigerator.

Nutritional Value (Amount per Serving):

Calories 61; Fat 0.1 g; Carbohydrates 16.8 g; Sugar 13.6 g; Protein 0.2 g; Cholesterol 0 mg

Marinara Sauce

Preparation Time: 10 minutes; Cooking Time: 18 minutes; Serve: 4

Ingredients:

- 1 lb tomatoes, diced
- 2 tbsp olive oil
- 4 oz vegetable stock
- 2 tbsp parsley, chopped
- 2 tbsp basil, chopped
- 1 carrot, diced
- 1 tbsp dried oregano
- 1 tbsp dried basil
- 6 garlic cloves, minced
- 1 large onion, diced
- Salt

Directions:

1. Add oil into the instant pot duo crisp and set pot on sauté mode.
2. Add garlic and sauté for 1 minute.
3. Add onion and dried herbs and sauté for 2-3 minutes.
4. Add tomatoes, fresh herbs, carrots, and stock and stir well.
5. Seal the pot with pressure cooking lid and cook on high pressure for 15 minutes.
6. Once done, allow to release pressure naturally for 10 minutes then release remaining pressure using a quick release. Remove lid.
7. Using blender blend sauce until getting desired consistency.

Nutritional Value (Amount per Serving):

Calories 115; Fat 7.5 g; Carbohydrates 12.2 g; Sugar 5.7 g; Protein 2.2 g; Cholesterol 0 mg

Classic Pasta Sauce

Preparation Time: 10 minutes; Cooking Time: 20 minutes; Serve: 8

Ingredients:

- 4 lbs fresh tomatoes, chopped
- 10 oz tomato paste
- 2 tbsp Italian seasoning
- 5 garlic cloves, peeled
- 5 medium carrots, chopped
- 2 large onions, diced
- 2 tsp sea salt

Directions:

1. Add tomatoes, garlic, carrots, and onions to the instant pot duo crisp. Stir well.
2. Sprinkle Italian seasoning and salt on top of tomatoes mixture.
3. Seal the pot with pressure cooking lid and cook on high pressure for 20 minutes.
4. Once done, allow to release pressure naturally for 10 minutes then release remaining pressure using a quick release. Remove lid.
5. Blend sauce using immersion blender until smooth. Add tomato paste and blend again.
6. Serve immediately and enjoy.

Nutritional Value (Amount per Serving):

Calories 114; Fat 1.7 g; Carbohydrates 23.8 g; Sugar 14.1 g; Protein 4.4 g; Cholesterol 2 mg

Cherry BBQ Sauce

Preparation Time: 10 minutes; Cooking Time: 15 minutes; Serve: 6

Ingredients:

- 2 1/2 cups cherries, pitted
- 1 tbsp fresh rosemary, chopped
- 2 1/2 tbsp maple syrup
- 1/2 tsp paprika
- 1 tsp cinnamon
- 2 tsp ginger, minced
- 2 1/2 tbsp apple cider vinegar
- 10 oz can tomatoes, diced
- 2 garlic cloves, minced
- 1 medium onion, chopped
- 2 tbsp olive oil
- Pepper

- Salt

Directions:
1. Add oil into the instant pot duo crisp and set pot on sauté mode.
2. Add garlic and onion and sauté for 3-5 minutes.
3. Add remaining ingredients and stir everything well.
4. Seal the pot with pressure cooking lid and cook on high pressure for 10 minutes.
5. Once done, release pressure using a quick release. Remove lid.
6. Blend sauce using immersion blender until smooth.
7. Pour in air-tight container and store in the refrigerator.

Nutritional Value (Amount per Serving):
Calories 372; Fat 5 g; Carbohydrates 80.7 g; Sugar 7.4 g; Protein 1.7 g; Cholesterol 0 mg

Fresh Cherry Jam

Preparation Time: 10 minutes; Cooking Time: 5 minutes; Serve: 25
Ingredients:
- 4 cups fresh cherries, pitted
- 1/8 cup water
- 1/4 tsp ginger
- 1/2 tsp nutmeg
- 1 tsp cinnamon
- 1/4 cup honey
- 1/2 cup sugar

Directions:
1. Add all ingredients into the instant pot duo crisp and stir everything well.
2. Seal the pot with pressure cooking lid and cook on high pressure for 5 minutes.
3. Once done, release pressure using a quick release. Remove lid.
4. Mash the cherries using a potato masher. Set pot on sauté mode and cook until jam thickens.
5. Pour in air-tight container and store in the refrigerator.

Nutritional Value (Amount per Serving):
Calories 68; Fat 0 g; Carbohydrates 17.1 g; Sugar 6.8 g; Protein 0.1 g; Cholesterol 0 mg

Easy Peach Jam

Preparation Time: 10 minutes; Cooking Time: 11 minutes; Serve: 15
Ingredients:
- 2 lbs fresh peaches, pitted and chopped
- 2 tbsp fresh lemon juice
- 1/2 cup brown sugar

Directions:
1. Add all ingredients into the instant pot duo crisp and stir well and let it roast for 5 minutes.
2. Seal the pot with pressure cooking lid and cook on high pressure for 6 minutes.
3. Once done, release pressure using a quick release. Remove lid.
4. Stir well and blend jam using an immersion blender until getting desired consistency.
5. Set pot on sauté mode and cook the jam for 3-5 minutes.
6. Pour in air-tight container and store in the refrigerator.

Nutritional Value (Amount per Serving):
Calories 27; Fat 0.1 g; Carbohydrates 6.7 g; Sugar 6.6 g; Protein 0.2 g; Cholesterol 0 mg

Slow Cooked Pear Sauce

Preparation Time: 10 minutes; Cooking Time: 8 hours; Serve: 8
Ingredients:
- 4 lbs pears, chopped
- 1/4 cup honey
- 10 whole cloves
- 1 cinnamon stick

- 2 oranges, peeled and chopped

Directions:
1. Add pears, cloves, cinnamon sticks, and oranges into the instant pot duo crisp.
2. Seal the pot with pressure cooking lid and select slow cook mode and cook on low pressure for 8 hours.
3. Once done then remove the lid and allow to cool sauce slightly.
4. Strain sauce through a sieve in a bowl. Add honey and stir well.
5. Pour in air-tight container and store in the refrigerator.

Nutritional Value (Amount per Serving):
Calories 212; Fat 2 g; Carbohydrates 54 g; Sugar 35.3 g; Protein 1.8 g; Cholesterol 0 mg

Cranberry Pear Sauce

Preparation Time: 10 minutes; Cooking Time: 3 minutes; Serve: 8
Ingredients:
- 15 oz fresh cranberries
- 1 tsp fresh ginger, grated
- 1 cup of water
- 3/4 cup honey
- 4 pears, cored and diced

Directions:
1. Add all ingredients into the instant pot duo crips. Stir well.
2. Seal the pot with pressure cooking lid and cook on high pressure for 3 minutes.
3. Once done, allow to release pressure naturally for 10 minutes then release remaining pressure using a quick release. Remove lid.
4. Pour in air-tight container and store in the refrigerator.

Nutritional Value (Amount per Serving):
Calories 187; Fat 0.2 g; Carbohydrates 47.1 g; Sugar 38.2 g; Protein 0.5 g; Cholesterol 0 mg

Flavorful Strawberry Jam

Preparation Time: 10 minutes; Cooking Time: 6 minutes; Serve: 8
Ingredients:
- 1 lb fresh strawberries, quartered
- 2 tsp cornstarch
- 1/4 cup water
- 1/2 cup sugar

Directions:
1. Add strawberries and sugar into the instant pot duo crisp and set pot on sauté mode.
2. Cook strawberries on sauté mode until sugar is melted.
3. Seal the pot with pressure cooking lid and cook on high pressure for 1 minute.
4. Once done, allow to release pressure naturally for 10 minutes then release remaining pressure using a quick release. Remove lid.
5. In a small bowl, whisk together water and cornstarch and pour into the pot.
6. Set pot on sauté mode and cook the jam for 3-5 minutes.
7. Once the jam is cool then pour in air-tight container and store in the refrigerator.

Nutritional Value (Amount per Serving):
Calories 68; Fat 0.2 g; Carbohydrates 17.5 g; Sugar 15.3 g; Protein 0.4 g; Cholesterol 0 mg

Strawberry Chia Jam

Preparation Time: 10 minutes; Cooking Time: 6 minutes; Serve: 12
Ingredients:
- 2 lbs fresh strawberries, chopped
- 1/4 cup chia seeds
- 2 tbsp fresh lemon juice
- 3/4 cup sugar

Directions:
1. In a mixing bowl, add strawberries and sugar. Mix well and let sit for 30 minutes.

2. Transfer strawberry and sugar mixture into the instant pot duo crisp.
3. Add lemon juice and stir well.
4. Seal the pot with pressure cooking lid and cook on high pressure for 6 minutes.
5. Once done, allow to release pressure naturally. Remove lid.
6. Add chia seeds and stir well.
7. Once the jam is cool then pour in air-tight container and store in the refrigerator.

Nutritional Value (Amount per Serving):
Calories 75; Fat 0.4 g; Carbohydrates 18.6 g; Sugar 16.3 g; Protein 0.6 g; Cholesterol 0 mg

Easy Raspberry Jam

Preparation Time: 10 minutes; Cooking Time: 8 minutes; Serve: 6
Ingredients:
- 1 lb frozen raspberries
- 1 tbsp fresh lemon juice
- 1/2 cup honey

Directions:
1. Add raspberries, lemon juice, and honey into the instant pot duo crisp and stir well.
2. Seal the pot with pressure cooking lid and cook on high pressure for 8 minutes.
3. Once done, allow to release pressure naturally. Remove lid.
4. Once the jam is cool then pour in air-tight container and store in the refrigerator.

Nutritional Value (Amount per Serving):
Calories 164; Fat 0.1 g; Carbohydrates 43.1 g; Sugar 39.7 g; Protein 0.6 g; Cholesterol 0 mg

Mix Berry Jam

Preparation Time: 10 minutes; Cooking Time: 10 minutes; Serve: 10
Ingredients:
- 8 cups mixed berries
- 1/2 cup chia seeds
- 2 tsp vanilla
- 1 fresh lemon juice
- 1/2 cup maple syrup

Directions:
1. Add mixed berries, vanilla, lemon juice, and maple syrup into the instant pot duo crisp and mix well.
2. Seal the pot with pressure cooking lid and cook on high pressure for 6 minutes.
3. Once done, allow to release pressure naturally. Remove lid.
4. Lightly mash berries using a potato masher.
5. Set pot on sauté mode. Add chia seeds and stir well and cook on sauté mode until jam thickens. About 3-4 minutes.
6. Once the jam is cool then pour in air-tight container and store in the refrigerator.

Nutritional Value (Amount per Serving):
Calories 116; Fat 0.9 g; Carbohydrates 25 g; Sugar 17.6 g; Protein 1.1 g; Cholesterol 0 mg

Blueberry Jam

Preparation Time: 10 minutes; Cooking Time: 20 minutes; Serve: 8
Ingredients:
- 4 cup blueberries
- 1/4 tsp allspice
- 1/4 tsp ground cloves
- 1 tsp cinnamon
- 1 lemon juice
- 1 1/2 cups sugar

Directions:
1. Add all ingredients into the instant pot duo crisp and stir well.
2. Seal the pot with pressure cooking lid and select pressure cook mode and set timer for 6 minutes.

3. Once done, release pressure using a quick release. Remove lid.
4. Set pot on sauté mode and cook until liquid reduces and jam thickens, about 10-14 minutes.
5. Once the jam is cool then pour in air-tight container and store in the refrigerator.

Nutritional Value (Amount per Serving):
Calories 185; Fat 0.3 g; Carbohydrates 48.4 g; Sugar 44.8 g; Protein 0.6 g; Cholesterol 0 mg

Hot Jalapeno Sauce

Preparation Time: 10 minutes; Cooking Time: 2 minutes; Serve: 45
Ingredients:
- 1/2 lb fresh jalapeno peppers, cut ends and sliced
- 2 tsp garlic, minced
- 3/4 cup water
- 2 tbsp fresh lime juice
- 1/4 cup agave nectar
- 1/2 cup apple cider vinegar
- 2 tsp salt

Directions:
1. Add jalapenos, garlic, water, and salt into the instant pot duo crisp and stir well.
2. Seal the pot with pressure cooking lid and cook on high pressure for 2 minutes.
3. Once done, allow to release pressure naturally. Remove lid.
4. Add remaining ingredients and stir well. Blend the sauce using an immersion blender until smooth.
5. Once the sauce is cool then pour in air-tight container and store in the refrigerator.

Nutritional Value (Amount per Serving):
Calories 3; Fat 0.1 g; Carbohydrates 0.6 g; Sugar 0.2 g; Protein 0.1 g; Cholesterol 0 mg

Delicious BBQ Sauce

Preparation Time: 10 minutes; Cooking Time: 8 minutes; Serve: 8
Ingredients:
- 1 cup ketchup
- 1 tsp chili powder
- 1/4 tsp cumin
- 3/4 tsp paprika
- 1 tbsp adobo sauce
- 2 tsp apple cider vinegar
- 1/4 cup orange juice
- 1/4 cup honey
- 1 tsp garlic, chopped
- 1 onion, chopped
- 1 tsp olive oil
- 1/4 tsp pepper
- 1 tsp salt

Directions:
1. Add oil into the instant pot duo crisp and set pot on sauté mode.
2. Add garlic and onion and sauté for 3 minutes.
3. Meanwhile, whisk together the remaining ingredients and pour them into the instant pot and stir well.
4. Seal the pot with pressure cooking lid and cook on high pressure for 8 minutes.
5. Once done, release pressure using a quick release. Remove lid.
6. Blend sauce using blender until smooth.
7. Once the sauce is cool then pour in air-tight container and store in the refrigerator.

Nutritional Value (Amount per Serving):
Calories 81; Fat 0.8 g; Carbohydrates 19.5 g; Sugar 17.3 g; Protein 0.9 g; Cholesterol 0 mg

Peach BBQ Sauce

Preparation Time: 10 minutes; Cooking Time: 15 minutes; Serve: 8
Ingredients:
- 1 1/2 cups ketchup
- 1 tsp paprika

- 2 tbsp Dijon mustard
- 1 tsp garlic, chopped
- 1/2 cup onion, minced
- 1 tbsp adobo sauce
- 4 fresh peaches, peeled and halved
- 1/4 cup Worcestershire sauce
- 1/3 cup apple cider vinegar
- 2 tbsp honey
- 1/4 tsp pepper
- 1 tsp salt

Directions:
1. Add all ingredients into the instant pot duo crips and stir well.
2. Seal the pot with pressure cooking lid and cook on high pressure for 15 minutes.
3. Once done, allow to release pressure naturally for 5 minutes then release remaining pressure using a quick release. Remove lid.
4. Blend sauce using immersion blender until smooth.
5. Once the sauce is cool then pour in air-tight container and store in the refrigerator.

Nutritional Value (Amount per Serving):
Calories 108; Fat 0.5 g; Carbohydrates 26.1 g; Sugar 24 g; Protein 1.8 g; Cholesterol 0 mg

Peach Compote

Preparation Time: 10 minutes; Cooking Time: 2 minutes; Serve: 6
Ingredients:
- 4 peaches, peeled and chopped
- 2 tbsp water
- 1/2 tbsp cornstarch
- 1 tsp vanilla

Directions:
1. Add peaches, vanilla, and 1 tbsp water into the instant pot duo crisp and stir well.
2. Seal the pot with pressure cooking lid and cook on high pressure for 1 minute.
3. Once done, allow to release pressure naturally for 5 minutes then release remaining pressure using a quick release. Remove lid.
4. In a small bowl, whisk together 1 tbsp water and cornstarch and pour into the instant pot.
5. Set pot on sauté mode and cook peach compote for 1 minute or until thickened.
6. Serve immediately or store.

Nutritional Value (Amount per Serving):
Calories 44; Fat 0.3 g; Carbohydrates 10 g; Sugar 9.4 g; Protein 0.9 g; Cholesterol 0 mg

Strawberry Compote

Preparation Time: 10 minutes; Cooking Time: 4 minutes; Serve: 15
Ingredients:
- 2 lbs fresh strawberries, chopped
- 2 tbsp sugar
- 1 tbsp agave
- 1/3 cup orange juice

Directions:
1. Add all ingredients into the instant pot duo crisp and stir well.
2. Seal the pot with pressure cooking lid and cook on high pressure for 4 minutes.
3. Once done, allow to release pressure naturally. Remove lid.
4. Allow to cool completely before serving.

Nutritional Value (Amount per Serving):
Calories 32; Fat 0.2 g; Carbohydrates 7.9 g; Sugar 6 g; Protein 0.5 g; Cholesterol 0 mg

Easy Blueberry Compote

Preparation Time: 10 minutes; Cooking Time: 3 minutes; Serve: 6
Ingredients:
- 3 cups fresh blueberries
- 1 tsp cinnamon
- 1 tsp vanilla
- 2 tbsp fresh lemon juice
- 1/4 cup maple syrup
- Pinch of salt

Directions:
1. Add all ingredients into the instant pot duo crisp and stir well.
2. Seal the pot with pressure cooking lid and cook on high pressure for 3 minutes.
3. Once done, allow to release pressure naturally for 10 minutes then release remaining pressure using a quick release. Remove lid.
4. Set pot on sauté mode and cook until compote thickens.
5. Allow to cool completely then serve or store.

Nutritional Value (Amount per Serving):
Calories 80; Fat 0.3 g; Carbohydrates 19.8 g; Sugar 15.2 g; Protein 0.6 g; Cholesterol 0 mg

Pear Compote

Preparation Time: 10 minutes; Cooking Time: 2 minutes; Serve: 4

Ingredients:
- 3 pears , peeled, cored and diced
- 1/2 tsp ground ginger
- 1 tsp cinnamon
- 1/4 cup water

Directions:
1. Add all ingredients into the instant pot duo crisp and stir well.
2. Seal the pot with pressure cooking lid and cook on high pressure for 2 minutes.
3. Once done, allow to release pressure naturally for 5 minutes then release remaining pressure using a quick release. Remove lid.
4. Allow to cool completely. Serve or store.

Nutritional Value (Amount per Serving):
Calories 93; Fat 0.2 g; Carbohydrates 24.5 g; Sugar 15.3 g; Protein 0.6 g; Cholesterol 0 mg

Sweet & Spicy BBQ Sauce

Preparation Time: 10 minutes; Cooking Time: 7 minutes; Serve: 12

Ingredients:
- 16 oz tomato sauce
- 1/4 cup tomato paste
- 1/3 cup honey
- 1/4 cup molasses
- 3 tbsp Worcestershire sauce
- 1/2 cup apple cider vinegar
- 1/4 cup water
- 1 tsp paprika
- 1 tsp garlic, minced
- 1/2 cup onion, chopped
- 1 tbsp olive oil
- 1/4 tsp pepper
- 1/2 tsp salt

Directions:
1. Add oil into the instant pot duo crisp and set pot on sauté mode.
2. Add onions and sauté for 2 minutes.
3. Add paprika and garlic and sauté for a minute.
4. Turn off the sauté mode. Add remaining ingredients and stir everything well.
5. Seal the pot with pressure cooking lid and cook on high pressure for 5 minutes.
6. Once done, release pressure using a quick release. Remove lid.
7. Blend sauce using immersion blender until smooth.
8. Serve or store.

Nutritional Value (Amount per Serving):
Calories 81; Fat 1.3 g; Carbohydrates 17.4 g; Sugar 14.8 g; Protein 0.9 g; Cholesterol 0 mg

Peach Apple Sauce

Preparation Time: 10 minutes; Cooking Time: 7 minutes; Serve: 8

Ingredients:
- 5 apples, peel, core, and dice
- 4 peaches, peel, core, and dice

- 2 tbsp honey
- 1/2 tsp cinnamon
- 1 tbsp fresh lemon juice
- 1/4 cup apple juice
- 1/8 tsp salt

Directions:
1. Add all ingredients into the instant pot duo crisp and stir well.
2. Seal the pot with pressure cooking lid and cook on high pressure for 7 minutes.
3. Once done, allow to release pressure naturally for 10 minutes then release remaining pressure using a quick release. Remove lid.
4. Blend sauce using an immersion blender until smooth.
5. Once the sauce is cool then pour in air-tight container and store in the refrigerator.

Nutritional Value (Amount per Serving):
Calories 122; Fat 0.5 g; Carbohydrates 31.6 g; Sugar 26.6 g; Protein 1.1 g; Cholesterol 0 mg

Pumpkin Applesauce

Preparation Time: 10 minutes; Cooking Time: 20 minutes; Serve: 8
Ingredients:
- 7 apples, peel, core, and dice
- 1 cup pumpkin puree
- 1/2 cup water
- 1 tbsp honey
- 1/2 tsp cinnamon
- 1 tbsp pumpkin pie spice
- Pinch of salt

Directions:
1. Add apples, water, honey, cinnamon, pumpkin pie spice, and salt into the instant pot duo crisp. Stir well.
2. Seal the pot with pressure cooking lid and cook on high pressure for 6 minutes.
3. Once done, allow to release pressure naturally for 2 minutes then release remaining pressure using a quick release. Remove lid.
4. Add pumpkin puree and stir well. Lightly mash the applesauce using a potato masher.
5. Serve hot or store.

Nutritional Value (Amount per Serving):
Calories 123; Fat 0.5 g; Carbohydrates 32.2 g; Sugar 23.5 g; Protein 0.9 g; Cholesterol 0 mg

Chunky Raspberry Applesauce

Preparation Time: 10 minutes; Cooking Time: 10 minutes; Serve: 10
Ingredients:
- 7 apples, peel, core, and dice
- 2 cups raspberries
- 1/2 tsp ginger
- 1 tsp cinnamon
- 1 tbsp fresh lemon juice
- 3/4 cup water

Directions:
1. Add all ingredients into the instant pot duo crisp and stir well.
2. Seal the pot with pressure cooking lid and cook on high pressure for 5 minutes.
3. Once done, release pressure using a quick release. Remove lid.
4. Lightly mash sauce using a potato masher.
5. Serve and enjoy.

Nutritional Value (Amount per Serving):
Calories 95; Fat 0.5 g; Carbohydrates 24.8 g; Sugar 17.4 g; Protein 0.8 g; Cholesterol 0 mg

Quick Cranberry Applesauce

Preparation Time: 10 minutes; Cooking Time: 5 minutes; Serve: 8
Ingredients:
- 2 cups fresh cranberries
- 4 lbs apples, peel, core, and slice

- 1/2 tsp ground cloves
- 1/4 cup fresh lemon juice

Directions:
1. Add all ingredients into the instant pot duo crisp and stir well.
2. Seal the pot with pressure cooking lid and cook on high pressure for 5 minutes.
3. Once done, allow to release pressure naturally. Remove lid.
4. Blend sauce using immersion blender until desired consistency gets.
5. Serve or store in an air-tight container.

Nutritional Value (Amount per Serving):
Calories 75; Fat 0.3 g; Carbohydrates 18.1 g; Sugar 12.8 g; Protein 0.4 g; Cholesterol 0 mg

Easy Rhubarb Compote

Preparation Time: 10 minutes; Cooking Time: 5 minutes; Serve: 4
Ingredients:
- 8 rhubarb stems, rinse, peel, and cut into 1-inch pieces
- 2 cinnamon sticks
- 1 tsp ginger, grated
- 1/2 cup water
- 1 cup of sugar

Directions:
1. Spray instant pot duo crisp from inside with cooking spray and set on sauté mode.
2. Add rhubarb and sauté for 2-3 minutes.
3. Add sugar and stir until sugar is melted. Once sugar is melted then add cinnamon, ginger, and water and stir well.
4. Seal the pot with pressure cooking lid and cook on high pressure for 2 minutes.
5. Once done, allow to release pressure naturally. Remove lid.
6. Discard cinnamon sticks. Once compote cools then store in the refrigerator before serving.

Nutritional Value (Amount per Serving):
Calories 243; Fat 0.5 g; Carbohydrates 62.3 g; Sugar 52.7 g; Protein 2.3 g; Cholesterol 0 mg

Mixed Berry Compote

Preparation Time: 10 minutes; Cooking Time: 5 minutes; Serve: 4
Ingredients:
- 1 lb mixed berries, fresh or frozen
- 2 tbsp liquid whey
- 1/2 cup sugar

Directions:
1. Add mixed berries and sugar in the inner pot of instant pot duo crisp and let it sit for 10 minutes.
2. Add liquid whey and stir well.
3. Seal the pot with pressure cooking lid and cook on high pressure for 5 minutes.
4. Once done, allow to release pressure naturally for 10 minutes then release remaining pressure using a quick release. Remove lid.
5. Once compote is cool then pour in air-tight container and store in the refrigerator.

Nutritional Value (Amount per Serving):
Calories 232; Fat 0 g; Carbohydrates 38.2 g; Sugar 33.9 g; Protein 21.8 g; Cholesterol 0 mg

Chia Peach Jam

Preparation Time: 10 minutes; Cooking Time: 15 minutes; Serve: 12
Ingredients:
- 2 cups ripe peaches, remove pit and mashed
- 2 tbsp chia seeds
- 1 tsp vanilla
- 2 tsp fresh lemon juice
- 2 tbsp maple syrup

Directions:

1. Add peaches, vanilla, lemon juice, and maple syrup into the inner pot of instant pot duo crisp and stir well.
2. Seal the pot with pressure cooking lid and cook on high pressure for 2 minutes.
3. Once done, allow to release pressure naturally. Remove lid.
4. Blend jam using immersion blender until smooth.
5. Add chia seeds and stir well. Set pot on sauté mode and cook for 3-5 minutes.
6. Once the jam is cool then pour in air-tight container and store in the refrigerator.

Nutritional Value (Amount per Serving):
Calories 43; Fat 1.5 g; Carbohydrates 6.6 g; Sugar 4.4 g; Protein 1 g; Cholesterol 0 mg

Chicken Broth

Preparation Time: 10 minutes; Cooking Time: 60 minutes; Serve: 3 quarts
Ingredients:
- 3 3/4 lbs chicken legs
- 3 quarts water
- 1 bay leaf
- 1 large onion, diced
- 4 garlic cloves, smashed
- 2 tbsp salt

Directions:
1. Add all ingredients into the inner pot of instant pot duo crips.
2. Seal the pot with pressure cooking lid and select pressure cook mode and cook on high pressure for 60 minutes.
3. Once done, allow to release pressure naturally. Remove lid.
4. Strain broth in containers and store in the fridge.

Nutritional Value (Amount per Serving):
Calories 461; Fat 16 g; Carbohydrates 10 g; Sugar 8 g; Protein 58 g; Cholesterol 0 mg

Turkey Stock

Preparation Time: 10 minutes; Cooking Time: 45 minutes; Serve: 2 quarts
Ingredients:
- 1 cooked turkey carcass, chopped
- 10 cups water
- 1 bay leaf
- 1/4 cup parsley
- 2 fresh thyme sprigs
- 1 tsp black peppercorns
- 2 carrots, chopped
- 1 leek, sliced
- 2 celery sticks, chopped
- 6 garlic cloves, smashed
- 1 onion, quartered

Directions:
1. Add all ingredients into the inner pot of instant pot duo crisp.
2. Seal the pot with pressure cooking lid and cook on high pressure for 45 minutes.
3. Once done, allow to release pressure naturally. Remove lid.
4. Strain stock in containers and store in the fridge.

Nutritional Value (Amount per Serving):
Calories 200; Fat 0 g; Carbohydrates 8 g; Sugar 8 g; Protein 40 g; Cholesterol 0 mg

Vegetable Stock

Preparation Time: 10 minutes; Cooking Time: 30 minutes; Serve: 2 1/2 quarts
Ingredients:
- 1 leek, chopped
- 2 carrots, peeled and chopped
- 2 celery ribs, chopped
- 2 onions, chopped
- 12 cups water
- 1 tsp black peppercorns
- 2 bay leaves
- 1 fresh thyme sprigs
- 2 fresh rosemary sprigs
- 1/4 cup parsley

- 3 garlic cloves, smashed

Directions:
1. Add all ingredients into the inner pot of instant pot duo crisp.
2. Seal the pot with pressure cooking lid and cook on high pressure for 30 minutes.
3. Once done, allow to release pressure naturally. Remove lid.
4. Strain stock in containers and store in the fridge.

Nutritional Value (Amount per Serving):
Calories 100; Fat 20 g; Carbohydrates 20 g; Sugar 20 g; Protein 0 g; Cholesterol 0 mg

Perfect Chicken Stock

Preparation Time: 10 minutes; Cooking Time: 40 minutes; Serve: 2 quarts
Ingredients:
- 2 lbs chicken carcasses
- 9s cups water
- 2 bay leaves
- 1 tsp black peppercorns
- 1 tsp dried rosemary
- 3 garlic cloves
- 1 celery stalk, chopped
- 2 carrots, peeled and chopped
- 1 onion, diced
- 1/4 cup parsley
- 2 tsp salt

Directions:
1. Add all ingredients into the inner pot of instant pot duo crisp.
2. Seal the pot with pressure cooking lid and cook on high pressure for 40 minutes.
3. Once done, allow to release pressure naturally. Remove lid.
4. Strain stock in containers and store in the fridge.

Nutritional Value (Amount per Serving):
Calories 78; Fat 4.5 g; Carbohydrates 5.9 g; Sugar 5.7 g; Protein 5.5 g; Cholesterol 0 mg

Beef Bone Broth

Preparation Time: 10 minutes; Cooking Time: 1 hour 30 minutes; Serve: 2 1/2 quarts
Ingredients:
- 3 lbs beef bones
- 12 cups water
- 2 bay leaf
- 1 tbsp apple cider vinegar
- 1 onion, quartered
- 6 garlic cloves, smashed
- 2 celery ribs, chopped
- 2 carrots, peeled and chopped
- 1 tsp sea salt

Directions:
1. Preheat the oven to 425 F.
2. Arrange beef bones on baking tray and roast in preheated oven for 30 minutes. Turn bones halfway through.
3. Add all ingredients into the inner pot of instant pot duo crisp.
4. Seal the pot with pressure cooking lid and cook on high pressure for 60 minutes.
5. Once done, allow to release pressure naturally. Remove lid.
6. Strain stock in containers and store in the fridge.

Nutritional Value (Amount per Serving):
Calories 384; Fat 13.7 g; Carbohydrates 9.1 g; Sugar 7 g; Protein 48.5 g; Cholesterol 0 mg

Chapter 9: Desserts

Delicious Apple Crisp

Preparation Time: 10 minutes; Cooking Time: 10 minutes; Serve: 4

Ingredients:

- 5 apples, peel and cut into bite-size pieces
- 1 tsp maple syrup
- 1/4 cup brown sugar
- 3/4 cup rolled oats
- 1/4 cup flour
- 1/4 cup butter
- 1 1/2 tsp cinnamon
- 1/4 tsp nutmeg
- 1/2 cup water
- 1/4 tsp salt

Directions:

1. Spray instant pot duo crisp from inside with cooking spray.
2. Add apple pieces into the pot. Sprinkle nutmeg, cinnamon, and maple syrup on top of apples.
3. Pour water over apple mixture.
4. Add butter in microwave-safe bowl and microwave until butter is melted.
5. Add oats, brown sugar, flour, and salt in melted butter and mix well.
6. Spread oat mixture evenly over apple mixture.
7. Seal the pot with pressure cooking lid and cook on high pressure for 5 minutes.
8. Once done, allow to release pressure naturally. Remove lid.
9. Seal the pot with air fryer lid and select air fry for 4 minutes.
10. Top with vanilla ice-cream and serve immediately.

Nutritional Value (Amount per Serving):
Calories 375; Fat 13.2 g; Carbohydrates 65.6 g; Sugar 39 g; Protein 3.8 g; Cholesterol 31 mg

Almond Coconut Cake

Preparation Time: 10 minutes; Cooking Time: 40 minutes; Serve: 8

Ingredients:

- 2 eggs, lightly beaten
- 1/2 cup heavy whipping cream
- 1/4 cup butter, melted
- 1 tsp vanilla
- 1 tsp baking powder
- 1/3 cup Swerve
- 1/2 cup shredded coconut
- 1 cup almond flour

Directions:

1. Spray a 6-inch baking dish with cooking spray and set aside.
2. In a mixing bowl, mix together almond flour, shredded coconut, sweetener, and baking powder.
3. Add egg, heavy cream, butter, and vanilla and mix until well combined.
4. Pour batter into the prepared dish and cover dish with foil.
5. Pour 2 cups of water into the inner pot of instant pot duo crisp then place steamer rack in the pot.
6. Place baking dish on top of the steamer rack.
7. Seal the pot with pressure cooking lid and cook on high pressure for 40 minutes.
8. Once done, allow to release pressure naturally for 10 minutes then release remaining pressure using a quick release. Remove lid.
9. Carefully remove the baking dish from the pot and let it cool for 20 minutes.
10. Slice and serve.

Nutritional Value (Amount per Serving):
Calories 197; Fat 17.9 g; Carbohydrates 4.5 g; Sugar 0.5 g; Protein 4.8 g; Cholesterol 66 mg

Choco Coconut Cupcake

Preparation Time: 10 minutes; Cooking Time: 10 minutes; Serve: 4
Ingredients:
- 1 egg, lightly beaten
- 2 tbsp coconut flour
- 2 tbsp cocoa powder
- 1/2 tsp vanilla
- 1/4 cup maple syrup
- 1/2 cup sun butter
- Pinch of salt

Directions:
1. In a bowl, whisk together sun butter, egg, vanilla, maple syrup, and salt.
2. Add coconut flour and cocoa powder and stir to combine.
3. Pour batter into the silicone muffin molds and place in instant pot air fryer basket. Place basket in the pot.
4. Seal the pot with air fryer lid and select bake mode and cook at 350 F for 10 minutes.
5. Serve and enjoy.

Nutritional Value (Amount per Serving):
   Calories 107; Fat 2.5 g; Carbohydrates 19.8 g; Sugar 12.4 g; Protein 2.7 g; Cholesterol 41 mg

Delicious Brownies Cupcake

Preparation Time: 10 minutes; Cooking Time: 20 minutes; Serve: 6
Ingredients:
- 2 eggs, lightly beaten
- 1 zucchini, shredded and squeeze out all liquid
- 1/4cup almond milk
- 1/4 cup maple syrup
- 1 cup sun butter
- 1/4 cup coconut flour
- 1/2 cup cocoa powder

Directions:
1. In a large bowl, mix together sun butter, milk, eggs, and maple syrup.
2. Add coconut flour, zucchini, and cocoa powder and stir until combined.
3. Pour batter into the silicone muffin molds and place in instant pot air fryer basket. Place basket in the pot.
4. Seal the pot with air fryer lid and select bake mode and cook at 350 F for 20 minutes.
5. Serve and enjoy.

Nutritional Value (Amount per Serving):
   Calories 151; Fat 5.8 g; Carbohydrates 29.9 g; Sugar 12.3 g; Protein 5.4 g; Cholesterol 56 mg

Creamy Choco Pots

Preparation Time: 10 minutes; Cooking Time: 15 minutes; Serve: 6
Ingredients:
- 5 egg yolks
- 4 tbsp sugar
- 1/2 cup milk
- 1 1/2 cups heavy cream
- 8 oz chocolate, melted
- Pinch of salt

Directions:
1. Add milk and cream in a saucepan and bring to simmer over medium-low heat.
2. In a bowl, whisk together sugar, egg yolks, and salt.
3. Slowly add egg yolks mixture in milk mixture and whisk constantly.
4. Add melted chocolate and whisk until combined.
5. Pour mixture into the 6 ramekins.
6. Pour 1 1/2 cups of water into the inner pot of instant pot duo crisp then place steamer rack in the pot.
7. Place ramekins on top of the steamer rack.

8. Seal the pot with pressure cooking lid and cook on high for 6 minutes.
9. Once done, allow to release pressure naturally. Remove lid.
10. Remove ramekins from the pot and let it cool completely then place in the refrigerator for 4 hours.
11. Top with whipped cream and serve.

Nutritional Value (Amount per Serving):
Calories 391; Fat 26.5 g; Carbohydrates 32.8 g; Sugar 28.5 g; Protein 6.4 g; Cholesterol 226 mg

Choco Cheesecake

Preparation Time: 10 minutes; Cooking Time: 40 minutes; Serve: 8
Ingredients:
- 2 eggs
- 1 lb cream cheese
- 1/2 cup sugar
- 3 tbsp butter, melted
- 3 tbsp sugar
- 4.5 oz graham crackers
- 10 oz chocolate, melted

Directions:
1. Spray cheesecake pan with cooking spray and line with parchment paper.
2. Add 3 tbsp sugar and graham crackers into the food processor and process until crumble. Add butter and mix well.
3. Add cracker mixture into the prepared cake pan and spread evenly and press down with a spatula. Place in refrigerator for 30 minutes.
4. In a large bowl, add cream cheese and sugar and beat until smooth.
5. Add one by one egg in cheese mixture and stir well. Add melted chocolate and stir to combine.
6. Pour batter on top of crust and spread well.
7. Pour 2 cups of water into the inner pot of instant pot duo crisp then place steamer rack in the pot.
8. Place cake pan on top of the steamer rack.
9. Seal the pot with pressure cooking lid and cook on high for 15 minutes.
10. Once done, release pressure using a quick release. Remove lid.
11. Carefully remove cake pan from the pot and let it cool completely then place in the refrigerator for 5 hours.
12. Slice and serve.

Nutritional Value (Amount per Serving):
Calories 560; Fat 37.3 g; Carbohydrates 48.5 g; Sugar 37 g; Protein 9.5 g; Cholesterol 123 mg

Blueberry Bread Pudding

Preparation Time: 10 minutes; Cooking Time: 30 minutes; Serve: 6
Ingredients:
- 2 eggs, beaten
- 4 bread slices, cut into cubes
- 1/2 tsp vanilla
- 1/2 cup fresh blueberries
- 2 cups warm milk
- 1/2 tsp cinnamon
- 1/3 cup brown sugar
- 1/4 cup almonds, sliced
- 1/4 tsp salt

Directions:
1. Spray casserole dish with cooking spray and set aside.
2. In a bowl, mix together bread, almonds, and blueberries.
3. In another bowl add eggs, vanilla, cinnamon, salt and brown sugar and stir until combined.
4. Pour egg mixture over bread mixture and mix well.

5. Pour bread mixture into the prepared dish and cover dish with foil.
6. Pour 3 cups of water into the inner pot of instant pot duo crisp then place steamer rack in the pot.
7. Place dish on top of the steamer rack.
8. Seal the pot with pressure cooking lid and cook on low for 20 minutes.
9. Once done, release pressure using a quick release. Remove lid.
10. Serve warm and enjoy.

Nutritional Value (Amount per Serving):
Calories 140; Fat 5.4 g; Carbohydrates 17.9 g; Sugar 13.3 g; Protein 5.9 g; Cholesterol 61 mg

Chocolate Chip Pudding

Preparation Time: 10 minutes; Cooking Time: 15 minutes; Serve: 6
Ingredients:
- 2 eggs
- 1 egg yolk
- 3 tbsp cocoa powder
- 3/4 cup sugar
- 4 tbsp butter
- 1/2 cup chocolate chips, semisweet
- 1 1/4 cups half and half
- 1 tsp vanilla
- 2 tbsp cornstarch
- 1/4 cup brown sugar

Directions:
1. Spray 6 ramekins with cooking and set aside.
2. In a bowl, beat together sugar and butter until smooth.
3. Add one by one egg and beat until combined.
4. Sift together cocoa powder and cornstarch and add into the bowl and beat until combined.
5. Add half and half and vanilla and stir until combined.
6. Pour batter into the prepared ramekins and top each with chocolate chips.
7. Cover ramekins with foil. Pour 2 cups of water into the inner pot of instant pot duo crisp then place steamer rack in the pot.
8. Place ramekins on top of the steamer rack
9. Seal the pot with pressure cooking lid and cook on low for 10 minutes.
10. Once done, release pressure using a quick release. Remove lid.
11. Once it cool then place in the fridge for 4 hours.
12. Serve and enjoy.

Nutritional Value (Amount per Serving):
Calories 373; Fat 20.2 g; Carbohydrates 45.6 g; Sugar 38.4 g; Protein 5.5 g; Cholesterol 132 mg

Simple Rice Pudding

Preparation Time: 10 minutes; Cooking Time: 10 minutes; Serve: 6
Ingredients:
- 1 cup of rice
- 1/4 tsp cinnamon
- 1 tsp vanilla extract
- 1/3 cup sugar
- 3 cups of milk
- 2 tbsp ghee

Directions:
1. Add ghee into the inner pot of instant pot duo crisp and set pot on sauté mode.
2. Add milk and bring to boil. Add rice stir well.
3. Seal the pot with pressure cooking lid and cook on high for 10 minutes.
4. Once done, allow to release pressure naturally. Remove lid.
5. Stir in vanilla and sugar.
6. Sprinkle cinnamon and serve.

Nutritional Value (Amount per Serving):
Calories 255; Fat 7 g; Carbohydrates 41.9 g; Sugar 16.7 g; Protein 6.2 g; Cholesterol 21 mg

Sliced Apples

Preparation Time: 10 minutes; Cooking Time: 3 minutes; Serve: 6
Ingredients:

- 3 large apples, peeled, cored and halved
- 1/2 tsp ground cardamom
- 1 cup apple cider
- 1/2 cup sugar
- 1/2 tsp vanilla
- 1-inch cinnamon stick

Directions:
1. Add all ingredients into the inner pot instant pot duo crisp and stir well.
2. Seal the pot with pressure cooking lid and cook on high for 3 minutes.
3. Once done, release pressure using a quick release. Remove lid.
4. Serve and enjoy.

Nutritional Value (Amount per Serving):
Calories 144; Fat 0.3 g; Carbohydrates 38 g; Sugar 32.8 g; Protein 0.4 g; Cholesterol 0 mg

Vanilla Tapioca Pudding

Preparation Time: 10 minutes; Cooking Time: 9 minutes; Serve: 4
Ingredients:

- 1/2 cup pearl tapioca
- 1/2 tsp vanilla
- 2 egg yolks
- 1/2 cup sugar
- 1/2 cup milk
- 1 1/2 cups water
- 1/4 tsp salt

Directions:
1. Add water and tapioca in the inner pot of instant pot duo crisp and stir well.
2. Seal the pot with pressure cooking lid and cook on high for 9 minutes.
3. Once done, allow to release pressure naturally. Remove lid.
4. Add salt and sugar and stir well.
5. In a bowl, whisk together milk and egg yolk and pour in the pot through a strainer.
6. Set pot on sauté mode and cook mixture starts to boil, stir constantly.
7. Turn off the pot. Add vanilla and stir well.
8. Allow to cool completely. Place pudding in the refrigerator for 2 hours before serving.
9. Serve and enjoy.

Nutritional Value (Amount per Serving):
Calories 206; Fat 2.9 g; Carbohydrates 43.7 g; Sugar 27.1 g; Protein 2.7 g; Cholesterol 107 mg

Pumpkin Brown Rice Pudding

Preparation Time: 10 minutes; Cooking Time: 25 minutes; Serve: 6
Ingredients:

- 1 cup brown rice, rinse and soak for 30 minutes
- 1 tsp pumpkin pie spice
- 1 cup pumpkin puree
- 1-inch cinnamon stick
- 1/2 tsp vanilla
- 1/2 cup maple syrup
- 1/2 cup water
- 3 cups of milk
- 1/8 tsp salt

Directions:
1. Add water and milk into the inner pot of instant pot duo crisp and stir well.
2. Add cinnamon, rice and salt and stir well.
3. Seal the pot with pressure cooking lid and cook on high for 20 minutes.
4. Once done, allow to release pressure naturally. Remove lid.

5. Set pot on sauté mode. Add pumpkin pie spice, maple syrup and pumpkin puree and cook for 3-5 minutes.
6. Turn off heat. Add vanilla and stir well.
7. Top with whipped cream and serve.

Nutritional Value (Amount per Serving):
Calories 263; Fat 3.6 g; Carbohydrates 52.2 g; Sugar 22.6 g; Protein 6.9 g; Cholesterol 10 mg

Choco Coconut Rice Pudding

Preparation Time: 10 minutes; Cooking Time: 7 minutes; Serve: 6
Ingredients:
- 1 cup Arborio rice
- 1/2 tsp vanilla
- 2 cups of water
- 2 tbsp butter
- 1/3 cup sugar
- 3/4 cup coconut, shredded
- 14 oz coconut milk
- Chocolate syrup

Directions:
1. Add butter into the inner pot of instant pot duo crisp and set pot on sauté mode.
2. Add rice and sauté for 1 minute.
3. Add vanilla and water and stir well.
4. Seal the pot with pressure cooking lid and cook on high for 6 minutes.
5. Once done, release pressure using a quick release. Remove lid.
6. Add coconut milk, sugar, and shredded coconut, stir well.
7. Drizzle rice pudding with chocolate syrup and serve.

Nutritional Value (Amount per Serving):
Calories 518; Fat 23.7 g; Carbohydrates 74.1 g; Sugar 38.8 g; Protein 5 g; Cholesterol 10 mg

Delicious Fruitcake

Preparation Time: 10 minutes; Cooking Time: 60 minutes; Serve: 6
Ingredients:
- 1/2 lb dried mixed fruit
- 2 cups self-rising flour
- 1/2 tsp baking powder
- 2 cups fruit juice

Directions:
1. Spray a baking dish with cooking spray and set aside.
2. In a bowl, mix together fruit juice and dried mixed fruit and soak overnight.
3. Add flour and baking powder in dried fruit mixture and fold well.
4. Pour batter into the prepared dish.
5. Pour 1 1/2 cups water into the inner pot of instant pot duo crisp then place steamer rack in the pot.
6. Place baking dish on top of the steamer rack.
7. Seal the pot with pressure cooking lid and cook on high for 60 minutes.
8. Once done, allow to release pressure naturally. Remove lid.
9. Slice and serve.

Nutritional Value (Amount per Serving):
Calories 227; Fat 0.6 g; Carbohydrates 50.5 g; Sugar 8.1 g; Protein 4.9 g; Cholesterol 0 mg

Quinoa Pudding

Preparation Time: 10 minutes; Cooking Time: 17 minutes; Serve: 2
Ingredients:
- 1/2 cup quinoa, rinsed and drained
- 1/4 cup condensed milk
- 2 1/2 cups milk
- 2 tsp ghee
- 1/4 tsp cardamom powder
- 2 tbsp almonds, chopped

Directions:

1. Add ghee into the inner pot of instant pot duo crisp and stir well.
2. Add quinoa and sauté for 2 minutes. Add milk and stir well.
3. Seal the pot with pressure cooking lid and cook on high for 10 minutes.
4. Once done, allow to release pressure naturally. Remove lid.
5. Add cardamom, condensed milk, and almonds. Stir well.
6. Set pot on sauté mode and cook for 3-5 minutes.
7. Serve and enjoy.

Nutritional Value (Amount per Serving):

Calories 504; Fat 19.4 g; Carbohydrates 64.5 g; Sugar 34.8 g; Protein 20.3 g; Cholesterol 49 mg

Cherry Rice Pudding

Preparation Time: 10 minutes; Cooking Time: 20 minutes; Serve: 6

Ingredients:

- 1 cup black rice, rinsed
- 1/2 cup cherries, dried
- 2 eggs
- 1 tsp vanilla
- 3/4 cup half and half
- 1 tbsp butter
- 1 1/2 cups water
- 1/2 cup sugar
- 1 cup milk
- Pinch of salt

Directions:

1. Add butter, water, rice, and salt into the inner pot of instant pot duo crisp and stir well.
2. Seal the pot with pressure cooking lid and cook on high for 20 minutes.
3. Once done, allow to release pressure naturally. Remove lid.
4. Add sugar and milk and stir well.
5. Set pot on sauté mode and add vanilla, half and half and eggs. Stir constantly until begins to boil.
6. Turn off heat. Add cherries and stir well.
7. Stir and serve.

Nutritional Value (Amount per Serving):

Calories 251; Fat 7.9 g; Carbohydrates 40.6 g; Sugar 18.9 g; Protein 5.5 g; Cholesterol 75 mg

Cinnamon Chocolate Cake

Preparation Time: 10 minutes; Cooking Time: 30 minutes; Serve: 6

Ingredients:

- 2 large eggs
- 4 tbsp butter, melted
- 1 tsp baking powder
- 1 tsp cayenne pepper
- 1 tsp ground cinnamon
- 4 tbsp cocoa powder
- 1 1/2 cups flour
- 2 cups hot water
- 1 cup milk
- 1/4 cup powdered sugar
- Pinch of salt

Directions:

1. Spray a baking dish with cooking spray and set aside.
2. In a bowl, beat eggs.
3. In another bowl, mix together baking powder, cinnamon, cocoa powder, flour, salt, sugar, and cayenne,
4. Slowly add dry ingredients into the egg and fold well.
5. Add milk and butter stir to combine.
6. Pour batter into the prepared dish.
7. Pour hot water into the inner pot of instant pot duo crisp then place steamer rack in the pot.

8. Place baking dish on top of the steamer rack.
9. Seal the pot with pressure cooking lid and cook on high for 30 minutes.
10. Once done, release pressure using a quick release. Remove lid.
11. Serve and enjoy.

Nutritional Value (Amount per Serving):
Calories 256; Fat 11 g; Carbohydrates 33.8 g; Sugar 7.1 g; Protein 7.5 g; Cholesterol 86 mg

Creamy Coconut Rice Pudding

Preparation Time: 10 minutes; Cooking Time: 20 minutes; Serve: 6
Ingredients:
- 1 cup rice, rinsed and drained
- 1 tsp vanilla
- 1 1/4 cups water
- 2 cups almond milk
- 4 tbsp maple syrup
- 1/2 cup coconut cream
- Pinch of salt

Directions:
1. Add all ingredients except coconut cream and vanilla into the inner pot of instant pot duo crisp and stir well.
2. Seal the pot with pressure cooking lid and cook on high 20 minutes.
3. Once done, allow to release pressure naturally. Remove lid.
4. Add coconut cream and vanilla and stir well.
5. Serve and enjoy.

Nutritional Value (Amount per Serving):
Calories 379; Fat 24.1 g; Carbohydrates 39.2 g; Sugar 10.7 g; Protein 6.9 g; Cholesterol 0 mg

Coconut Almond Risotto

Preparation Time: 10 minutes; Cooking Time: 5 minutes; Serve: 4
Ingredients:
- 1 cup Arborio rice
- 1/4 cup sugar
- 1 cup of coconut milk
- 2 cups almond milk
- 1/4 cup coconut flakes, toasted
- 1 1/2 tsp vanilla

Directions:
1. Add coconut milk and almond milk into the inner pot of instant pot and then set a pot on sauté mode.
2. Stir milk constantly and bring to boil.
3. Add rice and stir well.
4. Seal the pot with pressure cooking lid and cook on high for 5 minutes.
5. Once done, release pressure using a quick release. Remove lid.
6. Stir in vanilla and sugar.
7. Top with coconut flakes and serve.

Nutritional Value (Amount per Serving):
Calories 379; Fat 16.3 g; Carbohydrates 54.6 g; Sugar 15 g; Protein 4.7 g; Cholesterol 0 mg

Chocolate Cake

Preparation Time: 10 minutes; Cooking Time: 20 minutes; Serve: 6
Ingredients:
- 3 eggs
- 1 cup almond flour
- 1 tsp baking powder
- 1/4 cup walnuts, chopped
- 1/4 cup cocoa powder
- 1/4 cup powdered sugar
- 1/4 cup coconut oil
- 1/3 cup heavy whipping cream

Directions:

1. In a mixing bowl, add all ingredients and whisk until combined.
2. Spray baking dish with cooking spray. Pour batter into the baking dish.
3. Pour 2 cups water into the inner pot of instant pot duo crisp then place steamer rack in the pot.
4. Place baking dish on top of the steamer rack.
5. Seal the pot with pressure cooking lid and cook on high for 20 minutes.
6. Once done, allow to release pressure naturally. Remove lid.
7. Serve and enjoy.

Nutritional Value (Amount per Serving):
Calories 305; Fat 26.2 g; Carbohydrates 12.2 g; Sugar 5.2 g; Protein 8.8 g; Cholesterol 91 mg

Easy Coconut Pumpkin Pudding

Preparation Time: 10 minutes; Cooking Time: 14 minutes; Serve: 4
Ingredients:
- 4 cups pumpkin, cubed
- 1/2 cup brown sugar
- 1/2 cup almond milk
- 2 tbsp ghee
- 2 tbsp raisins
- 1/2 cup desiccated coconut
- 2 tbsp almonds, chopped
- 1/2 tsp cardamom powder

Directions:
1. Add ghee into the inner pot of instant pot duo crisp and set pot on sauté mode.
2. Add pumpkin and sauté for 2-3 minutes. Add almond milk and stir well.
3. Seal the pot with pressure cooking lid and cook on high for 5 minutes.
4. Once done, release pressure using a quick release. Remove lid.
5. Mash pumpkin using the potato masher.
6. Set pot on sauté mode. Add sugar and cook for 2-3 minutes.
7. Add remaining ingredients and stir well and cook for 2-3 minutes.
8. Serve and enjoy.

Nutritional Value (Amount per Serving):
Calories 332; Fat 18 g; Carbohydrates 44.5 g; Sugar 29.7 g; Protein 4.5 g; Cholesterol 16 mg

Easy Vanilla Peach Cake

Preparation Time: 10 minutes; Cooking Time: 30 minutes; Serve: 6
Ingredients:
- 14.5 oz can peaches in juice, cut peaches in half
- 1 cup of water
- 1/4 cup butter, cut into cubes
- 1/2 box vanilla cake mix

Directions:
1. Spray baking dish with cooking spray.
2. Add peaches into the baking dish. Sprinkle cake mix over the peaches.
3. Spread butter on top of cake mix. Cover baking dish with foil.
4. Pour water into the inner pot of instant pot duo crisp. Place steamer rack into the pot.
5. Place baking dish on top of the steamer rack.
6. Seal the pot with pressure cooking lid and cook on high for 25 minutes.
7. Once done, allow to release pressure naturally for 10 minutes then release remaining pressure using a quick release. Remove lid.
8. Remove aluminum foil from the baking dish.
9. Seal the pot with air fryer lid and select broil mode and cook for 5 minutes.
10. Serve and enjoy.

Nutritional Value (Amount per Serving):
Calories 205; Fat 7.7 g; Carbohydrates 34.4 g; Sugar 21.3 g; Protein 0.5 g; Cholesterol 20 mg

Cinnamon Apple Crisp

Preparation Time: 10 minutes; Cooking Time: 9 minutes; Serve: 4
Ingredients:

- 2 cups apples, peeled and chopped
- 1/4 cup brown sugar
- 1/4 tsp cornstarch
- 1/2 tsp vanilla
- 1/4 tsp cinnamon
- For topping:
- 1 tsp vanilla
- 1/4 cup brown sugar
- 1/3 cup flour
- 2 tbsp butter
- Pinch of salt

Directions:

1. Spray an oven-safe baking dish with cooking spray.
2. Add apples, cornstarch, vanilla, brown sugar, and cinnamon into the prepared dish and stir to combine.
3. Pour 1 cup of water into the inner pot of instant pot duo crisp then place steamer rack in the pot.
4. Place baking dish on top of the steamer rack.
5. Seal the pot with pressure cooking lid and cook on high for 4 minutes.
6. Once done, release pressure using a quick release. Remove lid.
7. Mix together topping ingredients and sprinkle over apple mixture.
8. Seal the pot with air fryer lid and select broil mode and cook for 5 minutes.
9. Serve and enjoy.

Nutritional Value (Amount per Serving):
Calories 218; Fat 6.1 g; Carbohydrates 41.5 g; Sugar 29.3 g; Protein 1.5 g; Cholesterol 15 mg

Sweetened Rice Pudding

Preparation Time: 10 minutes; Cooking Time: 7 minutes; Serve: 8
Ingredients:

- 2 cups of rice
- 6 1/2 cups milk
- 2 cinnamon stick
- 10 oz condensed milk
- 1/2 cup sugar
- Pinch of salt

Directions:

1. Add 6 cups of milk, sugar, rice, cinnamon sticks, and salt into the inner pot of instant pot duo crisp and stir well.
2. Seal the pot with pressure cooking lid and cook on high for 2 minutes.
3. Once done, allow to release pressure naturally. Remove lid.
4. Add condensed milk and stir well.
5. Set pot on sauté mode and cook for 5 minutes.
6. Stir in remaining milk and serve.

Nutritional Value (Amount per Serving):
Calories 433; Fat 7.5 g; Carbohydrates 79.9 g; Sugar 40.8 g; Protein 12.7 g; Cholesterol 28 mg

Oats Cookies

Preparation Time: 10 minutes; Cooking Time: 15 minutes; Serve: 3
Ingredients:

- 1 cup quick oats
- 2 tbsp milk
- 2 ripe bananas, mashed
- 2 tbsp coconut shredded

Directions:

1. Add all ingredients into the mixing bowl and mix until combined.
2. Line instant pot air fryer basket with parchment paper or foil.

3. Spoon cookie dough onto parchment paper. Place air fryer basket in the pot.
4. Seal air fryer basket with air fryer lid and select bake mode and cook at 350 F for 15 minutes.
5. Serve and enjoy.

Nutritional Value (Amount per Serving):
Calories 198; Fat 3.6 g; Carbohydrates 38.8 g; Sugar 12 g; Protein 4.9 g; Cholesterol 1 mg

Baked Pineapple Slices

Preparation Time: 10 minutes; Cooking Time: 10 minutes; Serve: 2
Ingredients:

- 2 pineapple slices
- 1/2 tsp cinnamon
- 1/4 cup brown sugar

Directions:
1. Add cinnamon and brown sugar in a zip-lock bag and mix well.
2. Add pineapple slices in the zip-lock bag and shake well to coat. Seal bag and place in the fridge for 30 minutes.
3. Spray instant pot air fryer basket with cooking spray.
4. Place pineapple slices in the air fryer basket and place basket in the pot.
5. Seal the pot with air fryer lid and select bake mode and cook at 350 F for 20 minutes. Turn pineapple slices halfway through.
6. Serve and enjoy.

Nutritional Value (Amount per Serving):
Calories 152; Fat 0.2 g; Carbohydrates 39.9 g; Sugar 33.9 g; Protein 0.9 g; Cholesterol 0 mg

Creamy Apple Rhubarb Pudding

Preparation Time: 10 minutes; Cooking Time: 15 minutes; Serve: 6
Ingredients:

- 1 cup Arborio rice
- 2 rhubarb stalks, chopped
- 1/2 apple, peeled and chopped
- 1/2 cup water
- 1 cinnamon stick
- 1 tsp vanilla
- 1 1/2 cup milk
- 1 tsp cinnamon

Directions:
1. Add all ingredients into the inner pot of instant pot duo crisp and stir well.
2. Seal the pot with pressure cooking lid and cook on high for 15 minutes.
3. Once done, release pressure using a quick release. Remove lid.
4. Stir well and serve.

Nutritional Value (Amount per Serving):
Calories 161; Fat 1.5 g; Carbohydrates 31.9 g; Sugar 5 g; Protein 4.3 g; Cholesterol 5 mg

Blueberry Muffins

Preparation Time: 10 minutes; Cooking Time: 15 minutes; Serve: 4
Ingredients:

- 1 egg
- 3/4 cup blueberries
- 1/2 tsp vanilla
- 2 tbsp erythritol
- 1 tsp baking powder
- 2/3 cup almond flour
- 3 tbsp butter, melted
- 1/3 cup almond milk

Directions:
1. Add all ingredients into the large bowl and mix until combined.
2. Pour batter into the silicone muffin molds.
3. Place in instant pot air fryer basket and place basket in the pot.

4. Seal the pot with air fryer lid and select bake mode and cook at 320 F for 15 minutes.
5. Serve and enjoy.

Nutritional Value (Amount per Serving):
   Calories 268; Fat 23.5 g; Carbohydrates 17.3 g; Sugar 11 g; Protein 6.1 g; Cholesterol 64 mg

Vanilla Pumpkin Pudding

Preparation Time: 10 minutes; Cooking Time: 20 minutes; Serve: 6
Ingredients:
- 2 eggs
- 1/2 cup almond milk
- 1/2 tsp vanilla
- 1/2 tsp pumpkin pie spice
- 14 oz pumpkin puree
- 1/4 cup sugar

Directions:
1. Grease 6-inch baking dish with cooking spray and set aside.
2. In a large bowl, whisk eggs with remaining ingredients.
3. Pour mixture into the prepared dish and cover with foil.
4. Pour 1 1/2 cups of water into the inner pot of instant pot duo crisp then place a steamer rack in the pot.
5. Place dish on top of the steamer rack.
6. Seal the pot with pressure cooking lid and cook on high for 20 minutes.
7. Once done, allow to release pressure naturally for 10 minutes then release remaining pressure using a quick release. Remove lid.
8. Carefully remove dish from the pot and let it cool completely then place in the refrigerator for 5 hours before serving.
9. Serve and enjoy.

Nutritional Value (Amount per Serving):
   Calories 122; Fat 6.4 g; Carbohydrates 15 g; Sugar 11.3 g; Protein 3.1 g; Cholesterol 55 mg

Cinnamon Bread Pudding

Preparation Time: 10 minutes; Cooking Time: 15 minutes; Serve: 2
Ingredients:
- 3 eggs, beaten
- 4 cups bread cube
- 3 tbsp raisins
- 1 cup almond milk
- 1/2 tsp cinnamon
- 1/2 tsp vanilla
- 1 tsp olive oil
- Pinch of salt

Directions:
1. Place bread cubes in the oven-safe casserole dish.
2. In a bowl, mix remaining ingredients and pour over bread cubes. Cover dish with foil.
3. Pour 2 cups of water into the inner pot of instant pot duo crisp than place steamer rack in the pot.
4. Place casserole dish on top of the steamer rack.
5. Seal the pot with pressure cooking lid and cook on high for 15 minutes.
6. Once done, allow to release pressure naturally for 10 minutes then release remaining pressure using a quick release. Remove lid.
7. Serve and enjoy.

Nutritional Value (Amount per Serving):
   Calories 635; Fat 37.6 g; Carbohydrates 58.5 g; Sugar 12.7 g; Protein 11.5 g; Cholesterol 246 mg

Cranberry Coconut Pudding

Preparation Time: 10 minutes; Cooking Time: 20 minutes; Serve: 6
Ingredients:

- 1 cup brown rice, rinsed and drained
- 1/2 cup coconut milk
- 1 1/2 cups milk
- 1 cup cranberries
- 1/4 cup sugar
- 1/2 tsp cinnamon
- 1/2 cup water

Directions:
1. Add all ingredients into the inner pot instant pot duo crisp and stir well.
2. Seal the pot with pressure cooking lid and cook on high for 20 minutes.
3. Once done, allow to release pressure naturally. Remove lid.
4. Stir and serve.

Nutritional Value (Amount per Serving):
   Calories 233; Fat 6.9 g; Carbohydrates 38.4 g; Sugar 12.4 g; Protein 4.9 g; Cholesterol 5 mg

Vermicelli Pudding

Preparation Time: 10 minutes; Cooking Time: 3 minutes; Serve: 6
Ingredients:
- 1/3 cup vermicelli, roasted
- 2 tbsp ghee
- 1/4 cup cashews, slice
- 1/4 cup shredded coconut
- 1/4 cup raisins
- 1/4 cup almonds
- 1/4 cup sugar
- 5 cups of milk

Directions:
1. Add ghee into the inner pot of instant pot duo crisp and set pot on sauté mode.
2. Add cashews and almonds and sauté for a minute.
3. Add raisins, coconut, and vermicelli, 3 cups milk, and sugar. Stir well.
4. Seal the pot with pressure cooking lid and cook on high for 2 minutes.
5. Once done, allow to release pressure naturally. Remove lid.
6. Add remaining milk and stir well.
7. Serve and enjoy.

Nutritional Value (Amount per Serving):
   Calories 268; Fat 14.3 g; Carbohydrates 28.7 g; Sugar 21.9 g; Protein 9.1 g; Cholesterol 28 mg

Raspberry Cake

Preparation Time: 10 minutes; Cooking Time: 10 minutes; Serve: 8
Ingredients:
- 1/2 cup raspberries
- 5 egg yolks
- 1/4 cup heavy cream
- 1/2 cup coconut flour
- 1 tsp baking powder
- 3 tsp liquid stevia
- 1/4 cup butter
- 1/4 cup coconut oil
- 1/2 tsp vanilla

Directions:
1. Add all dry ingredients except raspberries in a large bowl and mix well.
2. Add all wet ingredients and beat using a blender until well combined.
3. Spray 6-inch spring-form baking dish with cooking spray.
4. Pour batter in the prepared baking dish and top with raspberries.
5. Pour 2 cups of water into the inner pot of instant pot duo crisp then place steamer rack in the pot.
6. Place baking dish on top of the steamer rack.
7. Seal the pot with pressure cooking lid and cook on high for 10 minutes.
8. Once done, release pressure using a quick release. Remove lid.
9. Serve and enjoy.

Nutritional Value (Amount per Serving):

Calories 192; Fat 17.6 g; Carbohydrates 6.7 g; Sugar 0.4 g; Protein 2.9 g; Cholesterol 152 mg

Chocolate Rice Pudding

Preparation Time: 10 minutes; Cooking Time: 15 minutes; Serve: 6

Ingredients:

- 2 eggs, beaten
- 1 cup rice, rinsed
- 2 tbsp cocoa powder
- 1/2 tsp vanilla
- 5 cups of coconut milk
- 1 tbsp coconut oil
- 1/2 cup sugar

Directions:

1. Add all ingredients into the inner pot of instant pot duo crisp and set pot on sauté mode. Stir constantly and bring to boil.
2. Seal the pot with pressure cooking lid and cook on high for 15 minutes.
3. Once done, allow to release pressure naturally. Remove lid.
4. Stir well and serve.

Nutritional Value (Amount per Serving):

Calories 681; Fat 51.9 g; Carbohydrates 53.5 g; Sugar 23.6 g; Protein 9 g; Cholesterol 55 mg

Choco Fudge

Preparation Time: 10 minutes; Cooking Time: 15 minutes; Serve: 8

Ingredients:

- 5 eggs
- 1/2 cup cocoa powder
- 1/2 cup dark chocolate, chopped
- 2 cups almond flour
- 1 tsp baking soda
- 1/2 tsp vanilla
- 2 tbsp erythritol
- 3/4 tsp baking powder
- 1/2 cup almond milk
- Pinch of salt

Directions:

1. Add all dry ingredients into the large bowl and mix to combine.
2. Add remaining ingredients and beat using a blender until well combined.
3. Pour 2 cups of water into the inner pot of instant pot duo crisp then place steamer rack in the pot.
4. Pour batter in the oven-safe baking dish and place on top of the steamer rack.
5. Seal the pot with pressure cooking lid and cook on high for 15 minutes.
6. Once done, release pressure using a quick release. Remove lid.
7. Serve and enjoy.

Nutritional Value (Amount per Serving):

Calories 311; Fat 23.4 g; Carbohydrates 17.7 g; Sugar 7.5 g; Protein 11.6 g; Cholesterol 105 mg

Delicious Lime Pudding

Preparation Time: 10 minutes; Cooking Time: 3 minutes; Serve: 4

Ingredients:

- 1/4 cup coconut milk
- 3/4 tsp lime zest, grated
- 1/2 tsp orange extract
- 1 tbsp swerve
- 1/4 cup heavy whipping cream
- 1/4 cup coconut cream
- 1 tsp agar powder
- 1 tbsp coconut oil

Directions:

1. Add coconut oil into the inner pot of instant pot duo crisp and set the pot on sauté mode.
2. Add coconut milk, whipping cream, and coconut cream to the pot and stir constantly.
3. Add orange extract, swerve and agar powder. Stir constantly and cook for 2-3 minutes.
4. Turn off the pot and pour pot mixture into the ramekins.

5. Sprinkle lime zest on top of each ramekin.
6. Place ramekins in the fridge for 1-2 hours.
7. Serve and enjoy.

Nutritional Value (Amount per Serving):
Calories 159; Fat 12.8 g; Carbohydrates 11.6 g; Sugar 10.1 g; Protein 0.7 g; Cholesterol 10 mg

Thai Coconut Rice

Preparation Time: 10 minutes; Cooking Time: 8 minutes; Serve: 4
Ingredients:
- 1 cup Thai sweet rice
- 14 oz coconut milk
- 1 1/2 cups water
- 1/2 tsp cornstarch
- 4 tbsp pure sugar cane
- Pinch of salt

Directions:
1. Add water and rice into the inner pot of instant pot duo crisp and stir well.
2. Seal the pot with pressure cooking lid and cook on high for 3 minutes.
3. Once done, allow to release pressure naturally. Remove lid.
4. Meanwhile, heat coconut milk, sugar, and salt into the saucepan over medium heat until the sugar is dissolved. Set aside.
5. Add the half coconut milk mixture into the rice and stir it well.
6. Seal the pot with pressure cooking lid and cook on high for 5 minutes.
7. Once done, release pressure using a quick release. Remove lid.
8. Serve and enjoy.

Nutritional Value (Amount per Serving):
Calories 299; Fat 26.7 g; Carbohydrates 16.3 g; Sugar 8.3 g; Protein 2.8 g; Cholesterol 0 mg

Buckwheat Cobbler

Preparation Time: 10 minutes; Cooking Time: 12 minutes; Serve: 6
Ingredients:
- 1/2 cup dry buckwheat
- 2 1/2 lbs apples, cut into chunks
- 1/4 tsp nutmeg
- 1/4 tsp ground ginger
- 1 1/2 tsp cinnamon
- 1 1/2 cups water
- 1/4 cup dates, chopped

Directions:
1. Add all ingredients into the inner pot instant pot duo crisp and stir well.
2. Seal the pot with pressure cooking lid and cook on high for 12 minutes.
3. Once done, release pressure using a quick release. Remove lid.
4. Stir well and serve.

Nutritional Value (Amount per Serving):
Calories 119; Fat 0.6 g; Carbohydrates 29.2 g; Sugar 14.4 g; Protein 2.1 g; Cholesterol 0 mg

Vanilla Strawberry Cobbler

Preparation Time: 10 minutes; Cooking Time: 12 minutes; Serve: 2
Ingredients:
- 1/2 cup strawberries, sliced
- 1 1/4 cup all-purpose flour
- 3/4 cup milk
- 1 1/2 tsp baking powder
- 1/2 cup sugar
- 1/2 tsp vanilla
- 1/3 cup butter

Directions:
1. In a mixing bowl, add all ingredients except strawberries and mix well.
2. Add strawberries and fold well.

3. Spray 3 ramekins with cooking spray then pour batter into the ramekins.
4. Pour 1 1/2 cups water into the inner pot of instant pot duo crisp then place steamer rack into the pot.
5. Place ramekins on top of the steamer rack.
6. Seal the pot with pressure cooking lid and cook on high for 12 minutes.
7. Once done, allow to release pressure naturally. Remove lid.
8. Serve and enjoy.

Nutritional Value (Amount per Serving):
Calories 807; Fat 33.5 g; Carbohydrates 118.8 g; Sugar 56.2 g; Protein 11.6 g; Cholesterol 89 mg

Cinnamon Peach Cobbler

Preparation Time: 10 minutes; Cooking Time: 10 minutes; Serve: 6
Ingredients:
- 20 oz can peach pie filling
- 1 1/2 tsp cinnamon
- 1/2 cup butter, melted
- 15 oz vanilla cake mix
- 1 tsp nutmeg

Directions:
1. Spray inner pot of instant pot duo crisp with cooking spray.
2. Add peach pie filling into the pot.
3. In a mixing bowl, mix together the remaining ingredients and sprinkle over peaches.
4. Seal the pot with pressure cooking lid and cook on high for 10 minutes.
5. Once done, release pressure using a quick release. Remove lid.
6. Serve and enjoy.

Nutritional Value (Amount per Serving):
Calories 453; Fat 15.5 g; Carbohydrates 78 g; Sugar 48.7 g; Protein 0.2 g; Cholesterol 41 mg

Pear Apple Crisp

Preparation Time: 10 minutes; Cooking Time: 10 minutes; Serve: 4
Ingredients:
- 2 pears, cut into chunks
- 4 apples, peel and cut into chunks
- 3/4 tsp cinnamon
- 1/4 cup date syrup
- 1 cup steel-cut oats
- 1 1/2 cup hot water

Directions:
1. Add all ingredients into the inner pot of instant pot duo crisp and stir well.
2. Seal the pot with pressure cooking lid and cook on high for 10 minutes.
3. Once done, allow to release pressure naturally. Remove lid.
4. Serve and enjoy.

Nutritional Value (Amount per Serving):
Calories 273; Fat 1.9 g; Carbohydrates 65.4 g; Sugar 37.7 g; Protein 3.8 g; Cholesterol 0 mg

Cherry Black Rice Pudding

Preparation Time: 10 minutes; Cooking Time: 22 minutes; Serve: 3
Ingredients:
- 2 eggs
- 1 cup black rice, rinsed
- 3/4 cup half and half
- 1/2 cup sugar
- 1 cup milk
- 1 tbsp butter
- 2/3 cup dried cherries
- 1 tsp vanilla
- 1 1/2 cups water
- 1/4 tsp salt

Directions:
1. Add rice, butter, salt, and water into the inner pot of instant pot duo crisp and stir well.

2. Seal the pot with pressure cooking lid and cook on high for 22 minutes.
3. Once done, allow to release pressure naturally. Remove lid.
4. Add milk and sugar and stir well.
5. Set instant pot on sauté mode cook until sugar is dissolved.
6. Whisk eggs with vanilla and half and half and pour through a strainer into the pot.
7. Stir constantly until begins to boil. Turn off the pot.
8. Add cherries and stir well and serve.

Nutritional Value (Amount per Serving):
Calories 406; Fat 15.7 g; Carbohydrates 57.9 g; Sugar 37.8 g; Protein 10.6 g; Cholesterol 149 mg

Apple Pie Pudding

Preparation Time: 10 minutes; Cooking Time: 5 minutes; Serve: 4
Ingredients:
- 4 cups of rice
- 1/4 cup raisins
- 1 tbsp apple pie spice
- 2 cup almond milk
- 3 1/2 cups apples, chopped
- 1/4 tsp cardamom
- 1 tbsp vanilla

Directions:
1. Add all ingredients into the inner pot of instant pot duo crisp and stir well.
2. Seal the pot with pressure cooking lid and cook on high for 5 minutes.
3. Once done, release pressure using a quick release. Remove lid.
4. Stir well and serve.

Nutritional Value (Amount per Serving):
Calories 1094; Fat 30.4 g; Carbohydrates 190.2 g; Sugar 30.4 g; Protein 16.8 g; Cholesterol 0 mg

Raspberry Pudding

Preparation Time: 10 minutes; Cooking Time: 30 minutes; Serve: 6
Ingredients:
- 2 cups raspberries
- 1/2 cup heavy cream
- 2 tbsp raspberry jam
- 1/4 cup sugar
- 2 cups of milk
- 1 cup of water
- 1/2 tsp vanilla
- 1 cinnamon stick
- 1 cup Arborio rice

Directions:
1. Set instant pot duo crisp on sauté mode.
2. Add water, sugar, jam, and milk into the pot and stir until sugar dissolved.
3. Add cinnamon stick, vanilla, and rice. Stir well.
4. Seal the pot with pressure cooking lid and cook on high for 30 minutes.
5. Once done, allow to release pressure naturally. Remove lid.
6. Add raspberries and cream and stir well.
7. Serve and enjoy.

Nutritional Value (Amount per Serving):
Calories 262; Fat 5.8 g; Carbohydrates 48 g; Sugar 16.9 g; Protein 5.6 g; Cholesterol 20 mg

Yogurt Custard

Preparation Time: 10 minutes; Cooking Time: 20 minutes; Serve: 6
Ingredients:
- 1 cup Greek yogurt
- 1 cup milk
- 1 cup condensed milk, sweetened
- 1 1/2 tsp cardamom powder

Directions:

1. Add all ingredients into the heat-safe bowl and stir to combine.
2. Cover bowl with foil. Pour 2 cups of water into the inner pot of instant pot duo crisp than place steamer rack in the pot.
3. Place bowl on top of the steamer rack.
4. Seal the pot with pressure cooking lid and cook on high for 20 minutes.
5. Once done, allow to release pressure naturally. Remove lid.
6. Carefully remove bowl from the pot and set aside to cool completely.
7. Place custard in refrigerator for 1 hour.
8. Serve and enjoy.

Nutritional Value (Amount per Serving):
Calories 211; Fat 6 g; Carbohydrates 31.4 g; Sugar 30.9 g; Protein 8.8 g; Cholesterol 22 mg

Chapter 10: 30-Day Meal Plan

Day 1

Breakfast-Kale Egg Muffins

Lunch-Flavorful Broccoli Cheese Soup

Dinner-Delicious Beef Roast

Day 2

Breakfast-Chicken Egg Breakfast Muffins

Lunch-Creamy Basil Tomato Soup

Dinner-Spicy Pulled Beef

Day 3

Breakfast-Zucchini Muffins

Lunch-Flavorful Fish Stew

Dinner-Tasty Beef Tacos

Day 4

Breakfast-Spinach Egg Bites

Lunch-Creamy Cauliflower Soup

Dinner-Coconut Beef Curry

Day 5

Breakfast-Bacon Egg Muffins

Lunch-Easy Chicken Soup

Dinner-Lime Garlic Steak Carnitas

Day 6

Breakfast-Spinach Tomato Egg Muffins

Lunch-Tasty Mexican Chicken Soup

Dinner-Chili Garlic Brisket

Day 7

Breakfast-Protein Breakfast Muffins

Lunch-Curried Chicken Soup

Dinner-Taco Pork Roast

Day 8

Breakfast-Spinach Cheese Quiche

Lunch-Buffalo Chicken Soup

Dinner-Flavorful Pork Chop

Day 9

Breakfast-Cheese Spinach Muffins

Lunch-Creamy & Tasty Chicken Soup

Dinner-Pulled Pork

Day 10

Breakfast-Rutabaga Noodles

Lunch-No Bean Beef Chili

Dinner-Cuban Pork

Day 11

Breakfast-Broccoli Cheese Muffins

Lunch-Vegan Cauliflower Soup

Dinner-Pork Tenderloin

Day 12

Breakfast-Tomato Basil Egg Muffins

Lunch-Chicken Broccoli Soup

Dinner-Tasty Chipotle Barbacoa

Day 13

Breakfast-Cheesy Egg Muffins

Lunch-Broccoli Asparagus Soup

Dinner-Easy Pork Roast

Day 14

Breakfast-Roasted Cauliflower

Lunch-Lemon Asparagus Soup

Dinner-Ranch Pork Chops

Day 15

Breakfast-Mushrooms & Green Beans

Lunch-Nutritious Asparagus Soup

Dinner-Pork Carnitas

Day 16

Breakfast-Italian Frittata

Lunch-Mushroom Leek Soup

Dinner-Pulled Pork

Day 17

Breakfast-Soy Garlic Chicken

Lunch-Healthy Pumpkin Soup

Dinner-Pork Patties

Day 18

Breakfast-Creamy Chicken

Lunch-Easy Mushroom Soup

Dinner-Herb Pork Tenderloin

Day 19

Breakfast-Mini Frittata

Lunch-Curried Pumpkin Soup

Dinner-Buttery Pork Chops

Day 20

Breakfast-Spinach Frittata

Lunch-Hearty Kale Sausage Pumpkin Soup

Dinner-Tasty Boneless Pork Chops

Day 21

Breakfast-Mushroom Frittata

Lunch-Spicy Mushroom Soup

Dinner-Chipotle Beef

Day 22

Breakfast-Tomato Mozzarella Quiche

Lunch-Creamy Celery Soup

Dinner-Delicious Picadillo

Day 23

Breakfast-Lemon Butter Brussels sprouts

Lunch-Creamy Coconut Zucchini Soup

Dinner-Lamb Patties

Day 24

Breakfast-Creamy Cauliflower Mashed

Lunch-Vegan Zucchini Soup

Dinner-Ranch Seasoned Pork Chops

Day 25

Breakfast-Spicy Cabbage

Lunch-Spinach Soup

Dinner-Meatballs

Day 26

Breakfast-Cajun Cheese Zucchini

Lunch-Vegan Carrot Soup

Dinner-Spicy Lamb Patties

Day 27

Breakfast-Spinach Feta Muffins

Lunch-Kale Beef Soup

Dinner-Chuck Roast

Day 28

Breakfast-Pesto Cheese Chicken

Lunch-Cabbage Beef Soup

Dinner-Tomato Beef Brisket

Day 29

Breakfast-Italian Tomato Frittata

Lunch-Easy Chicken Salsa Soup

Dinner-Balsamic Chuck Roast

Day 30

Breakfast-Breakfast Casserole

Lunch-Spring Chicken Soup

Dinner-Classic Pot Roast

Conclusion

The book contains different types of healthy and delicious recipes. The recipes written in this book are easy to understand and easy to prepare.

Made in the USA
Middletown, DE
18 February 2020